First World War

and Army of Occupation

War Diary

France, Belgium and Germany

57 DIVISION
170 Infantry Brigade
Loyal North Lancashire Regiment
1/5th Battalion (Territorial Force)
1 January 1918 - 7 May 1919

WO95/2979/1

The Naval & Military Press Ltd
www.nmarchive.com
Published in association with The National Archives

Published by

The Naval & Military Press Ltd

Unit 10 Ridgewood Industrial Park,

Uckfield, East Sussex,

TN22 5QE England

Tel: +44 (0) 1825 749494

www.naval-military-press.com

www.nmarchive.com

This diary has been reprinted in facsimile from the original. Any imperfections are inevitably reproduced and the quality may fall short of modern type and cartographic standards.

Contents

Document type	Place/Title	Date From	Date To
Heading	WO95/2979-1		
Heading	57th Division 170th Infy Bde 1-5th Bn Loy. Nth Lancs Jan 1918-May 1919		
War Diary	Portsmouth Camp	01/01/1918	01/01/1918
War Diary	Proven	02/01/1918	02/01/1918
War Diary	Wez Macquart Sector	03/01/1918	31/01/1918
Heading	War Diary Of 15th Battalion Loyal North Lancashire Regiment From 1st February 1918 To 28th February 1918 Volume 13		
War Diary	Wez Macquart	01/02/1918	03/02/1918
War Diary	Laundry Erquinghem	04/02/1918	05/02/1918
War Diary	Wez Macquart (Centre in Left)	06/02/1918	09/02/1918
War Diary	Hollebecque	10/02/1918	13/02/1918
War Diary	Neuf Berquin	14/02/1918	14/02/1918
War Diary	Cottes	15/02/1918	28/02/1918
Miscellaneous	Move Orders By Lieut-Col. C.L. Harford	13/08/1918	13/08/1918
Miscellaneous	Battalion Training Circular No 1	17/02/1918	17/02/1918
Operation(al) Order(s)	1/5th Bn. Loyal North Lancashire Regiment Operation Order No. 1	20/02/1918	20/02/1918
Miscellaneous	Battalion Training Order No. 3	20/02/1918	20/02/1918
Miscellaneous	Allotment Of Training Grounds	21/02/1918	21/02/1918
Miscellaneous	Proceedings Of A Conference Held At Battalion Headquarters	20/02/1918	20/02/1918
Operation(al) Order(s)	Battalion Order No. 3	26/02/1918	26/02/1918
Operation(al) Order(s)	Battalion Training Circular No. 2	22/02/1918	22/02/1918
Operation(al) Order(s)	Battalion Training Order No. 6	24/02/1918	24/02/1918
Miscellaneous	Allotment of Training Grounds For Monday 25th Feb 1918	25/02/1918	25/02/1918
Operation(al) Order(s)	Battalion Order No 2	25/02/1918	25/02/1918
Operation(al) Order(s)	Battalion Training Order No. 8	26/02/1918	26/02/1918
Operation(al) Order(s)	Battalion Training Order No. 5	28/02/1918	28/02/1918
Miscellaneous	Allotment Of Training Grounds	22/02/1918	22/02/1918
Operation(al) Order(s)	Battalion Operation Order No. 4	27/02/1918	27/02/1918
Miscellaneous	March Table To Accompany Battalion Operation Order No. 4		
Operation(al) Order(s)	Battalion Training Order No. 7	25/02/1918	25/02/1918
Miscellaneous	Allotment Of Training Grounds	26/02/1918	26/02/1918
Miscellaneous	Headquarters 57th Division	04/04/1918	04/04/1918
Heading	War Diary Of 1/5th Battalion Royal With Lancashire Regiment Period 1st March 1918 To 31st March 1918 Volume 14		
War Diary	Cottes	01/03/1918	01/03/1918
War Diary	Pont De Nieppe	02/03/1918	19/03/1918
War Diary	Right Sub Sector Fleurbaix	20/03/1918	26/03/1918
War Diary	Sailly-Sur Lys	27/03/1918	29/03/1918
War Diary	Wez Macquart (Centre)	30/03/1918	31/03/1918
War Diary	Sailly	31/03/1918	31/03/1918
Miscellaneous	(Continued)	00/00/1918	00/00/1918
Operation(al) Order(s)	Battalion Training Circular No 5		
Miscellaneous	Battalion Operation Order No. 5	03/03/1918	03/03/1918

Operation(al) Order(s)	Battalion Operation Order No. 6	10/03/1918	10/03/1918
Miscellaneous	Battalion Instructions No. 1	22/03/1918	22/03/1918
Operation(al) Order(s)	Battalion Operation Order No. 7	14/03/1918	14/03/1918
Operation(al) Order(s)	Battalion Operation Order No. 8	18/03/1918	18/03/1918
Operation(al) Order(s)	Corrigenda To Battalion Operation Order No. 8	18/03/1918	18/03/1918
Operation(al) Order(s)	1/5th Bn. L. N, Lancashire Regt. Order No. 8	25/03/1918	25/03/1918
Operation(al) Order(s)	1/5th Battalion Loyal North Lancashire Regiment Order No. 9	29/03/1918	29/03/1918
Operation(al) Order(s)	1/5th Battalion Loyal North Lancashire Regiment Order No. 10	31/03/1918	31/03/1918
Heading	57th Division 170th Infantry Brigade 1/5th Battalion The Loyal North Lancashire Regt April 1918		
Heading	War Diary Of 1/5th Battalion Loyal North Lancashire Regiment Period 1st April 1918 To 30th April 1918 Volume 15		
War Diary	Sailly-Sur-La-Lys	01/04/1918	01/04/1918
War Diary	Arrewage	02/04/1918	03/04/1918
War Diary	Warluzel	04/04/1918	05/04/1918
War Diary	Humbercourt	06/04/1918	08/04/1918
War Diary	Grenas	09/04/1918	09/04/1918
War Diary	Halloy	10/04/1918	12/04/1918
War Diary	Beaudricourt	13/04/1918	13/04/1918
War Diary	Authie	14/04/1918	16/04/1918
War Diary	Couin	17/04/1918	30/04/1918
Operation(al) Order(s)	1/5th Bn. Loyal North Lancashire Regiment Order No. 11	31/03/1918	31/03/1918
Operation(al) Order(s)	1/5th Battalion Loyal North Lancashire Regt. Order No 12	01/04/1918	01/04/1918
Operation(al) Order(s)	1/5th Battalion Loyal North Lancashire Regiment Order No. 13	05/04/1918	05/04/1918
Operation(al) Order(s)	1/5th Battalion Loyal North Lancashire Regiment Order No. 14	08/04/1918	08/04/1918
Miscellaneous	Amendment To 1/5th Battalion Loyal North Lancashire Regiment Order No 15		
Operation(al) Order(s)	1/5th Battalion Loyal North Lancashire Regiment Order No. 15	09/04/1918	09/04/1918
Miscellaneous	1/5th Battalion Loyal North Lancashire Regiment Instruction No. 3		
Miscellaneous	Amendment To 1/5th Bn. Loyal North Lancashire Regiment Order No. 17	30/04/1918	30/04/1918
Operation(al) Order(s)	1/5th Bn. Loyal North Lancashire Regiment Order No. 17	26/04/1918	26/04/1918
Miscellaneous	1/5th Bn. Loyal North Lancashire Regiment	26/04/1918	26/04/1918
Heading	War Diary Of 1/5th Battalion Loyal North Lancashire Regiment Period 1st May 1918 To 31st May 1918 Volume 15		
War Diary	Couin	01/05/1918	06/05/1918
War Diary	Beer Trench	07/05/1918	11/05/1918
War Diary	Coigneux	12/05/1918	13/05/1918
War Diary	Left Subsector	14/05/1918	14/05/1918
War Diary	Left Brigade Sector	15/05/1918	15/05/1918
War Diary	Gommecourt	16/05/1918	29/05/1918
War Diary	Coigneux	30/05/1918	31/05/1918
Operation(al) Order(s)	1/5th Bn. Loyal North Lancashire Regiment Operation Order No. 24	31/08/1918	31/08/1918

Operation(al) Order(s)	1/5th Bn. Loyal North Lancashire Regiment Operation Order No. 25	23/05/1918	23/05/1918
Operation(al) Order(s)	1/5th Bn. Loyal North Lancashire Regiment Operation Order No 25	31/05/1918	31/05/1918
Operation(al) Order(s)	1/5th Bn. Loyal North Lancashire Regiment Order No. 19	07/05/1918	07/05/1918
Operation(al) Order(s)	1/5th Bn. Loyal North Lancashire Regiment Order No. 19	08/05/1918	08/05/1918
Miscellaneous	1/5th Bn. Loyal North Lancashire Regiment Order No 19	06/06/1918	06/06/1918
Heading	War Diary Of 1/5th Battalion Loyal North Lancashire Regiment Period 1st June 1918 To 30th June 1918 Volume 14		
War Diary	Rosignol Farm	01/06/1918	07/06/1918
War Diary	Stout Trench	08/06/1918	23/06/1918
War Diary	Chateau de La Haie	27/06/1918	27/06/1918
War Diary	Couin	28/06/1918	29/06/1918
War Diary	Commecourt	30/06/1918	30/06/1918
Miscellaneous	Amendment No 1 To 1/5th Battalion Loyal North Lancashire Regiment Order No. 26	01/06/1918	01/06/1918
Operation(al) Order(s)	1/5th Bn. Loyal North Lancashire Regiment Order No. 26	01/06/1918	01/06/1918
Miscellaneous	Report On Raid 1/5th Bn. Loyal North Lancashire Regt. 3/4th June, 1918	04/06/1918	04/06/1918
Operation(al) Order(s)	1/5th Bn. Loyal North Lancashire Regiment Order No. 27		
Operation(al) Order(s)	1/5th Battalion Loyal North Lancashire Regiment Order No. 30	22/06/1918	22/06/1918
Operation(al) Order(s)	1/5th Bn. Loyal North Lancashire Regiment Order No. 38	28/06/1918	28/06/1918
Miscellaneous	1/5th Bn Loyal North Lancs. Regiment Order No. 30	25/06/1918	25/06/1918
Miscellaneous	War Diary		
Heading	War Diary Of 1/5th Battalion Loyal North Lancashire Regiment Period 1st July 1918 To 31st July 1918 Volume 18		
War Diary	Left Sector Left Division	01/07/1918	01/07/1918
War Diary	Front Gommecourt	01/07/1918	01/07/1918
War Diary	Vauchelles	02/07/1918	27/07/1918
Miscellaneous	Amendment To Report On raid1/5th Bn. Loyal North Lancashire Regiment	04/06/1918	04/06/1918
War Diary	Vauchelles	28/07/1918	29/07/1918
War Diary	Le Souich	30/07/1918	30/07/1918
War Diary	Hautville	31/07/1918	31/07/1918
Miscellaneous	Addenda to Battn Order N. 33		
Miscellaneous	1/5th Bn Loyal North Lancs Regt Order No. 33	01/07/1918	01/07/1918
Miscellaneous	L. Dean		
Operation(al) Order(s)	1/5th Battalion Loyal North Lancs. Regt. Order No. 36		
Miscellaneous	1/5th Bn. L. N. Lancashire Regiment.	30/07/1918	30/07/1918
Miscellaneous	6 Dv		
Heading	War Diary 1/5th L. N. Lancashire Regt. August 1918		
War Diary	Etrun	01/08/1918	01/08/1918
War Diary	Feuchy Sector	02/08/1918	07/08/1918
War Diary	Anzin-St-Aubin	08/08/1918	15/08/1918
War Diary	Blangy Line, Dc	16/08/1918	18/08/1918
War Diary	Feuchy	18/08/1918	20/08/1918
War Diary	Arras	21/08/1918	21/08/1918

War Diary	Anzin	22/08/1918	22/08/1918
War Diary	Wanquetin	23/08/1918	23/08/1918
War Diary	Sus-St-Leger	24/08/1918	25/08/1918
War Diary	Bailleulmont	26/08/1918	26/08/1918
War Diary	Hendecourt-Lez-Ransart	27/08/1918	27/08/1918
War Diary	Neuville Vitasse	28/08/1918	28/08/1918
War Diary	Riencourt Sector	29/08/1918	31/08/1918
Heading	War Diary 1/5th Loyal North Lancs. Regt. Sept 1918 Vol 38		
Heading	War Diary Of 1/5th Battalion Loyal North Lancashire Regt. Period 1st September To 30th September 1918 Volume 20		
War Diary	Riencourt Sector	01/09/1918	03/09/1918
War Diary	Hindenburg Support Line	04/09/1918	07/09/1918
War Diary	Drocourt-Queant Line	08/09/1918	09/09/1918
War Diary	Moeuvres	10/09/1918	13/09/1918
War Diary	Moeuvres Reserve	14/09/1918	16/09/1918
War Diary	Bullecourt	17/09/1918	18/09/1918
War Diary	Saulty	19/09/1918	25/09/1918
War Diary	Noreuil	26/09/1918	27/09/1918
War Diary	E 29 A	28/09/1918	28/09/1918
War Diary	F28a72	29/09/1918	29/09/1918
War Diary	F25b	30/09/1918	30/09/1918
Heading	On His Majesty's Service.		
Heading	War Diary Of 1/5th Bn Loyal North Lancashire Regt. Period 1st October To 31st October 1918 Volume 21		
War Diary	Proville	01/10/1918	04/10/1918
War Diary	F21d	05/10/1918	08/10/1918
War Diary	G.37 &4 57b NW	08/10/1918	08/10/1918
War Diary	G 8 9	09/10/1918	09/10/1918
War Diary	Sheet 57 C.N.E. D 29c.	11/10/1918	12/10/1918
War Diary	Calonne Ricouart	13/10/1918	13/10/1918
War Diary	Fosse (Ref Map Bethune Combined Sheet R21b & R22a)	15/10/1918	15/10/1918
War Diary	Fosse	16/10/1918	17/10/1918
War Diary	Radingham	18/10/1918	18/10/1918
War Diary	Le Canteleu	19/10/1918	19/10/1918
War Diary	Hellemmes (Sheet 36 Rizb & D)	20/10/1918	20/10/1918
War Diary	Le Grand Marais	21/10/1918	21/10/1918
War Diary	Templeuve (Sheet 37 H33b)	22/10/1918	24/10/1918
War Diary	Sheet 37 H36c75.75.	25/10/1918	28/10/1918
War Diary	Templeuve	29/10/1918	31/10/1918
Operation(al) Order(s)	170th Inf. Bde. Order No. 159	11/10/1918	11/10/1918
Miscellaneous	Rain No. 4		
Operation(al) Order(s)	1/5th Bn. Loyal North Lancashire Regt. Order No. 49		
Miscellaneous	Table "A" For Personnel Moving By Train No.4		
Miscellaneous	Table 'C' Detail of Transport Proceeding By Train No. 5		
Operation(al) Order(s)	1/5th Bn. Loyal North Lancashire Regiment. Order No. 50	13/10/1918	13/10/1918
Operation(al) Order(s)	170th Inf. Bde. Order No. 163	24/10/1918	24/10/1918
Miscellaneous	170th Inf. Bde. Order 162	24/10/1918	24/10/1918
Miscellaneous	O.C.2/5th K.O.R.L. Regt.	23/10/1918	23/10/1918
Operation(al) Order(s)	170th Inf. Bde. Order No. 166	27/10/1918	27/10/1918
Miscellaneous	O.C. "A" Company		
Operation(al) Order(s)	1/5 Battn Loyal N. Lancs Rgt Order No		
Miscellaneous	O.C. D Coy		

Miscellaneous	A Form Messages And Signals		
Operation(al) Order(s)	1/5th Bn Loyal N. Lancs Rgt Order No 58		
Operation(al) Order(s)	1/5th Bn. Loyal North Lancashire Regiment Order No. 59	30/10/1918	30/10/1918
Miscellaneous	War Diary		
Operation(al) Order(s)	1/5th Bn. Loyal North Lancashire Regt. Order No. 51	16/10/1918	16/10/1918
Operation(al) Order(s)	1/5th Bn. Loyal North Lancashire Regiment Order No. 55	26/10/1918	26/10/1918
Miscellaneous	War Diary		
Miscellaneous	1/5th L.N.L.R.	21/10/1918	21/10/1918
Miscellaneous	O.C. 1/5th L.N.L. Regt.	20/10/1918	20/10/1918
Miscellaneous	170th Infantry Brigade	20/10/1918	20/10/1918
Operation(al) Order(s)	1/5th Battalion Loyal North Lancashire Regt. Order No. 53	20/10/1918	20/10/1918
Operation(al) Order(s)	1/5th Battalion Loyal North Lancashire Regt. Order No. 50. (a)	17/10/1918	17/10/1918
Operation(al) Order(s)	1/5th Battalion Loyal North Lancashire Regt. Order No. 5	00/10/1918	00/10/1918
Miscellaneous	OC. HQ. Coy		
Miscellaneous	1/5th Bn Loyal North Lancashire Regiment	24/10/1918	24/10/1918
Miscellaneous	OC. HQ. Coy		
Diagram etc	Diagram Etc		
Map	Map		
Miscellaneous	Headquarters 170th Infantry Brigade	29/10/1918	29/10/1918
Miscellaneous	1/5th Bn. L. N. Lancashire Regiment	04/00/1918	04/00/1918
Miscellaneous	At 20,00 (1/1/18) And	01/01/1918	01/01/1918
Miscellaneous	O.C. Coy	04/10/1918	04/10/1918
Diagram etc	Diagram		
Miscellaneous	1/5th Loyal North Lancs. Regiment		
Miscellaneous	Narrative	10/10/1918	10/10/1918
Miscellaneous	O.C. 1/5th L.N.L. Regt. (b)	11/10/1918	11/10/1918
Heading	War Diary Of 1/5th Bn. Loyal North Lancashire Regt Period 1st November to 30th November 1918 Volume 22		
War Diary	Rue Franche (Sheet 37 M 11 b & c)	01/11/1918	01/11/1918
War Diary	Hellemmes	02/11/1918	30/11/1918
Operation(al) Order(s)	1/5th Bn. Loyal North Lancashire Regiment Order No. 60	31/10/1918	31/10/1918
Operation(al) Order(s)	1/5th Bn. Loyal North Lancashire Regiment Order No. 61	08/11/1918	08/11/1918
Operation(al) Order(s)	1/5th Bn. Loyal North Lancashire Regiment Order No. 62	10/11/1918	10/11/1918
Miscellaneous	H.Q.		
Operation(al) Order(s)	1/5th Bn. Loyal North Lancashire Regiment Order No. 63		
Heading	War Diary Of 1/5th Battn Loyal North Lancashire Rgt. Period 1st December To 31st December 1918 Volume 23		
War Diary	Hellemmes	01/12/1918	01/12/1918
War Diary	Bois D' Epinoy	02/12/1918	02/12/1918
War Diary	Agnez-Les-Duisans (Lens113 H 90.65)	03/12/1918	07/12/1918
War Diary	Agnez-Les-Duisans	08/12/1918	31/12/1918
Operation(al) Order(s)	1/5th Bn. Loyal North Lancashire Regiment Order No. 1	30/11/1918	30/11/1918
Miscellaneous	War Diary		
Operation(al) Order(s)	1/5 Bn. Loyal N. Lancs. Regt Order 2	01/12/1918	01/12/1918

Miscellaneous	War Diary		
War Diary	Agnez-Les-Duisans	01/01/1919	28/02/1919
Miscellaneous	1/5th Loyal North Lancs Regt. Education Time Table.	05/02/1919	05/02/1919
Heading	1/5th Battalion Loyal North Lancashire Regiment War Diary Month Ending 31st March ,1919.		
War Diary	Agnez Les Duisans	01/03/1919	30/04/1919
Heading	1/5th Bn Loyal North Lancs War Diary Vol 46		
War Diary	Agnez-Les-Duisans.	22/05/1919	31/05/1919
War Diary	Agnez-Les-Duisans.	15/05/1919	21/05/1919
War Diary	Agnez-Les-Duisans.	08/05/1919	14/05/1919
War Diary	Agnez-Les-Duisans.	01/05/1919	07/05/1919
Heading	57th Division 170th Infy Bde 2-5th Loy Nth Lancs 1915 Sep-1916 Feb 1917 Feb-1917 Dec To Div Pioneers		

WO 95/2979 (1)

57TH DIVISION
170TH INFY BDE

1-5TH BN LOY.NTH LANCS

JAN 1918-MAY 1919

FROM 55 DN 166 BDE

Instructions regarding War Diaries and Intelligence Summaries are contained in F. S. Regs., Part II. and the Staff Manual respectively. Title pages will be prepared in manuscript.

WAR DIARY
or
INTELLIGENCE SUMMARY.
(Erase heading not required.)

JANUARY 1918

Army Form C. 2118.

12

Place	Date	Hour	Summary of Events and Information	Remarks and references to Appendices
PORTSMOUTH CAMP. PROVEN	1/1/18	12 noon	Strength of Battalion 39 Officers 668 Other ranks	
	2/1/18	7.0 am	The Battalion left PORTSMOUTH CAMP, PROVEN, entrained at PROVEN STA. 8.0 am & moved by Rail to BAILLEUL where detrained & marched to, & encamped at, HOLLEBEQUE CAMP. STEENWERCK AREA.	
WEZMACQUART SECTOR.	3/1/18	9.0 am	The Battalion moved into the line and relieved the 44th Australian Bn. (11 Aust Bde 3rd Div) in Close Support of the WEZMACQUART SECTOR. 3 Coys in Subsid Line & 1 Coy in Fleuris Switch.	
WEZMACQUART SECTOR.	3/1/18 to 15/1/18		The Coy. of this Bn. Garrisoning FLEURIS SWITCH carried out intensive work in improving the defences of the Switch. The other 3 Coys worked under instructions of the Bn. Commander holding the front line Systems.	
—do—	15/1/18	10.30 pm	The Bn was relieved by the 7/s Bn K.O.R.L. Regt and moved to Billets in ERQUINGHEM as Bn in Reserve.	
—do—	20/1/18	5.30 am	The Bn relieved the 7/s Bn Kings Own R.L. Regt. in Close Support and carried out work in improving defences.	

(A7092) Wt W12839/M1293 75,0.0. 1/17. D. D. & L., Ltd. Forms/C.2118/14.

Instructions regarding War Diaries and Intelligence Summaries are contained in F. S. Regs., Part II. and the Staff Manual respectively. Title pages will be prepared in manuscript.

WAR DIARY
or
INTELLIGENCE SUMMARY.
(Erase heading not required.)

Army Form C. 2118.

JANUARY 1918

12

Place	Date	Hour	Summary of Events and Information	Remarks and references to Appendices
WEZMACQUART SECTOR.	23/1/18	5.30	The Bn. was relieved by 1/5 Bn. K.O.R.L. Regt. and occupied billets in ERQUINGHEM as Bn. in Brigade Reserve.	
	26/1/18	5.0.	The Bn. relieved the 1/5 Bn. Kings Own R.L. Regt in Close Support and carried on work on the defences of FLEURIE SWITCH.	
	29/1/18	5.30pm	The Bn. was relieved by 1/5 Bn. Kings Own R.L. Regt. and occupied billets in ERQUINGHEM as Battalion in Brigade Reserve.	
	31/1/18	12.noon	Strength of Bn. 37 officers 646 O.ranks.	

(A7092). Wt. W12839/M1293. 750,000. 1/17. D. D. & L., Ltd. Forms/C.2118/14.

Confidential

War Diary

of

1/5th Battalion Loyal North Lancashire Regiment

from 1st February 1918 to 28th February 1918.

Volume 15.

Instructions regarding War Diaries and Intelligence Summaries are contained in F. S. Regs., Part II. and the Staff Manual respectively. Title pages will be prepared in manuscript.

WAR DIARY
~~or~~
~~INTELLIGENCE SUMMARY.~~
(Erase heading not required.)

Army Form C. 2118.

Place	Date 1918.	Hour	Summary of Events and Information	Remarks and references to Appendices
	FEB.			
VIEZ MACQUART	1		Trenches. Enemy fairly active with M.T.M. Low visibility all day. At night Brigade on our left carried out a raid on the enemy trenches. Slight retaliation with Gas shells &c. on our sector. 12 hours afterwards 7 of our men began to suffer from effects of gas and were evacuated.	[illegible]
	2		Trenches. Fairly quiet day & night. Patrols did not meet any of enemy in N.M.L. and searched unsuccessfully for gap in enemy wire.	[illegible]
	3		Quiet day. At night relieved by 1/4th Loyal North Lanc. Regt.	[illegible]
LAUNDRY ERQUINGHEM	4		Billets – Rest. Brigade Reserve. Amalgamated with the 1/5th [illegible]	[illegible]
	5		Relieved 1/4th Loyal North Lanc. Regt.	[illegible]
VIEZ MACQUART (CENTRE & LEFT)	6		Trenches. Very quiet day. At night raid on Enemy Trenches by Brigade on left assisted by dummy barrage on our Sector. Retaliation not so severe as expected.	[illegible]
	7		Trenches. Quiet day & night.	[illegible]
	8		do. do.	[illegible]
	9		do. Relieved by 1/5th King's Own (R.L.) Regt. and proceeded to HOLLEBECQUE CAMP in Divisional Reserve.	[illegible]

A6945 Wt. W11422/M1160 350,000 12/16 D. D. & L. Forms/C./2118/14.

Instructions regarding War Diaries and Intelligence Summaries are contained in F. S. Regs., Part II. and the Staff Manual respectively. Title pages will be prepared in manuscript.

WAR DIARY or INTELLIGENCE SUMMARY.

(Erase heading not required.)

Army Form C. 2118.

Place	Date	Hour	Summary of Events and Information	Remarks and references to Appendices
HOLLEBECQUE	10		Divisional Reserve, and cleaning up camp	AP
-do-	11		-do- and revetting round Huts for protection against Aerial Bombs	AP
-do-	12		-do-	AP
-do-	13		Proceeded to NEUF BERQUIN by March Route	AP
NEUF BERQUIN	14		Proceeded to COTTES by Motor Lorries	AP
COTTES	15		Corps Reserve, and Battalion Training	AP
-do-	16		-do- -do-	AP
-do-	17		-do- -do-	AP
-do-	18		-do- -do- A & B Coy: Range Practice	AP
-do-	19		-do- -do-	AP
-do-	20		-do- -do-	AP
-do-	21		-do- -do- C & D Coy Range Practice, Reinforcements 56 O.R.	AP
-do-	22		-do- -do-	AP
-do-	23		-do- -do- Reinforcements 2 O.R.	AP
-do-	24		-do- -do-	AP
-do-	25		-do- -do- Company Range Practice	AP

A6945 Wt. W11422/M1160 350,000 12/16 D. D. & L. Forms/C./2118/14.

Instructions regarding War Diaries and Intelligence Summaries are contained in F. S. Regs., Part II. and the Staff Manual respectively. Title pages will be prepared in manuscript.

WAR DIARY
or
INTELLIGENCE SUMMARY.
(*Erase heading not required.*)

Army Form C. 2118.

Place	Date	Hour	Summary of Events and Information	Remarks and references to Appendices
COTTES	26		Corps Reserve, and Battalion Training, Reinforcements 1 & 6 R.	a.R.
-do-	27		-do- Brigade parade, Presentation of Medal Ribbons by Corps Comdr. ×	a.R.
-do-	28		-do- Inspection by Divisional Comdr. and March Past	a.R.

A6945 Wt. W11422/M1160 350,000 12/16 D. D. & L. Forms/C./2118/14.

Copy No. 10

SECRET.

MOVE ORDERS

By Lieut-Col. G. L. Harford,
Commdg. "D" Bn. L. N. Lancs. Regt.

Ref. Map, HAZEBROUCK 5A. 1/100,000.
" " 36A. 1/40,000

1. The Battalion will move by lorry from NEUF BERQUIN to COTTES to-morrow, the 14th inst.

2. The Battalion will be formed up in Column of Route at a Point L.28.d.2.2. (36A. 1/40,000.) - 5.I.45.21. (Hazebrouck) facing S.E. in the following order:-
"D", "C", "B", "A" & Headquarters at 9.55 a.m.

3. The head of the embussing point will be at the Cross Roads 5.I.4[illegible].71. (Hazebrouck) - L.28.d.5.5. (Sheet 36A.). Busses facing West.

4. (a) The Battalion will assemble on the S. side of the road and where possible clear of it.
(b) The Battalion will be divided into groups of 25, comprising one lorry load, six of these groups should occupy 40 yds. of roadspace.
(c) Company Commanders will detail an Officer to take charge of each group, and an Officer or senior N.C.O. to take charge of each lorry - the above will be given the destination of the Battalion, in writing in case of breakdown.
(d) No N.C.O. or man will leave the lorries without permission.

5. On arrival at the debussing point the men will debus as quickly as possible, and will immediately clear off the road to the right hand side. Companies will not fall in or move along the road on which the debussing takes place until the bus convoy is clear of the road.

6. Billets and Horse - Lines will be left scrupulously clean, and a certificate ~~that~~ to that effect will be handed to the Adjutant on parade.

7. Companies will report when settled down in billets, giving location of Company Headquarters.

(Signed) A. Runciman. 2/Lieut.,
Act. Adjt.,
"D" Bn. L. N. Lancashire Regiment.

Issued at 6-35 p.m. 13/9/18. Copies as under:-

1. H.Q. 170th Bde.
2 -5. All Companies.
6. Quartermaster.
7. Transport Officer.
8. R. S. M.
9. File.
10. War Diary

BATTALION TRAINING CIRCULAR NO. 1.

1. The Brigade Rifle Range at T.9.c.&d. has been allotted to this Battalion as follows:-
February 18th, 21st & 25th.

2. Companies will use this range, in turn, commencing with "A" & "B" Companies to-morrow, the 18th inst. "C" & "D" Companies will fire on the 21st inst.

"A" & "C" Companies.	Commence Firing 9 a.m.
	Cease Firing 12-30 p.m.
"B" & "D" Companies.	Commence Firing 12-30 p.m.
	Cease Firing 4 p.m.

Further orders will be issued for the use of the range on the 25th inst.

3. Markers will be provided as follows:-
4 Officers, 4 Senior N.C.Os. and 64 Other Ranks. These will be found by "B" Company for marking for "A" Company and by "A" Company for marking for "B" Company.
Markers for "A" Company will be in the butts at 8-30 a.m. to-morrow, the 18th inst. Markers for "B" Company will change over as quickly as possible on completion of shooting by "A" Company.
The same arrangements will hold good for "C" & "D" Companies on the 21st inst.

4. The following practices will be fired by "A" & "B" Companies on the 18th inst., and by "C" & "D" Companies on the 21st inst:-
1. 5 rounds Grouping 100^{x}
2. 10 rounds Application. 200^{x}
3. 10 " " " 300^{x}
4. 10 rounds Snapshooting at 200^{x} & 300^{x}.
5. 15 rounds rapid at 300^{x} (Time allowed 60 seconds).

5. Dress. Battle Order - Haversacks on back. No pack to be carried.

6. Ammunition will be provided on the range.

7. Telephones. The Battalion Signal Officer will arrange for signal communication to be established between the Butts and Firing Points. The line laid for to-morrow (Monday) will be a permanent one for the use of the Brigade whilst in the ST HILAIRE AREA. Telephones will be taken to and from the range.

8. Meals. Dinners will be served to men under Company arrangements. Men remaining in the Butts as Markers will carry haversack rations.

9. Butt Memos. & Company Commanders Rolls will be made out by each Company, and the score of every Officer, N.C.O. and man recorded. A copy of this will be forwarded to Battalion Headquarters on completion of each day's firing.

10. Companies will parade at full strength; all men employed on Battalion Headquarters, The Quartermaster's Dept., Transport, Band, etc., will fire with their respective Companies.

11. Range discipline will be maintained and every precaution taken to avoid accidents.

12. Owing to range difficulties the Right Hand Range has only a firing point at 300^{x}. This may however be used for grouping practice by improvising a firing point at about 80^{x} range. Oil Sheets will be used for this purpose.

13. Companies firing in the afternoon will do at least 30 minutes P.T. in the morning and spend the remainder of the time prior to marching to the range in cleaning up.

14. Training programmes will be altered to comply with these instructions.

15. Company Commanders are reminded of the extreme importance of musketry at the present time. The greatest care and attention must be given to men who are backward and require coaching. Rapid Loading and Firing are points which require special attention.
N.C.Os. & men should be given every encouragement by their Company and Platoon Commanders to become thoroughly efficient marksmen.

B. H. Harrison
Capt. & Adjt.,
1/5th Bn. L. N. Lancashire Regt.

Issued at 4-30 p.m. 17/2/18. Copies to:-

1-4. All Companies.
5. Quartermaster.
6. Transport.Officer.
7. Signal Officer.

SECRET. 1/5TH BN. LOYAL NORTH LANCASHIRE REGIMENT Copy No.10...

OPERATION ORDER NO. 1.

::::::::::::::::::::::::::::::::::::

1. As this Brigade is liable to be called upon to reinforce certain parts of the XV Corps front while in the ST HILAIRE Area, the following instructions are issued and will be observed in the event of emergency.

2. The Battalion will move by lorry or March route according to circumstances.

3. In the event of the Battalion moving by lorry:-
(a) Transport will move under BrigadeTransport Officer, orders for which will be issued later.
(b) Lewis Guns will be carried by the Lewis Gun Sections in the lorries.
(c) Each man will carry one blanket. The remaining blanket will be carried under arrangements to be made by Headquarters 170th Infantry Brigade. These will be notified later.

4. In the event of the battalion moving by march route:-
(a) Transport will march immediately in rear of the battalion.
(b) The two blankets per man will be carried under arrangements to be made by Headquarters 170th Infantry Brigade. These will be notified later.

5. Dress. Fighting Order with great coats.
Company Commanders will make the necessary arrangements for collecting packs and handing same in to the Quartermaster's Stores before starting.

6. Lieut-Col. C. L. Harford will be in charge of the Brigade Column when on the line of march as far as L.33.d.7.7.

7. Acknowledge.

B. H. Hanson

Captain,
Adjutant,
1/5th Bn. L. N. Lancashire Regiment.

20/2/18.

Issued to:- 170th Bde.
All Companies.
Quartermaster.
Transport Officer.
Commanding Officer.
File.
War Diary.

BATTALION TRAINING ORDER NO. 3.

1. The attached table shows the allotment of training areas to companies for to-morrow 21st., inst.

2. "C" and "D" Companies will fire on the Brigade Range in accordance with Battalion Training Circular No. 1.d/d. 17/2/18 with the exception of practice No. 4, snapshooting, which cannot be carried out to-morrow owing to lack of necessary targets.

3. Ammunition will be provided on the range. The Transport Officer will arrange for 1 G.S. Limber to report at the Quartermaster's Stores at 8.15 a.m. to draw ammunition and convey it to the range. He will also detail a limber to report at the range at 4.30p.m. to bring back surplus ammunition &c.

4. **Telephones.** The attention of the Battalion Signal Officer is directed to para 7 of Battalion Training Circular No. 1.

5. Meals will be served under Company arrangements. Personnel of Battalion Headquarters, Q.M. Dept., Transport &c.&c. will take haversack rations or hand their mid-day rations to their respective Company Cooks in accordance with instructions issued by their respective Company Commanders.

6. Companies will parade at full strength, all men employed on Battalion Headquarters, Q.M. Dept., Transport, Band, Runners, Signallers and Officers Servants will shoot with their respective companies. The Quartermaster and Transport Officer will be held responsible that all men of "C" and "D" Companies employed in their respective departments are warned for this parade.

7. There will be no battalion parade to-morrow at 12.30p.m. The Commanding Officer will probably see "A" and "B" Companies march past on their way from training grounds to billets on conclusion of the morning's work.

B. H. Hawson
Captain,
Adjutant,
1/5th Bn. L. N. Lancashire Regiment.

20/2/18.

Issued to:-

All Companies.
Quartermaster.
Transport Officer.
Signal Officer.
War Diary.
File.
Spare.

ALLOTMENT OF TRAINING GROUNDS FOR THURSDAY, 21ST. Feb. 1918.

Coy.	Brigade Range. T.11.a.	100^x Range at T.10.d.8.2.	100^x Range at N.28.d.2.2.	Battalion Parade Ground.
A.	-	9a.m. - 12noon.	-	12 noon - 1p.m.
B.	-	-	9a.m. - 1p.m.	-
C.	9a.m. - 12.30p.m.	-	-	-
D.	12.30p.m.- 4p.m.	-	-	-

Proceedings of a Conference held at
Battalion Headquarters on Wednesday, 20th February, 1918.

---

1. Present. Commanding Officer, Acting 2nd in Command, Adjutant, Company Commanders and Transport Officer.

2. The question of dress of men during training was discussed and the following conclusions arrived at:-
   (a) For attack practice. Fighting Order (No packs, haversacks on back.)
   (b) Marching to & from Training Areas, men should be allowed to carry their packs slung. Steel helmets are not to be carried unless specially ordered.
   (c) Marching Order parades. All men in full marching order complete with Box Respirator. Pack to be strapped on. Steel helmets to be carried on packs.

3. Formations to be adopted in case of troops being attacked by hostile aircraft. Right and Left hand files to break ranks and line the hedge or ditch on the side of the road on which they are marching, and to remain perfectly still.
Men are to be cautioned against looking upwards on these occasions. This is to be practised when marching to & from Company Training Grounds.

4. The Divisional Commander will inspect the Battalion on the Battalion Parade ground on Thursday, 28th February. Particular attention was directed to the general turnout of the personnel and transport for this inspection. All buttons and buckles to be well polished, packs and equipment to be scrupulously clean and well fitted.
All men to have their hair cut.
Pack animals to parade with Transport under the Transport Officer.
Notification has since been received from Headquarters 170th Bde. that Steel Helmets will be worn by all ranks and box respirators will not be carried on this occasion.

5. Reconnaissance of the area at present occupied by the 12th Division to be carried out by Officers and N.C.Os. of all Companies. Headquarters 170th Infantry Brigade are being asked to furnish transport for this purpose.

6. The attention of all present was again directed to the fact that working parties under R.E. supervision were still regarded as "fatigues". It must be borne in mind that it is the duty of all Officers to dispel any such ideas existing amongst the men and to impress upon all concerned that work on defensive positions was just as important as taking an objective in an attack.

7. Anti-gas training was discussed and the necessity of at least 10 minutes training in the use of Box Respirators every day emphasised. This is to take place during the morning's training daily.

8. Recent enemy tactics have shewn that he is in the habit of attacking after a comparatively short bombardment of our wire and trenches, most of the destructive work being carried out by Medium & Heavy Trench Mortars. It is therefore of the greatest importance that all concerned take particular note of any increase in hostile T.M. activity or any unusual occurrence in connection with wire cutting or trench destruction, and report same to Battalion Headquarters with the least possible delay.

9. All Officers to know the Defence Schemes and Schemes for local counter attacks of the units on their immediate flanks. Liason between Officers of different Companies is to be encouraged, especially between Companies of the Battalions on our flanks. This not only gives greater confidence to all concerned, but also increases the "Entente" between units. Liason is one of the secrets of all succesful operations.

10. In the event of bombs being dropped by Hostile Aircraft, Battalion Headquarters should be informed at once, together with the approximate

(10). locality and time dropped.

11. (a) Additional Lewis Guns for "AA" Defence are shortly being issued to Battalions at the rate of one per Company. Two of these are already in possession and will be issued to Companies when the Battalion goes into the line.
(b) The idea of this is to avoid Lewis Guns sited for defensive purposes being taken away from their positions in order to deal with hostile aircraft. One of these guns will always be detailed for duty on the transport lines.
(c) The personnel for these guns will consist of 1 N.C.O. & 3 men; these will be obtained by withdrawing 1 O.R. from the L.G. Section of each platoon.
(d) Magazines for these guns will be issued at the rate of 10 magazines per gun.

12. (a) The necessity for more attention being paid to the uniformity of dress throughout the Battalion was discussed and emphasized by the Commanding Officer.
(b) Puttees will be worn in the regulation way only, and Company Commanders will take immediate steps to stop the habit at present existing amongst certain men of "crossing" their puttees.
(c) Caps are to be worn as issued and not turned into a "Gor blimey" affair, as is at present the custom with many of the men. Caps are to be worn set straight on the head and <u>not</u> on one side at a rakish angle. Men are to carry and turn themselves out as soldiers, and to be reminded of the fact that they are wearing the King's Uniform and that there is only one way of doing this, i.e., the correct one.

13. Cleaning of equipment was discussed and the conclusion arrived at that the most satisfactory and cheapest method of cleaning was to scrubb all webbing with Soap and water and sand, no "blanco" being applied. This will in future be adopted by all Companies.

14. The roads outside billets at present leave much to be desired in the way of cleanliness. Paper, cigarette covers, etc., litter the place. This practice is to cease. Companies will be held responsible for the cleanliness of roads outside their respective billets.

15. (a) Saluting. The importance of saluting in the correct method was again emphasized by the Commanding Officer. Several N.C.Os. & men, and in some cases Officers, are still apparently ignorant of the correct method of either giving or returning a salute. Company Commanders will give this matter their personal attention.
(b) Subaltern Officers should be instructed that when on parade they will invariably salute their Company Commander or any Senior Officer when either being spoken to or speaking to them.
(c) The practice of returning salutes with a stick is forbidden.

16. The attention of all Company Commanders was directed to the importance of enforcing the immediate compliance of orders, however trivial, by any senior authority.

17. The Company Orderly Corporals do not appear to understand their duties. Any "light duty" men left at their disposal should be employed to the very best advantage, e.g., cleaning of billets, cookers, general sanitation, and should not be employed on one job alone. "Light Duty" men are generally slackers and should not be given any encouragement to remain as such. Orderly Corporals should invariably know the whereabouts of their respective Companies.

B. A. Harrison

Capt. & Adjt.,
1/5th Bn. L. N. Lancashire Regt.

Issued to:- O.C. "A" Coy. The Quartermaster.
O.C. "B" Coy. Transport Officer.
O.C. "C" Coy. File.
O.C. "D" Coy. War Diary.

BATTALION ORDER NO. 3.

1. The Divisional Commander will inspect the Battalion on Thursday, 28th February, 1918, at 11 a.m., when he will select the best turned out and drilled Company for his prize of a Silver Bugle.

2. (a) The Battalion will be drawn up in line, facing South, on the parade ground of the 2/5th King's Own (R.L.) Regt. at N.35.a.5.2.
   (b) Companies will rendezvous at the road junction at T.5.d.35.85. at 10 a.m. in the following order:-
   "A", "B", "C" & "D".
   (c) The Band will parade and play the Battalion to the parade ground. On arrival they will take up their position in rear of the Battalion.
   (d) The Regimental Sergeant Major and one Marker per Company will report to the Adjutant on the parade ground at 10 a.m. Markers will be required to know the exact number of men on parade of their respective Companies.
   (e) Unless orders are issued to the contrary the Transport will not parade.
   (f) Companies will not be sized, but will be fallen in by Platoons and Sections.

3. The following will be the programme adopted:-
   (a) The Divisional Commander will be received with the "General Salute", after which the Battalion will "slope arms" and be inspected by the G.O.C.
   (b) The Battalion will march past in Column of Platoons.
   (c) The Battalion will then carry out such drill as the G.O.C. may direct.

4. Dress. Dress will be marching order. Steel Helmets will be worn on the head. Box Respirators will not be carried.

5. All Specialists, Signallers, Scouts, Runners, etc., will parade with their respective Companies.

6. Company Commanders will render parade states showing the exact number of men on and off parade. The employment or other cause of men being off parade will be shewn. Parade States must reach the Orderly Room by 8-45 a.m. on the 28th inst.

7. Particular attention is directed to the contents of the mens packs being in exact accordance with regulations, and to the fitting of equipment and to the state of rifles.

8. Officers will parade as for the Corps Commander's parade to-morrow, the 27th inst.

B. L. Hamer
Capt. & Adjt.,
1/5th Bn. L. N. Lancashire Regt.

Issued at 8-30 p.m. 26/2/18. Copies to:-

1. O.C. "A" Coy.
2. O.C. "B" Coy.
3. O.C. "C" Coy.
4. O.C. "D" Coy.
5. Quartermaster.
6. Transport Officer.
7. Signalling Officer.
8. File.
9. War Diary.
10. Commanding Officer.

Copy No. 10

BATTALION TRAINING CIRCULAR No. 2.

1. The Commanding Officer considers that the time devoted to the training of Lewis Gun Sections in this battalion is at present insufficient. The efficiency of N.C.Os. and men in handling and using Lewis Guns is every bit as important as musketry.

2. Commencing to-morrow 23rd inst., the following procedure will be adopted throughout the battalion daily:-
Each Company will detail 1 Lewis Gun Section Complete with gun to report to the Lewis Gun Sergeant at Battalion Headquarters at 8.30 a.m.
This will make a total of 4 Lewis Gun Sections in the battalion who will concentrate on Lewis Gun Training and range work every day.

3. One of the 100^x ranges will be allotted daily by Battalion Headquarters for the exclusive use of Lewis Gunners for the following day.

4. In addition to the Lewis Gun Sergeant, instructors will be provided from Companies as follows:-

No.243251,	Corpl. Worsley.	"A" Company.
No.243917,	Corpl. Cobham.	"B" Company.
No.243366,	Corpl. Wardle.	"D" Company.

These N.C.Os. will report to Sergeant Benjamin at 8.30a.m. daily at Battalion Headquarters.

5. The Transport Officer will detail one G.S. Limber to report at Battalion Headquarters at 8.30 a.m. daily for the conveyance of Lewis Guns and S.A.A. to the range.

B. H. Harrison

Captain,
Adjutant,
1/5th Bn. L. N. Lancashire Regiment.

Issued at 2 p.m. 22/2/18. Copies to:-

No. 1. Bde. H. Q.
No. 2. O.C. "A" Coy.
No. 3. O.C. "B" Coy.
No. 4. O.C. "C" Coy.
No. 5. O.C. "D" Coy.
No. 6. Quartermaster.
No. 7. Transport Officer.
No. 8. Lewis Gun Sergeant.
No. 9. File.
No.10. War Diary.

Copy No........

BATTALION TRAINING ORDER NO.6.

1. Training Grounds and rifle ranges are allotted to Companies for to-morrow 25th inst., in accordance with the attached table.

2. (a) The Brigade Range at T.15.a. is at the disposal of the Battalion all day. This allows each Company to use it exclusively for two hours.

(b) In detailing men for musketry to-morrow, Company Commanders will pay particular attention to backward shots and to men who did not fire on the previous occasion this range was allotted to the Battalion. Company Commanders will arrange direct with the Quartermaster, Transport Officer and Signal Officer for employed men to attend. Men employed at Battalion Headquarters will be detailed by the Adjutant.

(c) Each company will provide its own markers.

(d) The Band will fire as a separate detail with "B" Company.

(e) Practices to be fired will be decided upon by Company Commanders previous to taking their Companies to the range.

(f) Men not firing on the Brigade Range will carry out ordinary training on any ground available and not already allotted.

3. Training programmes will be amended in accordance with the above.

4. 1 Lewis Gun Section per Company will parade at 8.30a.m. under Sergt. Benjamin in accordance with Battalion Training Circular No. 2.

5. Scouts & Snipers will parade under Lieut. G. B. Coldham.

6. There will be no battalion ceremonial parade and march past to-morrow, but companies will do at least 15 minutes ceremonial drill and handling of arms under their respective Company Commanders.

B. H. Hunter

Captain,
Adjutant,
1/5th Bn. L. N. Lancashire Regiment.

Issued at 6 p.m. 24/2/18, copies to:-

No.		No.	
1.	Bde. H.Q.	6.	Commanding Officer.
2.	O.C. "A" Coy.	7.	Sniping Officer.
3.	O.C. "B" Coy.	8.	Lewis Gun Sergeant.
4.	O.C. "C" Coy.	9.	War Diary.
5.	O.C. "D" Coy.	10.	War Diary.

ALLOTMENT OF TRAINING GROUNDS FOR MONDAY, 25th Feb. 1918.

Coy.	Brigade Range T. 15. a.	100xRange at T. 10. d. 8. 2.	100x Range at N. 28. d. 2. 2.	Bullet & Bayonet Course T. 17. a. 5. 9.	Battalion Parade Ground.
A.	8. 30a.m. - 10. 30am.	-	-	10. 30a.m. - 11. 30a.m.	11. 30a.m. - 12. 30p.m.
B.	10. 30a.m. - 12. 30p.m.	10. 30a.m. - 12. 30p.m. For those not on Bde. Range.	-	-	9a.m. - 10. 30a.m.
C.	12. 30p.m. - 2. 30p.m.	-	-	-	11. 30a.m. - 12. 30p.m.
D.	2. 30p.m. - 4. 30p.m.	Two hours work on any of these Training Grounds. Ground at T. 11. c. 6. 3 is also available.			
Scouts & Snipers.	-	9a.m. - 10. 30a.m.	-	10. 30a.m. - 11. 30a.m.	
	11. 30a.m. - 1 p.m. any ground suitable, at the discretion of Lieut. Coldham.				
Lewis Gun Sctns.	-	-	9a.m. - 1 p.m.	-	-

Copy No.......9

BATTALION ORDER NO. 2.

1.(a) The Corps Commander will present Medal Ribands to those recipients of immediate rewards who have not yet been presented with them. The names of these are:-

CAPTAIN CAMERON A.
CAPTAIN HEIN C.G.
2nd LIEUT. MITCHELL N.C.

242672, Sergt. Smith J.S.
242562, Sergt. Foster P.
242503, Sergt. Grimshaw A.
29741, A/Sgt. Glover W.
243368, Corpl. Wardle W.
13989, Corpl. Hodgson J.
243476, A/Cpl. Hamer W.
243312, L.Cpl. Berry J.
243172, L.Cpl. Cummins L.
242864, L.Cpl. Coward A.
244939, Pte. Marsden C.
242467, Pte. Stevens J.
244772, Pte. Dean F.
242879, Pte. Brabin R.

(b) The presentation will take place on the Parade ground of the 2/5th Bn. King's Own (R.L.) Regt. N.35.b.5.2. at 3 p.m. 27th February, 1918.

2.(a) Companies will rendezvous at the Road junction at T.5.d.35.85 at 2 p.m. on Wednesday 27th inst., in the following order:-
"A", "B", "C", "D".

(b) Companies will parade 130 N.C.Os. & men per Company. All Officers will parade.

3. Recipients will march to the parade ground at the head of the battalion and will report to the Adjutant immediately on arrival.

4. The following programme will be adopted:-
(a) When the Corps Commander is seen approaching the Brigade will be ordered to "Slope Arms".
(b) On arrival of the Corps Commander ~~at 'A'~~ the Brigade Commander will give the order "General Salute"- "Present Arms" and the Brigade massed bands will play the General Salute.
(c) The Brigade will then be ordered to "Slope Arms" and "Order Arms".
(d) The Corps Commander will then probably inspect the Brigade.
(e) The Presentation will commence after the inspection.
(f) After completion of the presentation the Corps Commander will take up his position at the saluting base.
The battalion will then march past with fixed bayonets in column of route.
(g) After the march past the battalion will continue its march direct to billets.

5. Dress. (a) Dismounted Officers (including Coy. Comdrs.) Regulation Gloves, Sam Browne Belts, Puttees.
(b) Mounted Officers will wear Field Boots or leggings and spurs.
(c) Sticks will not be carried.
(d) Other Ranks. Drill Order (i.e. Rifles, belt and sidearms only, steel helmets will not be worn).
Recipients. Officers as laid down in (a),(b),(c).
Other Ranks Belt and sidearms only.

6. Band. The Band will play the battalion to the parade ground, on arrival there it will be massed with the band of the 2/5th Bn. King's Own (R.L.) Regt. under the direction of Sergt. Cowburn.

7. A rehearsal of the above will take place to-morrow 26th inst., at 3.30p.m. Companies will rendezvous at 2.30p.m. at the road junction at T.5.d.35.85. The remainder of the above programme will be unchanged.

8. Particular attention is to be paid to the "turnout" for both the rehearsal and the actual parade. Men are to have their hair cut, belts to be tight and caps worn properly. Buttons and Badges to be thoroughly clean.

B. A. Hamer
Captain,
Adjutant,
1/5th Bn.L. N. Lancashire Regiment.

25/2/18.

Copies to:-

No. 1. O.C. "A" Coy.
2. O.C. "B" Coy.
3. O.C. "C" Coy.
4. O.C. "D" Coy.
5. O.C. H.Q. Coy.
No.6. R. S. M.
7. Signal Officer.
8. Commanding Officer.
9. War Diary.
10. File.

Copy No. 9.

BATTALION TRAINING ORDER NO. 8.

1. Training Programmes for to-morrow Wednesday 27th inst., are cancelled and the following substituted.

2. Companies will parade on the ground at T.10. central at 9.30 a.m. for Ceremonial Drill under the Commanding Officer.

3. (a) The Battalion will be drawn up in Mass facing South. There will be about 10 minutes Arms Drill, after which the battalion will March past in Column of Platoons.
(b) On reaching the AUCHY AU BOIS - ST HILAIRE Road Companies will form fours, right, lead on about 50 x and then wheel to the right and form up again in mass in their original positions. They will then march past again in Column of Platoons, after which they will proceed direct to their billets. The remainder of the morning will be spent in getting ready for the Ceremonial Parade and presentation of Medal Ribands by the Corps Commander in the afternoon.

4. One marker per Company will report to the Regimental Sergeant Major at T.10. central at 9.15a.m.

5. The band will parade and play the battalion past.

6. The afternoon programme will be carried out in accordance with Battalion Order No. 9, issued to all concerned yesterday the 25th inst.

7. Recipients will not wear their Medal Ribands for the Corps Commander's parade.

R. H. Hanson

Captain,
Adjutant,
1/5th Bn. L. N. Lancashire Regiment.

Issued at 7.30p.m. 26/2/18. Copies to:-

No.1. Bde. H.Q.
2. O.C. "A" Coy.
3. O.C. "B" Coy.
4. O.C. "C" Coy.
5. O.C. "D" Coy.
6. Sniping Officer.
7. R. S. M.
8. Lewis Gun Sergeant.
9. War Diary.
10. File.

Copy No. 9

BATTALION TRAINING ORDER NO. 5.

1. Training grounds for to-morrow, 23rd inst., are allotted to Companies in accordance with the attached table.

2. The 100^{x} range at N.28.d.2.2. is allotted solely for the use of Lewis Gunners under Sergt. Benjamin, vide Battalion Training Circular No.2.

3. Scouts & Snipers will parade under Lieut. G. B. Coldham. They will rejoin their respective Companies on the Battalion Parade Ground at 12.30p.m.

4. "A" & "B" Companies will carry out training in accordance with their respective programmes. "C" & "D" Companies will carry out training as laid down in their respective programmes of work for the 21st inst.

5. (a) All Companies will parade on the Battalion Parade Ground at 12.30 p.m. for 10 minutes arms drill under the Commanding Officer, after which they will march past.
   (b) One marker per Company will report to the Regimental Sergeant Major on the Battalion Parade Ground at 12-15p.m.

6. (a) The band will be on the Battalion Parade Ground at 12 noon and will play until 12-30p.m., when it will play the battalion past.
   (b) As soon as the last platoon of "D" Company is clear of the saluting base the Battalion will halt. The band will then proceed to take up its position in the Centre of the Column, between "B" & "C" Companies and play the Battalion back to billets.

7. After passing the cross-roads at T.11.a.2.2. Companies will proceed direct to private parade grounds and dismiss.

Capt. & Adjt.,
1/5th Bn. L. N. Lancashire Regiment.

Issued at 6.30p.m. 22/2/18 to:-

Copy No. 1. 170th Bde.
2. O.C. "A" Coy.
3. O.C. "B" Coy.
4. O.C. "C" Coy.
5. O.C. "D" Coy.
6. Commanding Officer.
7. Sniping Officer.
8. Lewis Gun Sergeant.
9. War Diary.
10. File.

ALLOTMENT OF TRAINING GROUNDS FOR SATURDAY 22/2/18.

Coy.	100^{x} Range T.10.d.2.2.	100^{x} Range N.20.d.2.2.	Bullet & Bayonet Course.	Ground at T.10.c.8.3.	Battalion Parade Ground.
A.	11.45 a.m. - 12.30p.m.	-	-	9 a.m. - 11.45a.m.	12.30p.m. - 1 p.m.
B.	-	-	11.15 a.m.- 12.30p.m.	-	9.30a.m.- 11.15a.m. 12.30p.m. - 1 p.m.
C.	-	-	9.30a.m. - 11.15a.m.	-	11.15a.m. - 1 p.m.
D.	9a.m. - 11.45a.m.	-	-	11.45a.m. - 12.30p.m.	12.30p.m. - 1 p.m.
1 L.G. Sectn. per Coy.	-	9 a.m. - 1 p.m.	-	-	-
Scouts & Snipers.	-	-	9a.m.- 9.30a.m.	-	12.30p.m.- 1 p.m.

Between 9.30a.m. and 12.30p.m. Scouts & Snipers may use any ground suitable for their training at the discretion of Lieut. Coldham.

Copy No. 10

BATTALION OPERATION ORDER No. [illegible]

1. The 1/5th Bn. L. [illegible] Lancashire Regt. will move to the PONT DE NIEPPE area on [illegible]th February and the 1st March, 191[illegible], in accordance with the attached March Table.

2. On arrival at PONT DE NIEPPE the Battalion will be called upon to supply Working Parties of a minimum strength of [illegible] Other Ranks for work on the [illegible] Line. Details of work will be issued later.

3. (a) The Battalion will move by lorry on the 1st March.
   (b) Transport will move by march route on [illegible]th February and 1st March. Transport of the [illegible]th L. N. L. Regt. and [illegible]th L. N. L. Regt. will be brigaded and come under the orders of Capt. [illegible] Osborne, Brigade Transport Officer, for the march to PONT DE NIEPPE.

4. The following distances will be maintained on the march:-

Between Battalions.	...	600 yds.
Between Coys.	...	100 yds.
Between Battn. and its transport.	...	100 yds.
Between transport of Battns.	...	400 yds.
Between every 6 transport vehicles.	...	25 yds.

5. All parade grounds, training grounds, Billets, Stables and Horse Standings will be left in a scrupulously clean condition. Receipts to this effect will be obtained in triplicate, two copies of which will be forwarded to Battalion Headquarters by 10 a.m. on the 2nd March.

6. The Battalion Signal Officer will detail two cyclist orderlies to report at Battalion Headquarters immediately on arrival at PONT DE NIEPPE. These orderlies will be required for duty at Brigade Headquarters until the 2nd March. Haversack rations will be taken to last them until Midday 2nd March.

7. Duties will be provided by Companies as follows:-

"A" Coy.	[illegible] O.R.	Traffic Control at [illegible]VILLE.
"B" Coy.	1 N.C.O. & [illegible] O.R.	-----------do-----------
"C" Coy.	[illegible] O.R.	Conservancy Duties, [illegible]VILLE.
"D" Coy.	1 N.C.O. & [illegible] O.R.	-----------do-----------

As far as possible unfit men should be selected for the above duties.
These details will report to Brigade Headquarters at [illegible] a.m. on the [illegible]th inst., and will be rationed up to March 2nd inclusive. They will be conveyed to the New Area by lorry. The names of those detailed will be forwarded to this Office by [illegible] a.m. on the [illegible]th inst.

8. (a) A Billeting Party, consisting of Lieut. [illegible] Faulkner, the 4 C.Q.M.S. and 1 N.C.O. from Battalion Headquarters, will report to the Staff Captain or his representative at Brigade Headquarters at [illegible] a.m. [illegible]th inst.
   (b) They will proceed by lorry and take over billets from Units of the 171st Infantry Brigade.
   (c) This party will not take bicycles.
   (d) The above party will meet the Battalion at the debussing point at PONT DE NIEPPE on the 1st March, and guide Companies to their respective billets.

9. Billeting parties from the 171st Infantry Brigade will take over the billets in this area to-morrow, [illegible]th inst. They will be accommodated by their opposite numbers in the Battalion. Every facility and assistance is to be rendered to these parties.

10. (a) All Area Stores, Training Material, etc. etc., with the exception of the Musketry Training Material already returned and the brooms issued by the Area Commandant, will be handed over by Companies to incoming Companies. Receipts will be obtained in triplicate and two copies forwarded to Battalion Headquarters by 10 a.m. on the 2nd March.
   (b) Brooms will be returned to the Quartermaster by 1 p.m. to-morrow [illegible]th inst., who will then hand them over to the Area Commandant, [illegible], and obtain receipt for same.

11. 3 Lorries are at the disposal of this Battalion for moving Stores, etc. The Quartermaster will detail a guide for these lorries to report at Brigade Headquarters at 6-45 a.m. on 1st March.

12. (a) All Officers Kits, Company Stores, etc., and 1 Blanket per man will be collected and stacked in the yard of the Quartermaster's Stores by [illegible] a.m. on the 1st March.
<u>Note</u> - as much kit, etc., as possible is to be sent to the Quartermaster's Stores on the night of the 28th inst.
(b) The two additional Lewis Guns will be handed over to the Quartermaster and conveyed by lorry.
(c) Companies will take their Camp Kettles on their respective lorries, these will not be handed over to the Quartermaster for carriage.
(d) All ranks will carry haversack rations for their midday meal on the 1st March.

13. O.C. 170th L.T.M.B. will hand over 1 handcart to the Quartermaster by 12 noon to-morrow, 28th inst., for conveyance to the new area. This handcart will be drawn by O.C. 170th L.T.M.B. the day following arrival at PONT DE NIEPPE.

[signature]

Capt. & Adjt.,
1/5th Bn. L. N. Lancashire Regt.

Issued at 4-30 p.m. 27/2/1[illegible]. Copies to:-

1. H.Q, 170th Bde. 7. Transport Officer.
2. O.C. "A" Coy. 8. L.G. Sergeant.
3. O.C. "B" Coy. 9. Commanding Officer.
4. O.C. "C" Coy. 10. War Diary.
5. O.C. "D" Coy. 11. File.
6. Quartermaster. 12. Spare.

MARCH TABLE TO ACCOMPANY BATTALION OPERATION ORDER NO. 4.

Serial No.	Date.	Unit.	Starting Pt.	Time passing Starting Pt.	Destination.	Route.
1.	[illegible]/3/18.	Tpt. of 1/5 L.[illegible]	[illegible]	9-6 a.m.	HAVERSKERQUE.	LILLERS-BUSNES - ST.VENANT.
2.	1/3/18.	1/5 L.[illegible].L. (less Tpt.)	Embus at T.[illegible].4.	Embus at [illegible]-20 a.m.	PONT DE NIEPPE.	LILLERS - ST.VENANT - X.25.c.Ad.
3.	1/3/18.	H.Q.Coy.	[illegible]	-[illegible] a.m.	---do--	---do---
		"A" Coy.	-----do----	-[illegible] a.m.	--do--	---do---
		"B" Coy.	-----do----	-[illegible] a.m.	--do--	---do---
		"C" Coy.	-----do----	-[illegible] a.m.	--do--	---do---
		"D" Coy.	-----do----	-[illegible] a.m.	--do--	---do---
4.	1/3/18.	Tpt. of 1/5 L.N.L.	[illegible]	[illegible] a.m.	--do--	MERVILLE-ESTAIRES-CROIX DU BAC.

Copy No......9.

BATTALION TRAINING ORDER NO.7.

1. Training Grounds and rifle ranges are allotted to Companies to-morrow in accordance with the attached table.

2. (a) Companies will parade on the Battalion Parade Ground at 10.30a.m. for Ceremonial Drill under the Commanding Officer.
(b) Each Company will detail one marker to report to the Regimental Sergeant Major on the Battalion Parade Ground at 10.15a.m.

3. One Lewis Gun Section per company will parade at 8.30a.m. under Sergt. Benjamin, in accordance with Battalion Training Circular No.2.

4. Scouts and Snipers will parade with their respective companies.

5. The Band will be on the Battalion Parade Ground at 10.15 a.m. They will play until 10.30a.m., after which they will play the battalion past.

6. Rehearsal for the Ceremonial Parade for the presentation of Medal Ribands by the Corps Commander will take place in the afternoon, in accordance with Battalion Order No.2 issued to companies to-day.

7. There will be no training after 11a.m. to-morrow. The time between 11a.m. and 1 p.m. will be entirely devoted to preparation and cleaning up for the afternoon parade.

A. H. Hawkes

Captain,
Adjutant,
1/5th Bn. L. N. Lancashire Regiment.

Issued at 7.30p.m. 25/2/18. Copies to:-

No. 1. Bde. H. Q.
2. O.C. "A" Coy.
3. O.C. "B" Coy.
4. O.C. "C" Coy.
5. O.C. "D" Coy.
6. Sniping Officer.
7. R. S. M.
8. Lewis Gun Sergeant.
9. War Diary.
10. File.

ALLOTMENT OF TRAINING GROUNDS FOR TUESDAY, 26th FEBRUARY, 1918.

Coy.	100' Range at T.10.d.[illegible].9.	Bullet & Bayonet Course.	Ground at T.11.c.[illegible].	Battalion Parade Ground.
A.	-	10a.m.-10.30a.m.	9a.m. - 10a.m.	10.30a.m.- 11 a.m.
B.	-	9a.m. - 9.30a.m.	9.30a.m. - 10.30a.m.	10.30a.m.- 11a.m.
C.	-	9.30a.m.-10a.m.	-	10a.m. - 11a.m.
D.	9a.m. - 10a.m.	-	-	10a.m. - 11a.m.
Lewis Gun Sctn.	10a.m. -11a.m.	-	-	-

Confidential

Headquarters
57th Division
—"—

1/5TH
LOYAL NORTH
LANCS. REGIMENT.
No. C. 152
Date 5-4-18

Forward War Diary of the Unit under my command, period 1/3/18 to 31/3/18.

[signature]

Lieut. Col.
Commdg. 1/5 L. N. Lancashire Regt.

4.4.18.

Confidential.

War Diary

of

1/5th Battalion Royal North Lancashire Regiment

Period 1st March 1918 to 31st March 1918.

Volume 14.

Vol 32

Army Form C. 2118.

Instructions regarding War Diaries and Intelligence Summaries are contained in F. S. Regs., Par. II. and the Staff Manual respectively. Title pages will be prepared in manuscript.

WAR DIARY
or
~~INTELLIGENCE~~ SUMMARY.
(Erase heading not required.)

Place	Date 1918	Hour	Summary of Events and Information	Remarks and references to Appendices
COTTES	Mar. 1		Conveyed by bus to PONT DE NIEPPE	
PONT DE NIEPPE	" 2		BILLETS. 200 men working parties, remainder cleaning billets &	
"	" 3		" ~~300~~ " SUNDAY " " ~~Training~~	
"	4		" 300 men Working Parties, remainder Training	
"	5		" 300 " " "	
"	6		" 300 " " "	
"	7		" 300 " " "	
"	8		" 300 " " "	
"	9		" 300 " " "	
"	10		" SUNDAY	
"	11		" 300 men Working Parties remainder Training	
"	12		" 300 " " "	
"	13		" 300 " " "	
"	14		" 300 " " "	
"	15		" 300 " "	
"	16		" 300 " "	

A6945 Wt. W11422/M1160 350,000 12/16 D. D. & L. Forms/C./2118/14.

Instructions regarding War Diaries and Intelligence Summaries are contained in F. S. Regs., Par. II. and the Staff Manual respectively. Title pages will be prepared in manuscript.

WAR DIARY
or
~~INTELLIGENCE SUMMARY.~~
(Erase heading not required.)

Army Form C. 2118.

Place	Date 1918	Hour	Summary of Events and Information	Remarks and references to Appendices
PONT DE NIEPPE	Mar 17		BILLETS SUNDAY	[illegible]
"	18		300 men Working Parties remainder Training	[illegible]
			Advance Parties proceeded to Right Subsector of FLEURBAIX Section	[illegible]
"	19		Relieved 6th Bn The BUFFS in the do do	
			Relief completed 2.25 am remainder of night very quiet	[illegible]
Right Subsection FLEURBAIX	20		TRENCHES Slight shelling of trenches during day. During night Enemy Artillery active on few localities in trenches. Small party of about 12 men attempted to raid RICHARD POST N 6 a 5505 Enemy driven off with the assistance of one of our patrols which reinforced the garrison of RICHARD POST, (our casualties - 2 wounded). The other patrol on the left front had nothing of interest to report.	[illegible]
"	21		TRENCHES Enemy Artillery continuously active from 4.30 am to 9 am on back areas with HE + gas. During rest of day intermittent shelling of back areas + trenches. Quiet during night. 3 Patrols out + nothing seen or heard of enemy	[illegible]

A6945 Wt. W11422/M1160 350,000 12/16 D. D. & L. Forms/C./2118/14.

Army Form C. 2118.

Instructions regarding War Diaries and Intelligence Summaries are contained in F. S. Regs., Par. II. and the Staff Manual respectively. Title pages will be prepared in manuscript.

WAR DIARY
or
~~INTELLIGENCE SUMMARY.~~

(Erase heading not required.)

Place	Date 1918	Hour	Summary of Events and Information	Remarks and references to Appendices
FLEURBAIX (Right Sub-Sector)	Mar 22		Trenches. Enemy Artillery active on left half of sector. At night 2 patrols out until 5 am. Nothing seen or heard of enemy. At 5.15 am Enemy carried out a silent raid on RICHARD POST. Estimated strength of enemy 25-30 men in 2 bombing parties with covering party in No Man's Land. After hand to hand fighting Enemy driven off, taking his casualties with him. Our casualties 1 killed + 3 wounded.	[illegible initials]
	23		Trenches. Enemy Artillery again fairly active during day. At night 2 patrols out reporting no signs of enemy.	[illegible initials]
	24		Trenches. At 4.30 am Artillery active on left Company Headquarters, and in the afternoon on the whole of the left half of the sector. At night 3 patrols out but no signs of enemy beyond seeing 4 men in enemy line for five minutes.	[illegible initials]
	25		Trenches. Quiet day + night. During night 3 patrols out but no signs of enemy.	[illegible initials]

A6945 Wt. W11422/M1160 350,000 12/16 D. D. & L. Forms/C./2118/14.

Instructions regarding War Diaries and Intelligence Summaries are contained in F. S. Regs., Part II. and the Staff Manual respectively. Title pages will be prepared in manuscript.

WAR DIARY

or

~~INTELLIGENCE SUMMARY.~~

(Erase heading not required.)

Army Form C. 2118.

Place	Date 1918	Hour	Summary of Events and Information	Remarks and references to Appendices
FLEURBAIX (Right Sub-Sector)	March 26		Trenches – Quiet day. At night relieved by 7/6th Bn. The King's (Liverpool) Regt.	
SAILLY-SUR-LYS	27		BILLETS – Working parties & reconnaissance of defence points etc.	
"	28		" do do	
"	29		Proceeded to Trenches and relieved the 2nd R. W. Fusiliers in the WEZ MACQUART (CENTRE) SECTOR. Quiet night. At 5 am morning of 30th Enemy patrol approached EILEEN POST & was driven off by rifle fire.	
WEZ MACQUART (CENTRE)	30		TRENCHES. Quiet day & night. At 5.15 am morning of 31st Enemy patrol again appeared in front of EILEEN POST & was driven off by rifle fire.	
	31		TRENCHES – Enemy artillery active throughout day on Trenches. At night relieved by the 10th Bn. The Lincolnshire Regt. Marched to billets at SAILLY.	
SAILLY			BATT. Strength 31st March 1918 – Officers 40, ORs 994	

A5834 Wt. W4973/M687 750,000 8/16 D. D. & L. Ltd. Forms/C.2118/13.

6. <u>(Continued)</u>. Another two Lewis Guns for "AA" defence, in addition to the two referred to above, will shortly be supplied to the battalion, this will give each Company 1 Lewis Gun which will be reserved exclusively for "AA" Defence. Further instructions regarding the Mounting and siting of these Guns will be issued in due course.

R. H. Hawson [signature]

Captain,
Adjutant,
1/5th Bn. L. N. Lancashire Regiment.

Issued at [illegible] p.m. [illegible].

Copies to:-

No. 1. Bde. H.Q.
2. O.C. "A" Coy.
3. O.C. "B" Coy.
4. O.C. "C" Coy.
5. O.C. "D" Coy.
6. Quartermaster.
7. Transport Officer.
8. Commanding Officer.
9. Lewis Gun Sergeant.
10. War Diary.
11. File.
12. Spare.

Copy No. 10

BATTALION TRAINING CIRCULAR NO. [illegible]

1. The following procedure with regard to work and training will be adopted whilst the Battalion is in the POST [illegible] area.

2. The Battalion has been called upon to supply working parties to a strength of [illegible] men daily for work under the supervision of the [illegible] Field Company R.E. These parties are required for wiring, and the construction of new trenches and strong points in the [illegible] Line of defence.

3. When Companies are detailed for work they will parade complete up to a total strength of [illegible] all ranks. Company and platoon commanders will parade with their respective Companies and platoons. All work set will be task work, parties may return to billets as soon as their respective tasks are completed to the satisfaction of the Supervising Officer R.E. or his representative.

4. Dress for all working parties will be F.S., Steel Helmets, Box Respirators, Rifle and one Bandolier S.A.A. On cold days leather jerkins may be worn.

5. The present strength of Companies permits one Company to be available one day in every four for training. Training will be carried out under the supervision of Company Commanders. A programme shewing the nature and place of training will be rendered to the Orderly Room on the day before each Company is due for training. Companies will carry out training in turn commencing with "A" Company on Monday [illegible]th March.

6. (a) Lewis Gun Training will be carried out under Sergt. Benjamin. Each Company will provide a class of [illegible] men, untrained in the use and handling of Lewis Guns, for this purpose daily.
The same men will attend each day, and by this means it will be possible to bring all Lewis Gun Sections up to strength and to maintain a reserve of trained men to take their places in the event of casualties. Men detailed for this class will report to Sergt. Benjamin at [illegible] a.m. daily, commencing to-morrow Monday, [illegible]th March.
Names of men selected will be forwarded to this Office by [illegible] a.m. to-morrow (Monday).
(b) In addition to the above the following N.C.Os. will be required as assistant instructors during the time the Battalion is in this area.

No. [illegible], Cpl. Worsley. "A" Coy.
No. [illegible], Cpl. Cobham. "[illegible]" Coy.
No. [illegible], Cpl. [illegible] "D" Coy.

(c) Two Lewis Guns will be mounted day and night for "AA" Defence at the following places.

[illegible]
[illegible]

Teams for manning these guns will be supplied as follows:-

1 N.C.O. and [illegible] men in each Company will be trained exclusively in "AA" duties.
These will be found by withdrawing 1 N.C.O. or man from each of the [illegible] existing Lewis Gun Sections in each Company, who will be replaced by one of the men to be trained as laid down in sub-para (a) above.
The additional Lewis Gun Sections thus formed will become part of their respective Company Headquarters and will be shewn as such on all states, returns, &c.
At present as the Battalion has only been supplied with two additional Lewis Guns for "AA" duties, "A" and "B" Companies and "C" and "D" Companies will alternately provide the necessary men for manning these two guns.
Arrangements for this will be made direct with Companies by the Lewis Gun Sergeant.

Copy No...9.....

BATTALION OPERATION ORDER NO. 6.

Ref. Sheet. 36 N.W. 36 A. 1:40,000.
HAZEBROUCK. 5.a. 1:100,000.

---

1. The following will be the action of the Battalion whilst in the PONT de NIEPPE Area in the event of the 170th Infantry Brigade being called upon to reinforce certain parts of the XV Corps front.

2. (a) On receipt of orders from 170th Infantry Brigade the battalion will move at once to NOUVEAU MONDE (G.27.c.36.N.W.) via CROIX du BAC, where it will be held in immediate readiness to move.
   (b) Transport will accompany the battalion.
   (c) The unexpended portion of the day's ration will be carried by all ranks.

3. Accomodation in NOUVEAU MONDE will be as follows:-
   G.27.c.5.2. - G.27.d.2.9.
   G.27.d.2.9. - G.34.b.7.0.
   Transport Lines will be North of the River LYS at G.10.b.
   All billeting will be very crowded owing to the restricted area.

4. Dress. Battle Order. Packs & Blankets will be handed in to the Quartermaster and stored in the vacated billets.

5. The following reconnaissances will be made in cases where Officers and N.C.Os. are not already well acquainted with the areas specified:-
   (i) All roads, approaches, and defences works in the 19th Division Area as far East as the line LAVENTIE - FLEURBAIX - L'ARMEE including the works recently constructed on the left bank of the River LYS and the NOUVEAU MONDE - BAC ST MAUR bridgeheads.
   (ii) The roads, approaches and works in the Northern part of the PORTUGUESE CORPS area as far East as the defences of the line from Road junction R.24.a.5.9. (BOUT DELVILLE Sheet 36.A.) inclusive - RIEZ BAILLEUL (5.I.[illegible]) CARTERS POST (5.I.9.5.) - LE DRUMEZ (J.04.55) - MUDDY LANE (5.J.01.60) COCKSAY HOUSE (J.15) inclusive. All references to HAZEBROUCK. 5 a. 1:100,000.

6. Application has been made to Headquarters 170th Infantry Brigade for the necessary transport to carry out these reconnaissances, details of which will be communicated to companies as soon as possible. In the meantime the roads and approaches to the L'ARMEE - FLEURBAIX line will be proceeded with.

B. H. Hamilton
Captain,
Adjutant,
1/5th Bn. L. N. Lancashire Regiment.

Issued at 6 p.m. 3/3/18. Copies to:-

No. 1. Bde. H.Q.
2. O.C. "A" Company.
3. O.C. "B" Company.
4. O.C. "C" Company.
5. O.C. "D" Company.
6. Quartermaster.
7. Transport Officer.
8. Commanding Officer.
9. War Diary.
10. File.
11. Spare.

Copy No.....9.....

BATTALION OPERATION ORDER NO.6.

Ref. Sheet. 36 N.W. 36A. 1:40,000.
HAZEBROUCK. 5a. 1:100,000.

---

1. On receiving the order to move Companies and Transport will act in accordance with Battalion Operation Order No.5 d/d. 3/3/18.

2. (a) Companies will parade at a time to be notified later as follows:- "A","B" and "C" Companies on the PONT de NIEPPE - LE BISET Road. The head of "A" Company to be at the Cross Roads at B.23.d.95.35. "D" Company will parade on the ground in front of the Church at B.23.b.10.25 and will follow in rear of "C" Company after the latter Company has passed the Cross Roads.
(b) Transport will parade at the Transport Lines and follow in rear of "D" Company.

3. 100^x distance will be maintained between Companies and between Transport and the rear of "D" Company on the march. There will also be a distance of 100^x between every six vehicles.

4. Packs, Greatcoats and Blankets will be labelled by Companies and handed in to the Quartermaster's Stores. Each Company will detail two men unfit for marching, to remain in charge of these stores. Pending further orders Officers kits will also be stored at the Quartermaster's Stores.

5. (a) Lieut. & Quartermaster R. P. Trees assisted by R.Q.M.S. Herbert will remain behind and be in charge of the Stores.
(b) All ranks remaining in PONT de NIEPPE will be in possession of 3 days rations.

6. Particular attention is directed to Paras. 2 and 4 of Battalion Operation Order No.5. All ranks will parade with Waterbottles filled.

7. The Band will parade with their instruments and will play on the March.

8. Officers Commanding Companies will ensure that every man is in possession of his full complement of ammunition (120 rounds).

B. H. Harrison
Captain,
Adjutant,
1/5th Bn. L. N. Lancashire Regiment.

Issued at 7-45p.m. 10/3/18.

Copies to:-

No1. Bde. H.Q.
2. O.C. "A" Company.
3. O.C. "B" Company.
4. O.C. "C" Company.
5. O.C. "D" Company.
6. Quartermaster.
7. Transport Officer.
8. Commanding Officer.
9. War Diary.
10. File.
11. Lt. & Q.M. Trees.
12. R. S. M.

SECRET. Copy No.....11

BATTALION INSTRUCTIONS NO. 1.

Issued in Conjunction with Battalion Operation Orders, Nos. 5 & 6.

::::::::::::::::::::::::::

1. Para. 8a of Battalion Operation Order No. 6 is cancelled and the following substituted:-
Companies will parade at a time to be notified later on the PONT DE NIEPPE - L'EPINETTE ROAD ready to march or embus, according to circumstances, with the head of the Column 50^x short of the Railway Crossing at B.28.b.3.8.
Companies will parade in the following order:- "A", "B", "C", "D".
Personnel detailed to proceed with Battalion Headquarters will march immediately in front of "A" Company.

2.(a) 33% of the Personnel will be left out of the line in accordance with Sec. XXX S.S.135.
The following Officers will accompany the Battalion:-

Battalion Headquarters.	Commanding Officer, Adjutant, Intelligence Officer, Signalling Officer, Medical Officer. (Other Ranks personnel of Battalion Headquarters to proceed with the Battalion will be detailed by the Adjutant.)
"A" Company.	Captain A. Johnson, 2nd Lieut. D.H.Provan, M.C. 2nd Lieut. N. Entwisle, 2nd Lieut. R.J. Johnston.
"B" Company.	Captain C.G.Hein, M.C., 2nd Lieut. W.T. Russell, 2nd Lieut. F.A. Wyles, 2nd Lieut. P. Gross.
"C" Company.	Captain P. Twaddle, 2nd Lieut. E.A. Hollinrake, M.C., 2nd Lieut. J. Collier, 2nd Lieut. G. Bell.
"D" Company.	Lieut. C. B. Coldham, Lieut. J.G. Maclagan, 2nd Lieut. J. E. Emery, 2nd Lieut. J. M. Arkieson.

All other Officers will proceed to the Transport Lines at NOUVEAU MONDE, with the following Other Ranks:-

A/C.S.M. Jones	"A" Coy.	
C.S.M. Barton.	"D" Coy.	
C.S.M. Hill	"D" Coy.	
L.Cpl.Heywood.	"B" Coy.	(Gas N.C.O.)
Sergt.Whitehead.	"A" Coy.	(Bombing Instructor).
Sergt.Benjamin.	"A" Coy.	(Lewis Gun Instructor).
Corpl. Hamer	"B" Coy.	----------do----------
Sergt. Leavis	"A" Coy.	Musketry Instructor.
L.Cpl. Hall	"D" Coy.	
L.Cpl. Brown	"A" Coy.	

and all Battalion Headquarters Personnel Not detailed to proceed to the line with the Battalion (Quartermaster's Dept., Pioneers, Police, etc.)

(b) Each Company will also detail 1 Sergeant, 1 Corpl., 1 Lance Corpl. & 3 Runners, and each Platoon 1 Rifle Bomber, 1 Scout & 2 Lewis Gunners to remain at the Transport Lines, making a total of 22 per Company, in addition to those named above.
The number of Signallers to be left out of the line will be arranged by the Signal Officer according to circumstances.

(c) 50% of the personnel at the Transport Lines will eventually be sent to the Divisional Wing, Corps Reinforcement Camp, at LINGHEM.

3. Transport. On arrival in the new area only Water Carts, Tool Carts and Mess Cart will accompany the Battalion; the remainder of the vehicles will proceed to the Transport Lines. Arrangements will be made for the water carts to be filled again immediately they are emptied. The tools from the tool limbers will be dumped near Battalion Headquarters, and the limbers returned to the Transport Lines immediately on arrival at NOUVEAU MONDE.

4. Lewis Guns. The 4 'AA' Lewis Guns will be issued to Companies on receipt of the orders to move, and will be carried in accordance with instructions contained in this Office No. A.689, d.6/3/18.

5. Cooking will be carried out under Company arrangements. The Quartermaster will arrange to supply Companies with such Camp Kettles, etc., as they require at once.

6. All public monies, etc., in possession of Companies will be handed over to Captain W. H. Satterthwaite forthwith.

R. H. Hanson
Capt. & Adjt.,
1/5th Bn. L. N. Lancashire Regiment.

Issued at 8-30 p.m. 21/3/18.   Copies to:-

1. H.Q. 170th Bde.
2. O.C. "A" Coy.
3. O.C. "B" Coy.
4. O.C. "C" Coy.
5. O.C. "D" Coy.
6. Quartermaster.
7. Commanding Officer.
8. Transport Officer.
9. R. S. M.
10. File.
11. War Diary.
12. Lt. & Q.M. R. F. Trees.

SECRET.

Copy No......

BATTALION OPERATION ORDER NO.7.

Ref Map. CROIX du BAC. 1:20,000.

1. The Battalion will relieve the 6th Bn. "The Buffs" on a date to be notified later (probably the 16th/17th March) in the line FLEURBAIX SECTION.

2. The following will be the dispositions of Companies on completion of relief:-

LINE.	Right.	"A" Coy.	H.Q's. at H.36.c.50.20.
	Left.	"D" Coy.	H.Q's. at CULVERT FARM I.25.c.3.3. and at H.36 Central.
SUPPORT.	Right.	"C" Coy.	H.Q's. at ELBOW FARM H.29.c.12.18.
	Left.	"B" Coy.	H.Q's. at COMMAND POST H.29.b.3.1.

Battalion Headquarters is at WYE FARM H.36.a.2.1.
Regimental Aid Post is at the TEMPLE H.36.a.6.0.
Quartermaster's Stores and Transport Lines are at G.10.b.20.10.

3. Boundaries. Battalion Boundaries are as follows:-
   Right. TINBARN TRAMLINE (inclusive) N.6.c.25.95 - H.28.d.35.00.
   Left. I.31.d.10.95 thence along ditch crossing TUI ROAD to I.31.a.89.80 - junction of CULVERT POST and MOAT FARM AVENUE I.25.c.25.45 - H.30.b.43.21.
   Inter-Company Boundary.
   Front line at H.36.d.75.00 - H.36.d.1.5.
   H.36.c.85.80 - thence N.W. along road to H.29.b.30.10.

4. Advance Parties.
   (a) Advance Parties consisting of 1 Officer and 4 N.C.O's. per Company and Sergt. Whitehead for Bn. H.Q's. Company will report to their opposite numbers of the 6th Bn. "The Buffs" at 3 p.m. on Friday 15th March.
   Representatives of "B" and "C" Companies will report direct at COMMAND POST and ELBOW FARM respectively, and those of "A" and "D" Companies and Bn. H.Q's. at WYE FARM where guides will be provided and conduct them to their respective sectors.
   (b) These parties will proceed in Battle Order and will remain in the line until the Battalion relief takes place.
   (c) They will take the unexpended portion of the day's ration and two days' rations in addition.
   (d) They will take over all Trench Stores - Maps - Aeroplane Photographs &c. and give receipts for same. A.F.B.3045 will be used and a copy will be sent to the Battalion Orderly Room by 10a.m. the day following relief.

5. Order of March. Bn. H.Q., "A", "D", "C" and "B" Companies.

6. Route. PONT de NIEPPE - Cross Roads at B.27.d.2.8 - ERQUINGHEM BRIDGE - RUE du MOULIN - Road junction H.16.c.5.7. - Cross roads H.22.b.90.05 - Cross Roads at SMITH'S VILLA H.29.c.95.90. On arrival at this point "B" and "C" Companies will proceed direct to their respective positions in Support.

7. Distance between Companies and platoons on the March will be as follows:- 500x between companies as far as road junction H.16.c.5.7. after which point 100x will be maintained between platoons.

8. Guides. Guides of the 6th Bn. "The Buffs" at the rate of one for every post in the line and one for every platoon in Support will meet Companies at the cross roads at H.29.c.95.90 and conduct them to their positions in the line.

. . . . . .

9. <u>Lewis Guns.</u> Lewis Guns will be carried by limber as far as cross roads H.29.b.95.90 from which point they will be carried by their respective sections.
Lewis Gun Pans will be taken into the line.
Lewis Gun Limbers will proceed immediately in front of their respective Companies. After being unloaded they will proceed direct to the new Transport Lines at G.10.b.2.1. via ELBOW FARM - FLEURBAIX - BAC ST MAUR and CROIX du BAC.
The Transport Officer will detail a N.C.O. to be in charge of these 4 limbers.

10. <u>Cooking Arrangements.</u> Companies will take Camp Kettles only into the line and support. All Cookers will remain at the Transport Lines. One Water Cart will proceed with "C" Company to ELBOW FARM. This will be filled daily.

11. <u>Transport.</u> The Transport Officer will detail one G.S. Limber per Company to convey Company Stores to the various dumps and one G.S. Limber and the Officers' Mess Cart for Bn. Headquarters. These 6 vehicles will follow 500^x in rear of "B" Company under a N.C.O. detailed by the Transport Officer.
The Transport less the vehicles mentioned above will proceed to G.10.b.2.1. via L'EPINETTE - CROIX du BAC Road.

12. <u>Handing over Billets &c.</u> All billets and Transport Lines are to be handed over in a scrupulously clean and sanitary condition. Receipts to be obtained for this from advanced party of incoming unit and a copy forwarded to the Battalion Orderly Room by 10a.m.on the day following relief.

13. <u>Relief.</u> Relief complete will be reported by using the Code Word "SPADE".

14. ACKNOWLEDGE.

W. A. Satterthwaite

Captain,
for Adjutant,
1/5th Bn. L. N. Lancashire Regiment.

Issued at 8 p.m. 14/3/18. Copies to:-

No. 1. Bde. H.Q.
2. O.C. 6th Bn."The Buffs".
3. O.C. "H.Q." Coy.
4. O.C. "A" Coy.
5. O.C. "B" Coy.
6. O.C. "C" Coy.
7. O.C. "D" Coy.
8. Commanding Officer.
9. Quartermaster.
10. Transport Officer.
11. Signal Officer.
12. Medical Officer.
13. Intelligence Officer.
14. R. S. M.
15. War Diary.
16. File.
17. Spare.
18. Spare.

S E C R E T.   Copy No. 15

BATTALION OPERATION ORDER NO. [illegible].

Ref. Sheet CROIX du BAC.   1:20,000.

1. The Battalion will relieve the 6th Bn. "The Buffs" Regt., in the line of the Right Sub-sector of the FLEURBAIX Section on the night 19th/20th March.

2. Lewis Gun Sections will relieve by day. Lewis Guns and pans will be conveyed by limber as far as Road Junction at H.16.b.05.55. Sections will move from PONT de NIEPPE at 10a.m. and proceed by route laid down in Bn. Operation Order No.7, para 6 - a distance of 250x will be maintained between Companies. 2/Lieut. Taylor ("B" Coy.) will be in charge of this party. Sergt. Benjamin will accompany this party.

3. Dress. Battle Order, Great Coats to be worn.

4. Move. The Battalion less Lewis Gun Sections will move in accordance with instructions contained in Bn. Operation Order No. 7 paras. 5 & 6. Battalion Headquarters will leave PONT de NIEPPE at 6.30p.m. followed by "A","D","C" and "B" Companies.
Distance to be maintained on the March:-500x between Companies, 100x between platoons after passing Road Junction at H.16.b.05.55.

5. Guides will be found by the 6th Bn. "The Buffs" as follows:-
   Bn. Headquarters 1 guide at Road Junction H.29.c.95.90.
   "A" Company - Post Guides at ELBOW FARM.
   "D" Company - " " at Road Junction H.29.c.95.90.
   "C" Company - Platoon Guides ELBOW FARM.
   "B" Company - " " at Road Junction H.29.c.95.90.

6. Blankets. Blankets will be rolled as per instructions received from the Quartermaster, and stacked at the Quartermaster's Stores by 9a.m. Company surplus stores will be handed over to the Quartermaster at 9 a.m.

7. Officers' Kits will be stacked at the Quartermaster's Stores by 11a.m.

8. Rations. Rations ~~xxxx~~ for the 20th inst., will be conveyed on the G.S. Limbers detailed in Bn. Operation Order No. 7, para. 11 and will be loaded by 5 p.m. They will proceed with their respective Companies to Company Dumps.

W H Satterthwaite
Captain,
for Adjutant,
1/5th Bn. L. N. Lancashire Regiment.

Issued at 8.45p.m. 18/3/18.   Copies to:-

No.1. 170th Infy. Bde. H.Q.
2. O.C. 6th Bn. "The Buffs".
3. O.C. "H.Q." Company.
4. O.C. "A" Company.
5. O.C. "B" Company.
6. O.C. "C" Company.
7. O.C. "D" Company.
8. Commanding Officer.
9. Quartermaster.
10. Transport Officer.
11. Signal Officer.
12. Medical Officer.
13. Intelligence Officer.
14. R. S. M.
15. War Diary.
16. File.
17. Spare.
18. Spare.

SECRET. Copy No....15

CORRIGENDA TO BATTALION OPERATION ORDER NO. 8.

1. Para. 2 is amended as follows:-
Only Nos. 1 & 2 of Lewis Gun Sections with their Guns and Pans will relieve by day. The balance of the personnel of Lewis Gun Sections will relieve by night. The remainder of the order will hold good including transportation.

2. Ref. para. 4 line 3 - for 6-30 p.m. read 9-30p.m.

W.H. Satterthwaite
Captain,
for Adjutant,
1/5th Bn. L. N. Lancashire Regiment.

Issued at 11.15p.m. 18/3/18, to all recipients of Battalion Operation Order No. 8.

SECRET. Copy No. 10

1/5th Bn. L. N. Lancashire Regt. ORDER NO. 8.

Reference Sheet 36 N.W. 1/20,000.

1. (a) The battalion will be relieved by "F" Bn. K.L.R. in the trenches to-morrow night, 26/27th March.
(b) The battalion will move to billets in SAILLY at present occupied by "F" Bn. K.L.R. on completion of relief.

2. (a) Advanced parties of "F" Bn. K.L.R. will come into the line to-day and will take over all trench stores, log books, aeroplane photographs, etc. Receipts will be obtained on A.F.W.3405, in triplicate, and 2 copies forwarded to Battalion Headquarters by 12 noon on the day following relief.
(b) All details of work in hand or proposed will also be handed over.

3. (a) Nos. 1 & 2 of L.G. Sections, with their guns, will come into the line to-morrow morning; guides to meet these parties will be at the cross roads H.29.c.95.90 at 6 a.m. to-morrow, and conduct them to their respective posts.
(b) Officers Commanding Companies will arrange for guides to meet the incoming battalion as follows:-
1 guide per platoon for the two Support Companies to be at ELBOW FARM at 9 p.m. to-morrow, 26th inst.
1 guide per post for the two Companies in the line - guides for Right Company at ELBOW FARM at 9 p.m; guides for Left Company at cross roads H.29.c.95.90 at 9 p.m.
All guides will be in possession of a slip of paper with the name or number and location of their respective post or platoon written thereon.

4. Companies will move out of the line independently as soon as they are relieved, a distance of 100^x between platoons will be maintained on the march. The following routes will be used:-
(a) For Companies in Support at ELBOW FARM & COMMAND POST via ELBOW FARM - Road Junction H.21.d.90.40 - Road Junction H.21.d.50.40 - Road Junction H.14.a.75.35.
(b) For Companies in the line. Left Half of Left Company via GREATWOOD AVENUE - Road Junction H.29.c.95.90 - thence as above.
Right Half of Left Company via BAY AVENUE - CITY ROAD - Road Junction H.29.c.95.90 - thence as above.
Right Company via TIN BARN AVENUE - ELBOW FARM - thence as above.
(c) Lieut. T. Hollis will arrange for 1 guide per platoon to meet Companies at Road Junction at H.14.a.75.35 to conduct troops to their respective billets.

5. (a) Lieut. T. Hollis will arrange for one N.C.O. for Battalion Headquarters and the 4 C.Q.M.Sergts. for Companies to take over billets from "F" Bn. K.L.R. to-morrow. Receipts as to cleanliness etc., will be given.
(b) 2nd Lieut. Runciman will proceed to SAILLY by 4 p.m. to-morrow, and will take over Battalion Headquarters and any Defence Schemes, Schemes for Reinforcing, Working Party details, etc.

6. (a) Transport will be provided as follows:-
Battalion Headquarters 1 G.S. Limber.
Mess Cart.
Each Company 1 G.S. Limber.
The Transport Officer will arrange with the Transport Officer of "F" Bn. K.L.R. for these vehicles to be placed at the disposal of the Battalion after the Stores, etc., of "F" Bn. K.L.R. have been brought up and unloaded.
(b) Companies will arrange for Company Stores, Officers kits, etc., to be stacked at dumps as follows:-
"C" & "B" Companies at ELBOW FARM & COMMAND POST respectively by 9 p.m. to-morrow. "A" & "D" Companies at TIN BARN DUMP & GREATWOOD AVENUE DUMP respectively by 9 p.m. to-morrow.

7. (10) All trenches, dugouts, etc., are to be handed over in a scrupulously clean and sanitary condition and receipts obtained in triplicate - 2 copies of which must reach Battalion Headquarters by 12 noon on the day following relief.

8. O.C. "C" Company will detail his "AA" Lewis Gun Section to proceed to G.11.b.5.4. by 4 p.m. to-morrow to take over a position in the Corps "AA" Defences from "F" Bn.K.L.R.

9. Commencing on the 27th March the Battalion will probably be called upon to find two Companies daily for work under the C.R.E. details of this work will be issued later.

10. 1 N.C.O. & 12 men with half a G.S. Limber will report to the Area Commandant, SAILLY, at 9 a.m. daily for Sanitary Work. This party will be found by the Company for duty.

11. Transport Lines and Quartermaster's Stores will not be exchanged.

12. (a) The Command of the Sector will pass to O.C. "F" Bn.K.L.R. on completion of relief.
(b) Companies will notify completion of relief to Battalion Headquarters, by runner, using the Code Word "BATH."

13. ACKNOWLEDGE.

R. H. Hamilton

Capt. & Adjt.,
1/5th Bn. L. N. Lancashire Regiment.

Issued at 6 p.m. 25/3/18.

Copies as under:-

1. H.Q. 170th Infy. Bde.
2. O.C. "F" Bn.K.L.R.
3. O.C."A" Company.
4. O.C."B" Company.
5. O.C."C" Company.
6. O.C."D" Company.
7. Quartermaster.
8. Transport Officer.
9. R. S. M.
10. War Diary.
11. File.
12. Commanding Officer.

SECRET. Copy No. 7.

1/5th Battalion Loyal North Lancashire Regiment
Order No. 9.

Reference Map, Sheet 36 N.W. 1/20:000.

1. The Battalion will relieve the 2nd Battn. R.W.F. in the Centre Sub Sector, WEZ MACQUART SECTION, to-night 29/30th March.

2.(a) Dispositions of Companies will be as follows:-

Front & Subsidiary Line.	"B" Company.	RIGHT.
	"D" Company.	CENTRE.
	"C" Company.	LEFT.
FLEURIE SWITCH (SPRING POST).	"A" Company.	

Front Line Companies are distributed in depth.

(b) Battalion Headquarters is at I.14.d.4.6. near DESOLANQUE FARM.

(c) Battalion Boundaries are:-

Northern. I.16.b.2.5. - I.9.a.7.0. - I.8.Central. - I.1.d.5.0.

Southern. I.21.a.9.7. - Junction of SALOP & S.S. Line - (CONNIE & DOROTHY POSTS inclusive) - Junction of WELLINGTON AVENUE & Subsidiary Line - FLEURIE POST, exclusive.

(d) It is presumed that the front line posts are held the same as when this Battalion was in the WEZ MACQUART Section before.

3. "A.A" Lewis Guns at present found by "A", "C" & "D" Companies for the Corps A.A. Machine Gun Defences will not be relieved, but will remain in their present positions until the Battalion comes out of the line again.

4. Lewis Guns and pans will be conveyed by limber.

5.(a) All ranks will proceed to the line as lightly equipped as possible, as it is probable that the Battalion will be relieved to-morrow night, 30/31st March.

(b) Officers kits, blankets, packs, will be collected and stored in the billets at present occupied by Companies, and a guard of 1 N.C.O. & 1 man left in charge.

(c) All ranks will carry two pairs of clean socks, one pair to be carried one sock in each trouser pocket, and the other pair in the greatcoat pockets.

6. Starting Point will be Cross Roads at H.13.c.1.8. Headquarters Coy. will pass the Starting Point at 6-45 p.m.

7.(a) Route. BAC ST MAUR - ERQUINGHEM - H.6.a.0.9. - H.6.d.7.7. - I.9.c.3.5.

(b) Order of March. Battn. H.Q'Rs., "C", "D", "B" & "A" Coys.

(c) A distance of 200x between platoons will be maintained throughout the march.

8. Gudies at the rate of 1 per platoon & 1 for Battalion Headquarters will meet ingoing troops at SANDBAG CORNER I.1.d.7.3. at 8-45 p.m. & conduct them to their respective posts.

9.(a) All trench stores, log books, Maps, etc., will be taken over on relief and receipts given.

(b) Billets are to be left in a scrupulously clean condition and receipts obtained.

(c) Copies of receipts for (a & b) to be forwarded to Battalion Headquarters, in duplicate, by 10 a.m. to-morrow, 30th March.

10. Transport will be provided as follows:-

(a) For Lewis Guns. 1 Limber for "C" & "D" Companies.
1 Limber for "A" & "B" Companies.
These two limbers will march with the leading platoons of "C" & "B" Companies respectively.

(b) For Companies, etc. 1 Limber per Company.
1 Limber and Mess Cart for Battn. H'Qrs.

(c) After unloading stores, etc., Transport vehicles will be at the disposal of the 2nd Battn. Royal Welsh Fusiliers to convey their stores, etc., to billets.

11. Gum Boot Store and Foot Washing Centre are at DESOLANQUE FARM I.14.d.3.8.
O.C. "B" Company will detail 1 N.C.O. & 2 men to be in charge of this place.

12. Transport Lines & Quartermaster's Stores will not move.

13.(a) Command of Sector will pass to O.C. 1/5th Bn. L. N. Lancashire Regt. on completion of relief.
(b) Companies will notify completion of relief to Battalion Headquarters, by runner, using the Code word "Good EGG."

14. ACKNOWLEDGE.

B. H. Hawson
Capt. & Adjt.,
1/5th Bn. L. N. Lancashire Regt.

Issued at 11-50 a.m. 29th March, 1918. Copies as under:-

1. Bde. H.Q.
2. O.C. 2nd Bn. R.W.F.
3. O.C. "A" Coy.
4. O.C. "B" Coy.
5. O.C. "C" Coy.
6. O.C. "D" Coy.
7. Commanding Officer.
8. Quartermaster.
9. Transport Officer.
10. R.S.M.
11. War Diary.
12. File.

SECRET. Copy No.....10

1/5th Battalion Loyal North Lancashire Regiment
Order No. 10.

::::::::::::::::::::::::::::::::::::

Ref. Map 36 N.W. 1/20,000.

1.(a) The Battalion will be relieved by the 10th Bn. Lincolnshire Regt.in the trenches to-night, 31st March/1st April,1918.
(b) Companies will occupy the same billets in SAILLY Sur La Lys on completion of relief as they did previous to coming into the line.

2. The personnel employed as Town Guard, ARMENTIERES, will be relieved by personnel of the 103rd Infantry Brigade by 12 noon to-day, 31st March.

3.(a) Gum Boot Stores, Foot Washing Centres, Trench & Area Stores, and all maps, log books,etc., will be handed over on relief.
(b) Trenches will be left in a scrupulously clean and sanitary condition.
(c) Receipts for (a) & (b) will be obtained, and two copies forwarded to Battalion Headquarters by 10a.m. on the day following relief.

4. Transport Lines and Quartermaster's Stores will not move.

5. Guides for incoming units at the rate of 1 for Battalion Headquarters and 1 for each post forward of the Subsidiary Line will rendezvous at H.5.d.1.9. at 7-45 p.m. to-day, and conduct incoming troops to their respective posts.

6. Companies will move out independently on completion of relief.

7.(a) Routes. "A" Company - LA VESEE - GRIS POT - Road junction H.17.d.51. 35 - ERQUINGHEM - BAC ST MAUR - Billets.
"B" Company - WINE AVENUE - Subsidiary Line - RATION FARM - LA VESEE, thence as for "A" Company.
"D" Company - COWGATE AVENUE - Subsidiary Line, thence as for "B" Company.
"C" Company - LEITH WALK - CHAPELLE D'ARMENTIERES - SANDBAG CORNER I.1.d.7.3.) - Road junction N.6.d.65.65 - Road junction B.30.c.35.12. - ERQUINGHEM - BAC ST MAUR - Billets.
(b) A distance of 200^x between platoons will be maintained on the march.

8.(a) Transport will be provided as follows:-
1 Limber for Lewis Guns of "A" & "C" Companies.
1 Limber for Lewis Guns of "B" & "D" Companies.
1 Limber per Company for Officers kit,stores, etc.
1 Limber & Mess Cart for Battalion Headquarters.
(b) All Officers kit, Company Stores, etc., will be stacked at dumps as follows:-
"A" Company at Company Headquarters SPRING POST I.7.d.6.2. at 8p.m.
"B" & "D" Companies at RATION FARM DUMP at 8 p.m.
"C" Company at LEITH WALK DUMP at 8 p.m.
Lewis Guns and pans of "A" Company will be collected at "A" Company Headquarters at 7-30p.m. after which the limber will proceed to Cross Roads CHAPELLE D'ARMENTIERES I.9.c.31.87. and pick up Lewis Guns and pans of "C" Company.
Lewis Guns and pans of "B" & "D" Companies will be collected at RATION FARM DUMP (I.19.b.9.5.) whence they will be conveyed by limber to billets.
(c) All transport arrangements will be mutually decided upon by Transport Officers of the two Battalions concerned.

9.(a) Command of the sector will pass to O.C. 10th Bn. The Lincolnshire Regiment on completion of relief.

(b) Companies will notify completion of relief to Battalion Headquarters by telephone and runner, using the Code Word "EASTER".

P. T. O.

10. ACKNOWLEDGE.

B. H. Hancock

Capt. & Adjt.,
1/5th Bn. L. N. Lancashire Regt.

Issued at 10 a.m. 31/3/18. Copies as under:-

1. Bde. H.Q.
2. O.C. 10th Bn. Lincolnshire Regt.
3. O.C. "A" Company.
4. O.C. "B" Company.
5. O.C. "C" Company.
6. O.C. "D" Company.
7. Quartermaster.
8. Transport Officer.
9. R. S. M.
10. War Diary.
11. File.
12. Commanding Officer.

57th Division
170th Infantry Brigade

WAR DIARY

1/5th BATTALION

THE LOYAL NORTH LANCASHIRE REGT

APRIL 1918

Vol 33

Confidential

War Diary of

1/5th Battalion Loyal North Lancashire Regiment

period 1st April 1918 to 30th April 1918

Volume 15.

Army Form C. 2118.

WAR DIARY
or
~~INTELLIGENCE SUMMARY.~~
(Erase heading not required.)

Instructions regarding War Diaries and Intelligence Summaries are contained in F. S. Regs., Part II. and the Staff Manual respectively. Title pages will be prepared in manuscript.

Place	Date 1918	Hour	Summary of Events and Information	Remarks and references to Appendices
	APRIL			
SAILLY-SUR-LA-LYS	1		Marched to ARREWAGE near MERVILLE, & billeted there	8
ARREWAGE	2		Rested at ARREWAGE and at night marched to CALONNE-SUR-LYS.	
	3		Entrained at 1 am (3/4/18) and detrained at 12 noon at MONDICOURT (N.E. of DOULLENS) Marched to WARLUZEL	8
WARLUZEL	4		BILLETS - Cleaning up + 3 hours' training	8
	5		" 3 hours' Training Reconnaissance and march to HUMBERCOURT.	8
HUMBERCOURT	6		" 2 hours Training	8
	7		" SUNDAY	8
	8		" Marched to GRENAS	8
GRENAS	9		" Marched to HALLOY	8
HALLOY	10		" 2 hours' Training	8
	11		" do. and Reconnaissance	8
	12		" Reconnaissance and marched to BEAUDRICOURT	8
BEAUDRICOURT	13		" Marched from BEAUDRICOURT to BOIS LALEAU AUTHIE	8
AUTHIE	14		BIVOUAC Reconnaissance + preparing bivouac ground	8

A5834 Wt. W4973/M687 750,000 8/16 D. D. & L. Ltd. Forms/C.2118/13.

Instructions regarding War Diaries and Intelligence Summaries are contained in F. S. Regs., Part II. and the Staff Manual respectively. Title pages will be prepared in manuscript.

WAR DIARY
or
~~INTELLIGENCE SUMMARY~~.
(Erase heading not required.)

Army Form C. 2118.

Place	Date 1918	Hour	Summary of Events and Information	Remarks and references to Appendices
	APRIL			
AUTHIE	15		BIVOUAC working parties digging trenches & Reconnaissance	S
"	16		" Moved to COUIN & Reconnaissance	S
COUIN	17		" Reconnaissance + working parties digging trenches	S
"	18		" " & Training	S
"	19. 20 } 21		" " & working parties digging trenches	S
"	22		" 3 Companies practising occupation of rear line trenches & 1 Company digging trenches.	S
"	23		" Reconnaissance + working parties digging trenches	S
"	24		" " "	S
"	25		" 1 Company Baths &c. 3 Companies working Parties	S
"	26		" 1 Company - Baths &c. 3 Companies working Parties	S
"	27		" 2 Companies Training 2 Companies working Parties	S
"	28		" 2 Companies - Musketry Competition . 2 Companies working parties	S
"	29		" 2 Companies - Musketry Competition . 2 Companies working parties.	S
"	30		" 4 best Platoons . Musketry Competition . ~~P~~ 1 Company Baths 2 Companies working parties	S

A5834 Wt. W4973/M687 750,000 8/16 D. D. & L. Ltd. Forms/C.2118/13.

SECRET. Copy No...... 10

1/5th Bn. Loyal North Lancashire Regiment
Order No. 11.

Reference Map. HAZEBROUCK 5a. 1/100,000.

1.(a) The Battalion will move from SAILLY to ARREWAGE to-morrow, 1st April, 1918, by march route.
(b) Transport will accompany the Battalion.

2. Order of March will be :- Headquarters Company, "A","B","C","D" Companies, Transport Section.

3. Dress. Marching Order; Steel Helmets to be carried on the pack. 120 rounds S.A.A. per man.

4.(a) The Band will accompany the Battalion and will play on the march.
(b) The Transport Officer will arrange to carry the packs and rifles of the band.

5. Distances will be maintained on the march as follows:-

Between Battalions	500x
Between Companies	100x
Between Battalion & Transport	100x.

6. The Battalion will parade with the head of the column at SAILLY cross roads at 11-15 a.m., ready to march off, with 100x between Companies.

7. Billeting Party, consisting of Lieut. J. Faulkner, the 4 C.Q.M. Sergeants and Sergt. Whitehead will report to the Staff Captain at the Area Commandant's Office, MERVILLE, at 9-30a.m. to-morrow, 1st April, 1918.
This party will be mounted on bicycles. Signal Officer will arrange for these to be provided.

8. The 3 "A.A" Lewis Guns of "A", "C" & "D" Companies at present employed on XV Corps A.A. Machine Gun Defences will rejoin their respective Companies at 10a.m. to-morrow, 1st April, if not previously relieved by incoming troops. Officers Commanding Companies concerned will be responsible for recalling these sections.

9. 1 Lorry will be provided for the move. This will be used to carry the necessary Battalion Stores, Quartermaster's Stores, etc.

10. All billets will be left in a scrupulously clean and sanitary condition, and receipts to this effect obtained from either the incoming unit or Billet Wardens. Two copies to be forwarded to Battalion Headquarters.

11. On arrival at ARREWAGE the Signal Officer will detail two cyclists orderlies to report to the Adjutant. These two orderlies will carry the unexpended portion of their day's rations and rations for April 2nd.

12. All Battalion & Company Stores, Officers' kits, etc., will be stacked outside Battalion & Company Headquarters by 8-30a.m. to-morrow, 1st April, when they will be collected under arrangements to be made by the Transport Officer.

13. All Companies will report, by runner, the location of their respective Headquarters immediately on arrival at ARREWAGE.

14. Haversack Rations will be carried by all ranks. Dinners will be served to the men on arrival at billets.

P. T. O.

10. ACKNOWLEDGE.

B. H. Hanson

Capt. & Adjt.,
1/5th Bn. L. N. Lancashire Regiment.

Issued at 7.15p.m. 31/5/18. Copies as under:-

1. Bde. H.Q.
2. O.C. "A" Company.
3. O.C. "B" Company.
4. O.C. "C" Company.
5. O.C. "D" Company.
6. Quartermaster.
7. Transport Officer.
8. Signalling Officer.
9. R. S. M.
10. War Diary.
11. File.
12. Commanding Officer.

SECRET.

Copy No. 11

1/5th Battalion Loyal North Lancashire Regt.
Order No. 12.

Ref. Map 36a, 1/40,000.

1. The Battalion will entrain at CALONNE Station Q.3.c.8.7. on April 2nd.

2.(a) "D" Company with one Cooker and team will proceed to CALONNE STATION and report to the R.T.O. at 12-40 p.m. to-morrow, 2nd April.
(b) This Company will act as a loading party for all Units and will entrain with the Cooker & Team on Train No. 90, under orders of Capt. W.H. Satterthwaite.

3.(a) The Transport Officer will arrange for breast ropes for horses trucks to be provided.
(b) Ropes for vehicles will be provided by the Railway.

4. Each Company will detail 1 Officer & 4 N.C.Os. to be responsible for discipline during the journey. All doors of covered trucks and carriages are to be kept closed, except when entrainment or detrainment is in progress.

5.(a) Advanced billeting party, consisting of 2nd Lieut. A. Runciman, Sergt. Willets, and the 4 C.Q.M.Sergeants will proceed on the first train. The above named N.C.Os. will report to 2nd Lieut. A Runciman at Battalion Headquarters at 2 p.m. to-morrow, 2nd April.
(b) This party will be mounded on bicycles; the Signal Officer will arrange for these to be provided.
(c) This party will report to the Staff Captain at CALONNE STATION at 3 p.m. to-morrow, 2nd April.
(d) They will carry TWO days rations in addition to the unconsumed portion for the 2nd April.
(e) They will report to the Staff Captain immediately after detrainment, and will not move from the detraining station without orders from him.

6.(a) Dress:- Marching Order, Steel Helmets will be worn. 120 rounds S.A.A. per man will be carried.
(b) One Blanket per man will be carried.
(c) The Battalion will move with a normal Field Service scale of Transport, no extra Transport will be provided; Baggage Wagons will entrain with the 1st Line Transport.

7.(a) Lewis Guns and 24 pans of S.A.A. per gun will be carried during the march and train journey by Lewis Gun Sections.

8. All billets will be left in a scrupulously clean and sanitary condition. Certificates to this effect will be obtained from the Billet Wardens in triplicate, and two copies forwarded to Battalion Headquarters.

9.(a) All ranks will entrain with filled water bottles. All Other Ranks will be provided with tea for their water bottles, this will be done under Company arrangements. A certificate that every N.C.O. and man has had his water bottle filled will be handed to the Adjutant at CALONNE STATION.
(b) All arrangements with regard to rations will be made by the Quartermaster. Sandbags for carrying rations may be obtained from the Quartermaster.

10.(a) The Battalion, less "D" Company and Transport, will parade with the head of the column at Road Junction K.14.b.15.95. at 10-5 p.m. to-morrow, 2nd April.
(b) Order of March:- Headquarters Company, A, B & C Companies.
(c) A distance of 100x between Companies will be maintained on the march.

11.(a) Transport, less one Cooker, plus Supply and Baggage Wagons, will parade in sufficient time as to ensure the head of the column passing the Brigade Starting Point in MERVILLE at K.29.d.2.7. at 9-25 p.m. to-morrow, 2nd April.
(b) All Company Stores, Officers Kit, Mess kit, etc., will be loaded on vehicles not later than 7-30 p.m. Companies may only put their Mess Box in the Mess Cart, any other articles will be refused.

12. On arrival in the new area Companies will immediately report their arrival in billets and location thereof to Battalion Headquarters by runner.

13. ACKNOWLEDGE.

B. H. Harrison

Capt. & Adjt.,
1/5th Bn. L. N. Lancashire Regt.

Issued at [illegible] p.m. [illegible]/4/18. Copies as under:-

1.	Bde. H.Q.	7.	Transport Officer.
2.	O.C. "A" Coy.	8.	Signal Officer.
3.	O.C. "B" Coy.	9.	R.S.M.
4.	O.C. "C" Coy.	10.	Commanding Officer.
5.	O.C. "D" Coy.	11.	War Diary.
6.	Quartermaster.	12.	File.

SECRET. Copy No....1...

1/5th Battalion Loyal North Lancashire Regiment
Order No. 13.

Reference Map, LENS, 1/100:000.

1. The Battalion will march to billets in COULLEMONT this afternoon.

2. Companies will parade on the WARLUZEL - HUMBERCOURT Road, ready to march off at 2-30 p.m. Head of Column to be at cross roads 4.F.61.70. at 2-30 p.m.

3. Order of March:- Headquarters Company, "D", "C", "B", "A" Companies, Transport Section.

4. The Band will parade immediately in rear of Headquarters Company.

5. Billets will be left in a scrupulously clean and sanitary condition, receipts obtained in triplicate and two copies forwarded to Battalion Headquarters.

6. Companies will report arrival in billets to Battalion Headquarters by runner, giving Map location of Company Headquarters.

7. Dress:- Marching Order, Steel Helmets to be worn. One Blanket per man to be carried.

8. Lewis Guns. Lewis Guns will be carried by the L.G. Sections. All Lewis Gun pans & S.A.A. will be carried on the limbers.

9. A distance of 100^{x} between Companies will be maintained on the march.

10. Companies will send billeting parties of 1 N.C.O. per platoon to proceed to COULLEMONT as soon as they have had their dinners. These parties will report to 2nd Lieut. D.H. Provan, M.C. in COULLEMONT at cross roads 4.F.62.52. at 3 p.m. and conduct them to billets.

B. H. Hawton
Capt. & Adjt.,
1/5th Bn. L. N. Lancashire Regt.

Issued at 12-15 p.m. 5/4/18. Copies to:-

1. H.Q. 170th Bde.
2. O.C. "A" Coy.
3. O.C. "B" Coy.
4. O.C. "C" Coy.
5. O.C. "D" Coy.
6. Quartermaster.
7. Transport Officer.
8. R.S.M.
9. Commanding Officer.
10. War Diary.
11. File.
12. Spare.

SECRET.   Copy No....11....

1/5th Battalion Loyal North Lancashire Regiment
Order No. 14.

Reference Map, LENS 11, 1/100:000.

1. The Battalion will move by march route to-day, 8th April, to GRENAS.

2. Route:- HUMBERCOURT - Road Junction 4.F.37.20. - Road Junction 4.F.57.15. - GRENAS.

3.(a) Order of March:- Headquarters Company, "A", "B", "C" "D" Companies, Transport Section.
(b) The Battalion will parade, ready to march off, with the head of the column at 4.F.48.40. at 1-30 p.m.
(c) A distance of 200x between Companies and 100x between "D" Company and Transport Section will be maintained on the march.

4. Dress:- Marching Order. Steel Helmets will be worn.

5.(a) Advanced billeting party, consisting of the 4 C.Q.M.Sergeants and Sergeant Willets under 2nd Lieut. D.H. Provan M.C., will proceed to GRENAS and take over billets from a Battalion of the 171st Brigade.
(b) This party will arrive at GRENAS by 9 a.m. to-day, 8th April.
(c) 2nd Lieut. D.H. Provan M.C. will report to the Staff Captain at the Area Commandant's Office, MONDICOURT, at 12 noon to-day to report on the billets.

6. One lorry will be provided to move Battalion Stores, Blankets, etc. The Quartermaster will detail a guide to meet this lorry. Lorry will arrive in HUMBERCOURT at 11 a.m. to-day.

7. All blankets will be rolled in bundles of 10, labelled by Companies, and handed to the Quartermaster's Stores by 10-30 a.m. to-day.

8. Billets will be left in a scrupulously clean and sanitary condition, and certificates obtained from either the billet warden or the incoming Unit in triplicate, and two copies forwarded to Battalion Headquarters.

9. On arrival in GRENAS, Companies will report when they are settled in billets, and Map Location of their Company Headquarters to Battalion Headquarters by runner.

10. ACKNOWLEDGE.

B.H. Hanson
Capt. & Adjt.,
1/5th Bn. L. N. Lancashire Regt.

Issued at 5-15 a.m. 8th April, 1918. Copies to:-

1. H.Q. 170th Bde.	7. Transport Officer.
2. O.C. "A" Coy.	8. O.C. Headquarters Coy.
3. O.C. "B" Coy.	9. Commanding Officer.
4. O.C. "C" Coy.	10. R.S.M.
5. O.C. "D" Coy.	11. War Diary.
6. Quartermaster.	12. File.

A. Dean

Amendment to 1/5th Battalion Loyal North Lancashire Regiment Order No. 15.

---

1. Reference para. 5 (a), Billeting Party will report to the Staff Captain at Village Warden's Office, AMPLIER, at 8-30 a.m. to-day, and not as therein stated.

2. The Battalion will be billeted in AMPLIER and not HALLOY.

3. ACKNOWLEDGE.

B.H. Hansom
Capt. & Adjt.,
1/5th Bn. L. N. Lancashire Regt.

Issued to all recipients of Order No. 15.

SECRET. Copy No....11..

1/5th Battalion Loyal North Lancashire Regiment
Order No. 15.

Reference Map. LENS 11. 1/100,000.

1. The Battalion will move by march route to-day, 9th April, to HALLOY.

2. Route:- GRENAS - HALLOY Road.

3.(a) Order of March:- Headquarters Company, "D", "C", "B", "A" Companies, Transport Section.
  (b) The Battalion will parade, ready to march off with the head of the column at Cross Roads 5.F.34.00. at 9-25 a.m.
  (c) A distance of 100x between Companies, and 100x between "A" Company and Transport Section will be maintained on the march.

4. Dress:- Marching Order. Steel Helmets will be worn.

5.(a) Advanced billeting party, consisting of the 4 C.Q.M.Sergeants and Sergt. Willets, under 2nd Lieut. D.H. Provan M.C., will proceed to HALLOY and report to the Town Major, HALLOY, at 9-30 a.m. This party will be mounted on bicycles.
  (b) Guides from this party will meet the Battalion at Cross Roads 5.F.14.55. at 10 a.m. and conduct Companies to their respective billets.

6.(a) One lorry will be provided to move Battalion Stores, Blankets, etc. The Quartermaster will detail one guide to report at Brigade Headquarters at 8 a.m. to-day to conduct lorry to Quartermaster's Stores.
  (b) All blankets, kits, etc., will be handed in to the Quartermaster's Stores by 8-15 a.m. to-day, 9th April.
  (c) Blankets will be rolled in bundles of 10 and labelled by Companies.

7. Billets will be left in a scrupulously clean and sanitary condition, and receipts obtained from the billet wardens in triplicate. Two copies to be forwarded to Battalion Headquarters.

8. On arrival in the HALLOY area Companies will report when they are settled in billets and Map Location of their respective Company Headquarters to Battalion Headquarters by runner.

9.(a) On completion of this move the 57th Division will be in Army Reserve.
  (b) The Battalion will be at 1 hour's notice to move from 8 a.m. - 12 noon daily, and at 3 hours notice for the remainder of the day.

10. Reveille. Battalion Routine Order No. 280, 4. 8/4/18, is cancelled. Reveille to-day, 9th April, will be at 5-30 a.m.

11. ACKNOWLEDGE.

[illegible signature]

Capt. & Adjt.,
1/5th Bn. L. N. Lancashire Regt.

Issued at 12-15 a.m. 9/4/18.

Copies to:-

1. H.Q. 170th Bde.
2. O.C. "A" Coy.
3. O.C. "B" Coy.
4. O.C. "C" Coy.
5. O.C. "D" Coy.
6. O.C. Headquarters Coy.
7. Quartermaster.
8. Transport Officer.
9. R.S.M.
10. Commanding Officer.
11. War Diary.
12. File.

SECRET.   Copy No..10......

1/5th Battalion Loyal North Lancashire Regiment
Instructions No. 3.
!!!!!!!!!!!!!!!!

OCCUPATION OF RED LINE.

Ref. Sheet 57.d. 1/40,000.

If the Brigade is ordered to occupy the Red Line, the following dispositions will be made:-

INFANTRY. 1. The 2/5th K.O.R.L.R. will defend the line from the point where it cuts the road (exclusive) at O.34.c.5.5. to the point where it cuts the road at O.11.a.2.4. (inclusive).

The 4/5th L.N.L.R. from road O.11.a.3.4. (exclusive) to the track (inclusive) at I.29.d.9.7.

Each Bn. with three Coys. each in depth in front and one in reserve.

The 1/5th L.N.L.R. will be in Brigade Reserve in O.3.c.

L.T.M. BATTY. 2. 1 Section in Reserve with Reserve Battalion.

BDE.H.Q. 3. Brigade Battle Headquarters will be at O.3.d.3.3.

SIGNALS. 4. Signal communication will be established by wire, runner and visual between the Battalion and Brigade Battle Headquarters.

LIAISON & INFORMATION. 5. (a) Company Commanders will arrange to establish forward observation posts to keep the Commanding Officer in touch with the situation in front.

(b) The Brigade Liaison Party (as already detailed) will report at Brigade Battle Headquarters.

AMMUNITION SUPPLY. 6. Ammunition will be carried as laid down in App. VII of Battalion Organisation with the exception that all Riflemen will carry 170 rounds S.A.A. and 2 Mills Bombs in his pockets. No rifle grenades need be carried unless the Commanding Officer specially wishes to do so.

Each Company will be accompanied by 2 pack animals, 1 carrying 30 drums L.G. Ammunition and 1 carrying 2 boxes S.A.A. The pack animals will be with Battalion Headquarters.

The Transport Officer will detail two S.A.A. Wagons and one Bomb Wagon and one L.G.S. Wagon (containing the balance of the L.G. Drums, viz, 16 per gun) to rendezvous at H.16.c.8.0. and report to the Brigade Transport Officer.

The above wagons will proceed via BEAUQUESNE to N.1 .d.3.9. where they will form a Brigade Ammunition Reserve under the Brigade Bombing Officer.

7. Instructions re Medical Arrangements and method of supply will be issued later.

A. Rennie [signature]   2nd Lieut.,
Act. Adjt.,
1/5th Bn. L. N. Lancashire Regt.

Issued on 10/4/18.   COPIES TO:-

1.	H.Q. 170th Bde.	7.	Transport Officer.
2.	O.C. "A" Coy.	8.	Signal Officer.
3.	O.C. "B" Coy.	9.	Commanding Officer.
4.	O.C. "C" Coy.	10.	War Diary.
5.	O.C. "D" Coy.	11.	File.
6.	Quartermaster.	12.	Spare.

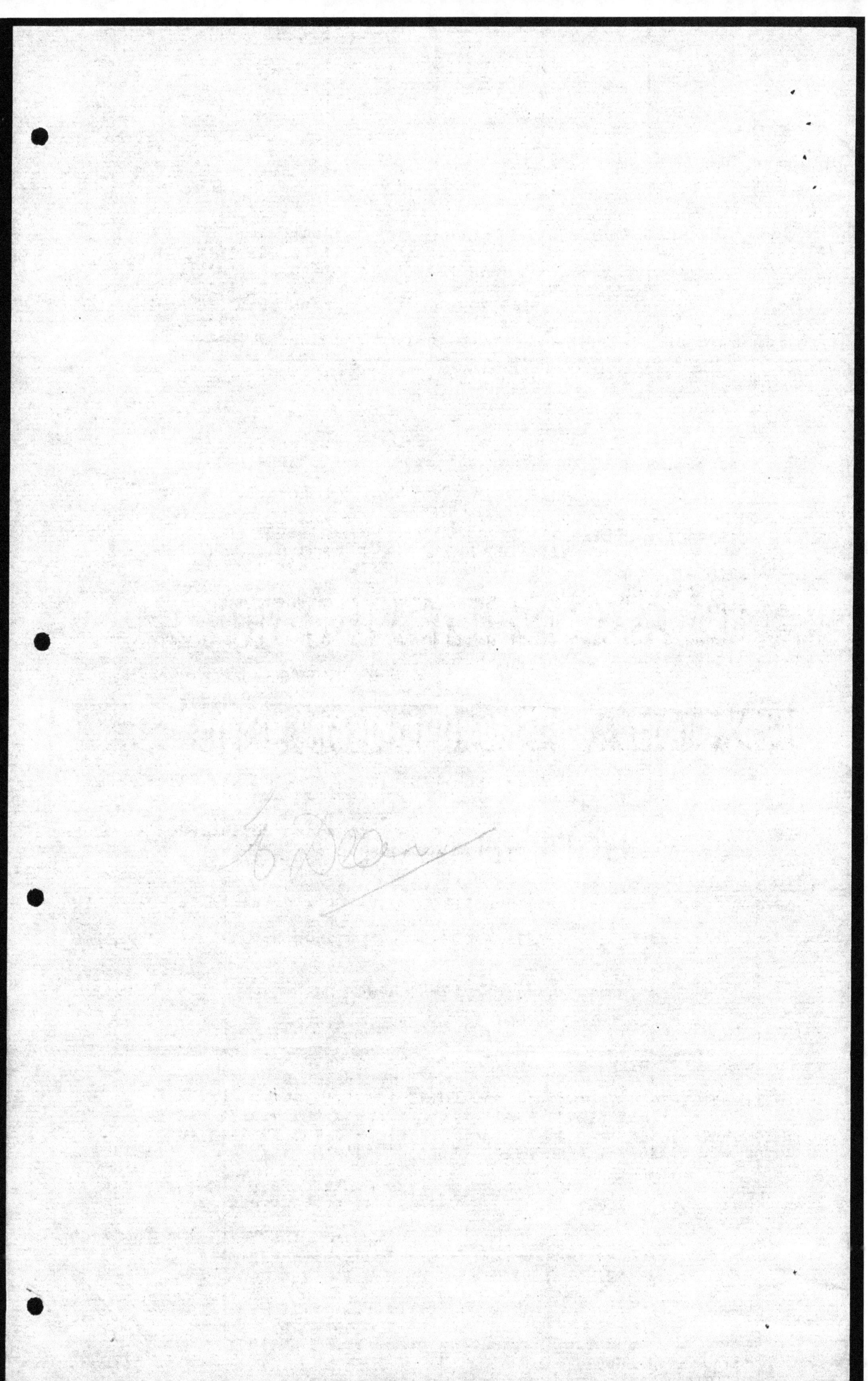

<u>SECRET</u>. Copy No.....5.

AMENDMENT TO 4/5TH BN . LOYAL NORTH
LANCASHIRE REGIMENT ORDER NO.17.

30/4/18.

1. <u>Para.2 (b)</u>. For facing N.E. read "facing S.E."
Add:-
(d) <u>Route</u>:- J.3.a.4.4. - J.11.d.6.0. via J.5.b.5.9. - D.27.c.3.3. - D.27.d.65.50 - D.28.d.80.15. - J.5.c.5.8. - J.11.a.5.9.
Transport accompanying Battalion to assembly position will move by road via COUIN and SOIGNEUX.
(e) The 2/4th Bn. L. N. Lancashire Regiment will have preceedence over all other Units of 170th Infantry Brigade.

2. <u>Para 12</u>.
When co-operating with tanks the following signals will be used:-
Infantry to tank. "Tank wanted here". Helmet raised on point of bayonet above the head.
Tank to Infantry. "Dont come here". Shovel raised and waved from manhole in top of tank.
(The latter signal means that the tank has encountered heavy rifle or M.G. Fire. On seeing it the infantry will work round and attack the position from which the fire is coming, from the flanks).

2nd Lieut.,
Act. Adjt.,
4/5th Bn. L. N. Lancashire Regiment.

Issued to all recipients of Bn. Order No. 17.

SECRET. Copy No.....6

1/5th Bn. Loyal North Lancashire Regiment
Order No. 17.

Reference Map, 57.D. N.E. Edtn. 4c. 1:20,000.

1. The enemy is expected to attack at an early date.

2.(a) On receipt of the order "Battle Positions" the Battalion will be formed up at the Battalion Alarm position J.2.a.4.4.

(b) Formation.
Lines of Companies in fours, facing N.E. 10 paces interval, ready to move to assembly position J.11.d. within 30 minutes of receipt of the orders.

(c) Dress:- Fighting Order.
Leather Jerkins will be worn.
W.P. Sheet carried.
Unexpended portion of day's rations.
2 Iron Rations.

3. The 33% personnel will be left behind and will be formed up under Major Anderson, who will march the party to the Camp of the 2/5th Bn. K.O.R.L. Regt. and report to Major Seward.

4. Battalion Liaison parties will report at Brigade Headquarters on receipt of the order "Battle Positions".

5.(a) The Transport Officer will detail 3 Mounted Orderlies to report to the Brigade Signal Officer at Brigade Headquarters on receipt of the order "Battle Positions". The horses will carry feeds.
He will be prepared to supply 2 Mounted Orderlies to Rear Brigade Headquarters.

(b) Company Commanders may take their horses with them to the Assembly Positions, but these horses will be sent back to the Transport Lines on arrival.

6. Ammunition will be carried as follows:-

(a) On the men as laid down in App.VII of Bn. Organization except that all Riflemen will carry 170 rounds of S.A.A. (50 rds. being in the Haversack).
At least one Mill's Bomb will be carried in the pocket.
Men of the Company 36 Grenade Squads will each carry 50 rds.S.A.A.
Two men will carry 1 discharger and 6 grenades.
Two men will carry 8 grenades.
Grenades will be carried in the Haversack Carriers.

(b) Each Company will carry flares and Very Lights that have been issued.

(c) Each Company will be followed by 2 Pack Animals, one carrying 32 drums of S.A.A., and one carrying 2 boxes of S.A.A.

7. A Dump has been formed at Battalion Headquarters. Companies will detail six men to report there to bring forward a supply of ammunition and bombs.

8. The following Transport will accompany the Battalion:-

(a) 1 Lewis Gun Limber (containing 272 filled pans).
2 Tool Wagons.
1 Water Cart.

(b) 3 S.A.A. Limbers (containing 22 boxes S.A.A. each) to report to the Brigade Transport Officer at Brigade Headquarters.
They will be sent by him to the Advanced Brigade Headquarters.

(c) After the initial issue of bombs, the bomb limbers will proceed to Rear Brigade Headquarters, where they will refill, after refilling the X wagonx will be sent by the Staff Captain to the Brigade Ammunition Reserve.

(d) As soon as the situation is clear a Brigade Ammunition Reserve will be formed near Advanced Brigade Headquarters, to which the 3 S.A.A. Limbers will proceed.

(e) 3 Lewis Gun Limbers of each Battalion will remain at the Wagon Lines, where they will be at the disposal of the Staff Captain, for supply of T.M. Ammunition and rations.

(f) All Transport other than that mentioned in para (a) above will remain at Battalion Transport Lines, under the Battalion Transport Officer who will act under orders of the Staff Captain.

8. Headquarters will be established as follows:-

Battalion Headquarters	J.17.b.70.80.
Officer Commanding 2 forward Companies.	J.15.b.6.7.
Regimental Aid Post.	J.18.a.05.95.

9. On the order "Battle Positions" being issued, Captain Myers, M.C. will report at Brigade Headquarters (J.1.b.4.7.) for Liaison duty with 172nd Infantry Brigade (H.Q. at D.17.a.6.3.)

10. Companies will send two runners on arrival in their assembly position to Battalion Headquarters.

11. ACKNOWLEDGE.

[signature]
2nd Lieut.,
Act. Adjt.,
26/4/18. 1/5th Bn. L. N. Lancashire Regiment.

Issued at 10 p.m. Copies to:-

1. O.C. "A" Company.
2. O.C. "B" Company.
3. O.C. "C" Company.
4. O.C. "D" Company.
5. O.C. "H.Q." Company.
6. Major Anderson.
7. Transport Officer.
8. Quartermaster.
9. R. S. M.
10. O.C. 2 forward Coys.
11. File.
12. War Diary.

SECRET. Copy No.....

1/5th Bn. Loyal North Lancashire Regiment.
Administrative Instruction to be read in conjunction with Battalion Order No.17.

1.(a) An extra Iron Ration will be issued to the men on receipt of the order "Battle Positions" or "Stand To".
(b) They will only actually be issued to the men going into action.
(c) Each man should then proceed to the line with:-
(i) Unexpended portion of the day's rations.
(ii) The following day's rations (iron).
(iii) The Iron Ration.
(d) Daily rations will be conveyed to the line in the normal way as far as possible. The Iron Ration will not be consumed without orders from an Officer.
(e) The Quartermaster and Transport Officer will keep in touch with the Battalion Headquarters in order to ascertain the most suitable routes, and positions to which rations are to be conveyed.

2. Collection of Blankets and Packs:-
Blankets will be rolled in bundles of 10 and stacked at the Q.M. Stores.
Packs will be clearly marked by the men, and stacked at the Q.M. Stores. The Quartermaster will arrange to have them stored at the Transport Lines as near the road as possible.

3.(a) Camp. All tents will be struck by the surplus personnel.
(b) The tents will be packed in their companies and stacked at Rear Brigade Headquarters.
(c) Latrines will be filled in.

4.(a) The Transport Lines will remain in their present position.
(b) One Baggage Wagon per unit will be loaded with Officers' Kits and stores which are not required, and returned to No.2 Company Divisional Train within an hour of the order "Battle Positions" being received.
One Baggage Wagon will remain with the unit in order to move Q.M. Stores, Orderly Room Stores and kits of Officers of the 33% personnel.
(c) Officers' Kits and Stores must be at the Q.M's. Stores ready to be loaded within 15 minutes of orders being received to move at any hour of the day or night.
(d) Whilst the Battalion is under 1 hours notice, Blankets will be rolled in bundles of 10 and packs ready to be stacked every morning shortly after Reveille.
(e) Officers' Valises will be rolled ready to be loaded on the wagon.

5.(a) The N.C.O. and 3 men already detailed for duty at the Stragglers Post, under 2nd Lieut. Ray will report to Brigade Headquarters on "Battle Positions" Order being received.
(b) 5 men from "A","B" and "C" Companies already detailed as Additional Stretcher Bearers will report to the Officer Commanding 3/2nd W. L. Fld. Amb., on "Battle Positions" being received.
Dress:- Fighting Order. (with rifles).
They will carry two days' rations and the Iron Ration.

[signature] 2nd Lieut.,
Act. Adjt.,
26/4/18. 1/5th Bn. L. N. Lancashire Regiment.

Issued at 10 p.m., to all recipients of Bn. Order No.17.

C.C. H.Q. Co.

Confidential

War Diary

1/5th Battalion Loyal North Lancashire Regiment

period 1st May 1918 to 31st May 1918

Volume 15.

VR 34

Army Form C. 2118.

Instructions regarding War Diaries and Intelligence Summaries are contained in F. S. Regs., Part II. and the Staff Manual respectively. Title pages will be prepared in manuscript.

WAR DIARY
or
~~INTELLIGENCE SUMMARY.~~

(Erase heading not required.)

Place	Date May	Hour	Summary of Events and Information	Remarks and references to Appendices
COUIN	1		Bivouac 2 Companies Working Party 2 Companies Training. Battalion Musketry Competition for best platoon in Battalion	S
	2		do 2 Companies Working Parties. 2 Companies Training & Baths	S
	3		do Brigade Musketry Competition for best platoon in Brigade. 2 Companies Working Parties 1 Company Training & Baths	S
	4		do 2 Companies with 1/5th Kings Own (R.L.) Regt. manning trenches with new dispositions. Remainder of Battalion - working parties	S
	5		do Reconnaissance of new line FONQUEVILLERS. Sunday Holiday ~~Companies Working parties~~	S
	6		do Reconnaissance. Relieved 1/6 MANCHESTER REGT.	S
BEER TRENCH	7		Trenches Working parties & improving trenches	S
	8		do do	S
	9		do do	S
	10		do do	S
	11		do do Relieved by 7/4 Loyal N. Lancs Regt.	S
COIGNEUX	12		Billets Rest & cleaning up	S
	13		do Baths & working parties. Relieved 2/6 The Kings (Liverpool) Regt. Casualties	S
LEFT SUBSECTOR LEFT BRIGADE SECTOR GOMMECOURT	14		Trenches Fairly quiet day & night 1	S
	15		" Very quiet day & night 3 patrols out. No contact with enemy -	S
	16		" do no patrols out 2	S

A5834 Wt. W4973/M687 750,000 8/16 D. D. & L. Ltd. Forms/C.2118/13.

Instructions regarding War Diaries and Intelligence Summaries are contained in F. S. Regs., Part II. and the Staff Manual respectively. Title pages will be prepared in manuscript.

WAR DIARY
or
~~INTELLIGENCE SUMMARY~~.
(Erase heading not required.)

Army Form C. 2118.

Place	Date May	Hour	Summary of Events and Information	Casualties	Remarks and references to Appendices
GOMMECOURT	17		Trenches Enemy Artillery active on Trenches. At night 3 patrols out. No contact with enemy		[illegible]
	18		" do do but quiet at night. do do		[illegible]
	19		" do Quiet during day but active at night do do	2	[illegible]
	20		" do do do 2 fighting patrols out but high visibility hindered good work	2/LT. BALFOUR Killed	[illegible]
	21		" do do & night Raid by 1 Officer + 40 men and by 1 Officer + 10 men. Both raids abandoned owing to inaccuracy of barrage	1	[illegible]
	22		" do active both day & night. Patrol found enemy post empty	2/LT MANTON wounded 1 missing 8 wounded	[illegible]
	23		" do. Quiet in day but activity at night so disorganised raiding party that raid had to be postponed.	12	[illegible]
	24		" do Very active during day. Raid by 1 Officer & platoon found 3 enemy posts all unoccupied. Patrol of 1 Officer + 10 men bombed by men in advance post in shellhole. Enemy bolted.	LT FAULKNER wounded 6 wounded	[illegible]
	25		" do. Very active day & night. No patrols out		[illegible]
	26		" do heavily bombarded our trenches all day. Gas shells on back areas at night. Enemy raid with 30-35 men on 2 of our posts. Raid repulsed leaving 1 dead & 1 wounded in our hands.	11	[illegible]
	27		" do fairly active during day Quiet at night	13	[illegible]

Instructions regarding War Diaries and Intelligence Summaries are contained in F. S. Regs., Part II. and the Staff Manual respectively. Title pages will be prepared in manuscript.

WAR DIARY
or
~~INTELLIGENCE SUMMARY.~~
(Erase heading not required.)

Army Form C. 2118.

Place	Date May	Hour	Summary of Events and Information	Casualties	Remarks and references to Appendices
GOMMECOURT	28		Trenches Very quiet – day & night	2/LT. HOLLINRAKE. M.C. wounded	[initials]
	29		" do do Relieved by 2/4 South Lancs Regt	4 wounded 6	[initials]
COIGNEUX	30		Billets Few shells in & around billets. At night, slept out in trenches	14	[initials]
	31		" Batt HQ & 2 Companies moved to ROSSIGNOL FARM. 2 Companies left in trenches near COIGNEUX. 1 Company preparing for raid; 3 Companies training		[initials]
			Battalion Strength – 1st May 1918 Officers 39. Men 972.		
			31st – – Officers 38. Men 863.		

A5834 Wt. W4973/M687 750,000 8/16 D. D. & L. Ltd. Forms/C.2118/13.

SECRET. Copy No. ..12....

1/5TH BN. LOYAL NORTH LANCASHIRE REGIMENT
OPERATION ORDER NO. 32.

Ref. Map Sheet 57.D. N.E. 1:20,000.

1. The Battalion will carry out two minor enterprise operations on the night 21/22nd inst. to secure identification.

FIRST ENTERPRISE.

2. (a) Strength of Party 2/Lieut. C.E. MANTON and 1 platoon of "D" Company plus 2 Lewis Gun Sections of "C" Company.
(b) Point of EXIT:- L.7.c.50.73.
(c) Objective:- Enemy post at L.7.c.42.52.
(d) ZERO HOUR (Time at which Artillery first opens fire 2 a.m.)

ARTILLERY PROGRAMME.

3. Zero - Zero+1 min. 18 pdrs. fire crash on line L.7.c. 10.20 - L.7.c.10.45 - L.7.c.30.20 - along road to L.7.c.00.50.
Zero+30 mins.-Zero 18 pdrs. fire as above. 4.5 Hows.
+33 mins. Intense on E. corner of ROSSIGNOL WOOD. at(K.12.b.50.15) and on Enemy M.G.Posts at L.7.d.20.60,L.7.d.15.30,L.7.d.25.45, L.8.c.50.25 and L.7.a.90. 5.
Infantry rush objective.
Zero+33 min -Zero 18 pdrs and 4.5 Hows. keep up medium
+40 min. rate of fire on above points.
Infantry returns to our lines by trench L.7.c.46.80.

LEWIS GUNS.

4. (a) Lewis Gun Post at L.7.a.35.10 will be prepared to silence enemy M.G. at L.7.c.50.75.
(b) Lewis Gun Post at L.7.a.1.3. will be pushed forward into sunken tramline or shell holes at about L.7.a.15.12. and will be prepared to silence enemy M.G. at L.7.c.20.75.
(c) A Lewis Gun Section will be pushed forward into shell holes and will be prepared to silence enemy M.G. at L.7.c.00.50.
(d) The above Lewis Gun Sections will remain in position until the Assaulting Parties have returned to our lines.

ACTION OF PLATOON.

5. (a) The Lewis Gun Section will operate in accordance with para. 4 (c) above.
(b) 1 Section will proceed along trench in a S.W. direction and will act as a Blocking Party at approx. L.7.c.37.62.
(c) 1 Section will be pushed forward and take up its position at about L.7.c.42.64.
(d) 1 Section will be pushed forward and take up its position at about L.7.c.44.58.
(e) The above sections and Lewis Gun Sections detailed in para 4 will be in their respective positions at ZERO minus 10 minutes.
(f) At ZERO plus 33 mins. the sections detailed in c & d above will rush the objective, after which withdrawal to our lines will be effected by the most favourable routes.

PASS WORD.

6. BLOODY.

SECOND ENTERPRISE.

7. (a) Will be carried out by a party consisting of Lieut. COLDHAM and 2 sections of "B" Company and will be carried out without Artillery Support except such as is afforded by that covering the first enterprise.
(b) Objective:- Enemy post at about L.7.a.15.40.
(c) This party will leave our lines at L.7.b.6.2. at 12 midnight.
(d) By Zero plus 25 minutes will be in a suitable position for rushing the objective at ZERO plus 33 minutes.
(e) Withdrawal to our lines will be effected by the most favourable routes.

PRISONERS &c. 8. Any identification obtained and number of prisoners will be wired immediately to Battalion Headquarters, prisoners and documents being conveyed sent there as soon as possible.

REPORTS. 9. Lieut. COLDHAM and 2nd Lieut. MANTON and Section Commanders of the 1st Enterprise Party will report to Battalion Headquarters as soon as possible immediately after their return in order to make their report.

MEDICAL ARRANGEMENTS. 10. 2nd Lieut. MANTON will arrange direct with O.C. "D" Company for additional Stretcher Bearers as required.

11. ACKNOWLEDGE.

2nd Lieut.,
Act. Adjt.,
1/5th Bn. L. N. Lancashire Regiment.

Issued at 8.10 p.m. 21/8/18. Copies as under:-

No. 1. Bde. H.Q.
2. Right Battalion.
3. Lieut. Manton.
4. Lieut. Coldham.
5. O.C. "D" Company.
6. O.C. "C" Company.
7. O.C. "B" Company.
8. Group Artillery (Left).
9. Commanding Officer.
10. War Diary.
11. File.
12. Spare.

SECRET.   Copy No.....

1/5TH BN. LOYAL NORTH LANCASHIRE REGIMENT
OPERATION ORDER NO. 83.

23/5/18.

Ref. Sheet 57 D. N.E. 1:20,000.

1. The Battalion will carry out an enterprise to-night with the object of capturing prisoners and obtaining identification.

2. Composition of Party - 1 Platoon under Lieut. GOLDHAM.

3. Objective - Enemy post L.8.a.[illegible].

ARTILLERY. 4. Artillery. 4.5 Hows. will fire on the following enemy M. G. Posts from Zero to Zero + 30 mins.

L.7.d.3.6.	1 How.
L.7.d.35.49.	1 How.
L.7.d.83.45.	2 Hows.
L.8.c.[illegible].	2 Hows.
L.8.b.[illegible].	2 Hows.
L.8.a.[illegible].	2 Hows.
FORK WOOD.	3 Hows.

5. Time of Exit of patrol - 12 midnight.

6. Point of Exit. - L.7.D.[illegible].

7. Zero Hour. (Time at which artillery opens and party rushes objective). - [illegible].30 a.m.

PASS WORD. 8. BACON.

PRISONERS &C. 9. Any identification obtained and number of prisoners will be wired immediately to Battalion Headquarters, prisoners and documents captured being sent there as soon as possible.

REPORTS. 10. Lieut. GOLDHAM will report to Battalion Headquarters as soon as possible immediately after his return in order to make his report.

MEDICAL ARRANGEMENTS. 11. Lieut. GOLDHAM will arrange direct with O.C. "B" Company for additional Stretcher Bearers as required.

12. ACKNOWLEDGE.

C. Blackburn

for Lieut., A/Adjt.,

1/5th Bn. L. N. Lancashire Regiment.

Issued at 4 p.m. 23/5/18. Copies as under:-

No. 1. Bde. H.Q.
2. Left Group Artillery.
3. Lieut. Goldham.
4. O.C. "B" Company.
5. Left Battalion.
6. Commanding Officer.
7. War Diary.
8. File.
9. Spare.

SECRET. Copy No. 11

1/5TH BN. LOYAL NORTH LANCASHIRE REGIMENT.
OPERATION ORDER NO. 25.

31/5/18.

1. The Battalion will move to the vicinity of ROSSIGNOL FARM at 1.0p.m. to-day.
Companies will move off by platoons at 5 minutes interval in the following order:-
Bn. H.Q., "A", "B", "C", "D".
Move to be completed by 2 p.m.

2. Company Commanders will notify Battalion Headquarters when they are settled in billets.

3. Huts, Billets, &c., will be left scrupulously clean and a certificate to this effect will be forwarded to the Battalion Orderly Room by 2.30p.m.

4. Dinners will be at 12 noon. Training Programme will be amended accordingly.

5. Battalion Headquarters will be established at ROSSIGNOL FARM at 2 p.m.

6. Officers' Kits and Mess Stores will be stacked at the Quartermaster's Stores by 2 p.m.

7. Orders regrding the Quartermaster's Stores and Transport will be issued later.

[signature]

A/Adjt.,
1/5th Bn. L. N. Lancashire Regiment.

Issued at 10 a.m. Copies to:-

1. Bde. H.Q.
2. O.C. "A" Company.
3. O.C. "B" Company.
4. O.C. "C" Company.
5. O.C. "D" Company.
6. Q. M.
7. T. O.
8. R. S. M.
9. H. Q. Company.
10. File.

A War Diary

SECRET. Copy No. 1.....

1/5TH. BN. LOYAL NORTH LANCASHIRE REGIMENT
ORDER NO. 19.

Ref: Sheet 57.D. N.E. 1/20:000.

1. In the event of attack, the Battalion will act as ordered by Brigade Headquarters.
The action of the Battalion in the event of attack will be as laid down in the following paras; any further action necessary will be ordered by Brigade Headquarters according to the situation.
2. Companies will be used either for the defence of BEER TRENCH or for counter attack, but will not advance E. of BEER TRENCH without orders from Battalion Headquarters.
3. Action if attack is indicated:-
(a) Should there be indication of enemy attack or on receipt of the message "TAKE PRECAUTIONS" from Battalion Headquarters, outposts will be at once placed in position in BEER TRENCH. These will consist of 4 L.G. Sections on each Company Front, with the remaining L.G. Sections in Reserve at the position of the Reserve Company.
(b) Companies will stand by and be prepared to man their defensive positions.
(c) Officers Commanding "A" & "D" Companies will detail a Liaison Officer to report to Headquarters 171st and 172nd Infantry Brigades respectively, to obtain information regarding the situation.
The above Headquarters are situated as follows:-
171st Infantry Brigade. E.28.d.1.8.
172nd Infantry Brigade. E.27.c.6.6.
(d) Should the Battalions on the front or flanks of the Brigade be attacked, the Companies will take up their defensive positions.
(e) All action will be reported immediately to Battalion Headquarters when an attack is threatened, if they have any parties away at work, if so where they are, or if they are all present.
4. Defence of BEER TRENCH. In case of attack:-
(a) BEER TRENCH will be occupied as a Defensive positionz by:-
1. "C" Company from K.3.c.4.3. to K.3.d.1.9. (approx.) with an advanced post of 1 Rifle Section at K.3.d.35.50. to effect a junction with the N.Z. Brigade in the night.
2. "B" Company from K.3.d.1.9. (approx.) to K.3.b.8.9. (approx.)
3. "A" Company from K.3.b.8.9. (approx.) to E.28.c.3.0.
(b) "D" Company will form a Defensive Flank from about E.28.c.9.8. to join with the FONQUEVILLERS Defences at about E.27.d.3.4. This Defensive Flank will be held by outposts and in case of necessity will be manned by the Reserve Company.
5. Nucleus Garrison. A nucleus garrison (gun and 3 O.R.) of all Lewis Gun Sections will be ready at any time to man the above positions in case of emergency.
6. Action of Working Parties.
(a) All working or carrying parties will proceed in fighting order. Companies will be at full strength (less nucleus Lewis Gunners). As much work as possible will be done during daylight.
(b) In the event of attack while they are away from their Battalion, working parties will take up a defensive position and the Officer in command of the party will at once report the strength of his party and position taken up to the nearest Battalion Headquarters of the Brigade in whose area he is working, and also by runner to his own Battalion Headquarters.
Parties will not return to their own Battalion without permission of the O.C. Battalion of the Brigade in the line to whom the Officer in charge has reported.
7. Accomodation of Companies in BEER TRENCH.
Dugouts and bivouacs of Companies in BEER TRENCH will be in the portion of trench they will occupy in case of holding it as a defensive position.
8. Counter-attack. Companies will be prepared to counter-attack on any part of the Divisional area as far E. as GOMMECOURT TRENCH on receipt of orders from Battalion Headquarters.
9. L.T.M. Battery. The L.T.M. Battery will place 2 Sections in position in BEER TRENCH forthwith, and will be under the orders of O.C. BEER TRENCH Battalion for tactical purposes.
These Sections will have positions sighted for the defence of this trench, and will also be prepared to move forward to support a counter-attack under the orders of the O.C. BEER TRENCH Battalion.

10. On receipt of the order "TAKE PRECAUTIONS" Battalion Liaison Party will report at Advanced Battalion Headquarters.
11. Ammunition Supply. Dumps are being established as follows:-
(a) In BEER TRENCH. S.A.A. 50,000 rds.
Near H.Q. BEER TR. BATTN. Bombs. 2,000.
(b) On receipt of the Order "TAKE PRECAUTIONS", the following transport will move under the Brigade Transport Officer to J.3.d.00.25. where it will form a Brigade Ammunition Reserve:-

S.A.A. Wagons. (32 boxes each).	3 per Battalion.
Bomb Wagon.	1.
Tool Wagons.	2 per Battalion.
Pack Animals.	8.

(c) Under Normal Conditions, the BEER TRENCH Battalion will have with it 44 drums per Lewis Gun Section.
(d) The Brigade Bombing Officer will be in charge of the Brigade Ammunition Reserve, and will arrange for wagons to be emptied and sent back to Rear Brigade Headquarters to refill in rotation.
(e) 3 L.G. Wagons of the Battalion will remain at the wagon lines, where they will be at the disposal of the Staff Captain for supply of T.M. Ammunition and rations.
(f) All transport, other than that mentioned in para. (b) above, will remain at the Battalion Wagon Lines under the Battalion Transport Officer, who will act under orders of the Staff Captain.
12. Advanced Brigade Headquarters will be established at J.3.b.78.60. at an hour which will be notified to units.
Rear Brigade Headquarters will remain at COUIN.
13. ACKNOWLEDGE.

2nd Lieut.,
Act. Adjt.,
1/5th Bn. L. N. Lancashire Regt.

Issued at 2-30 p.m. 7/5/18. Copies to:-

1. H.Q. Bde.
2. O.C. "A" Coy.
3. O.C. "B" Coy.
4. O.C. "C" Coy.
5. O.C. "D" Coy.
6. Capt. W.H. Satterthwaite.
7. Transport Officer.
8. War Diary.
9. File.
10. Spare.
11. Spare.

SECRET.   Copy No....1...

AMENDMENT NO. 1.
TO
1/5TH BN. LOYAL NORTH LANCASHIRE REGIMENT ORDER NO.19.

Delete Para. 4 (b) and substitute new para:-

"(b) A defensive flank will be formed on the left in the trench E.27.d.8.1. t o join with the FONQUEVILLERS defence about E.27.d1.8. This defensive flank will be held by outposts and in case of necessity be manned by the Res. Coy."

Para. 12. Fot "J.3.b.78.60." read "J.3. central.

2nd Lieut.,
Act. Adjt.,
8/5/18.   1/5th Loyal North Lancashire Regiment.

Issued at 11 a.m. Copies to all recipients of Bn. Order No.19.

Bn HQ

SECRET. Copy No.......

[illegible]th Bn. Loyal North Lancashire Regiment
Order No. [illegible].

Ref: Map Sheet [illegible]. [illegible] Edtn. [illegible] [illegible]/6/18.

1. The Battalion will relieve the [illegible]th Bn. "The Kings" Liverpool Regiment in Reserve in [illegible] SYSTEM on the [illegible]th inst. Relief to be complete by [illegible] p.m.

2. Dispositions. The dispositions will be as follows:-
"D" Company [illegible]th Bn.L.N.L. Regt. will occupy [illegible] LOCALITY.
"A" " " " " " " " [illegible] "
"C" " " " " " " " [illegible] "
"B" " " " " " " " [illegible] "
Bn. H.Qrs. " " " " " " "G" "

3. (a) Guides. Guides as under will meet Companies at the rendezvous junction of [illegible] and GUINNESS TRENCH, commencing with "D" Coy. at 3 p.m. followed by "A","C","B" and Headquarters at [illegible] hour intervals.
[illegible] guide per platoon.
1 guide Company Headquarters.
1 guide Battalion Headquarters.
(b) Companies will arrange to vacate their present positions in time to meet the guides at the above stated times.

4. Route.
(a) Companies will move by route to rendezvous under the least observation.
(b) Distance. A distance of [illegible] between sections will be maintained.

5. Advance Parties. The following Advance Parties will proceed and take over TRENCH STORES, Maps, &c., They will report at the Battn. Headquarters of the 2/6th (R.) Bn. "The King's" Liverpool Regt. at [illegible] noon on the [illegible]th June, 1918.
1 Sgt. for Battalion Headquarters.
1 Officer per Company.
[illegible] N.C.O. per Platoon.

6. Baggage, &c.
(a) All Company Stores, Officers' Mess Kits, &c. of "B" and "C" Companies and Bn. H.Qrs. will be stacked at CHATEAU DE LA HAIE by 2.30 p.m. ~~xx~~
They will be placed under the charge of a guard furnished by Battalion Headquarters.
(b) The Transport Officer will supply :-
1 Limber for "B" and "C" Companies.
1 Mess Cart for Bn. H.Qrs.
He will collect the baggage at [illegible] p.m. and convey it to the Notice Board S. of the Iron Gate on the [illegible] TRACK.
(c) After the limbers have been unloaded they will be loaded with baggage of the 2/6th (R.) Bn. "The King's" Liverpool Regt., which will be conveyed from the dump to the CHATEAU DE LA HAIE.
(d) "A" and "D" Companies will arrange to have their Stores, &c., carried to [illegible] TRENCH.

7. Trench Stores.
(a) All Trench Stores, Maps, &c. will be handed over to the incoming Unit and receipts obtained in duplicate, a copy will be forwarded to this Office by 9 a.m. the [illegible]th inst.
(b) All [illegible], &c. will be taken over from the 2/6th (R.) Bn. "The King's" Liverpool Regt. and receipt be given, a copy of which must reach this Office by 9 a.m. the [illegible] inst.

8. Cleanliness. All Billets, Trenches, and Shelters, &c., will be handed over scrupulously clean, a certificate to this effect will be obtained and a copy forwarded to this Office by [illegible] a.m. on the [illegible]th inst.

9. Completion of relief will be reported using the Code Word "SOAP".

10. ACKNOWLEDGE.

[signature] [illegible]/Lieut.,
A/Adjt.,
[illegible]th Bn. L.N. Lancashire Regiment.

Distribution:- As overleaf.

Issued at 3.[illegible]p.m. [illegible]/[illegible]/18. Copies to:-

1. Bde. H.Q.
2. 172nd. Infantry Bde.
3. O.C. "A" Company.
4. O.C. "B" Company.
5. O.C. "C" Company.
6. O.C. "D" Company.
7. O.C. "H.Q" Company.
8. Quartermaster.
9. Transport Officer.
10. 2/6th (R.) Bn. K.L.R.
11. Captain Catterthwaite.
12. War Diary.
13. File.

Confidential

War Diary

of

1st Battalion Loyal North Lancashire Regiment

Period 1st June 1918 to 30th June 1918

Volume 17.

Vol 35

Instructions regarding War Diaries and Intelligence Summaries are contained in F. S. Regs., Part II. and the Staff Manual respectively. Title Pages will be prepared in manuscript.

WAR DIARY

~~or~~

~~INTELLIGENCE SUMMARY~~

(Erase heading not required.)

Army Form C. 2118

Place	Date	Hour	Summary of Events and Information	Remarks and references to Appendices
Rossignol Farm	June 1		Billets & Trenches 3 Companies Training 1 Coy. training for Raid.	[illegible]
	2	-	do 3 " " 1 " " " " fixed for night of 2/3 cancelled owing to unforseen difficulties.	[illegible]
	3		do. Relieved 2/4 L.N.L – 2 Coys to Ban Dr. 1 Coy to Chateau de la Haie. C. Coy carried out raid on E. trenches in L 7.c. Heavy casualties inflicted on enemy. Our casualties 3 killed (including 2Lt. WISSETT) 7 wounded – 3 missing	[illegible]
	4		" 2 Coys. working parties. 1 Coy training – C Coy resting after raid at Rossignol Farm.	[illegible]
	5		" C. Coy. Relieved Coy. of 3/4 L.N.L at CHATEAU – 2 Coys. working parties 1 Coy. training	[illegible]
	6		" 2 Coys working – 2 Coys. training.	[illegible]
	7		" RELIEF of 2/6 The King's (LIVERPOOL) in STOUT TR. as Battn. in Reserve – Right Brigade Sector.	[illegible]
			Casualties in Bees Trench – Captain W.H. Satterthwaite (KILLED) Lieut Hollis, Lieut Edwards (WOUNDED) 2 OR's wounded.	

1875 Wt. W593/826 1,000,000 4/15 J.B.C. & A. A.D.S.S./Forms/C. 2118.

Instructions regarding War Diaries and Intelligence Summaries are contained in F. S. Regs., Part II. and the Staff Manual respectively. Title Pages will be prepared in manuscript.

WAR DIARY
or
~~INTELLIGENCE SUMMARY~~
(Erase heading not required.)

Army Form C. 2118

Place	Date	Hour	Summary of Events and Information	Remarks and references to Appendices
STOUT TRENCH	June 8th to	23rd	Battalion occupying the Reserve Sector in Stout Trench - Right Brigade Sector. 3 Coys working - D Coy. carrying party.	
			General work on the TRENCHES - improving trenches and dug-outs in each Coy sector. Opening out of disused trenches GOMMECOURT and MUSKETEER - Trenches widened and deepened and drained.	[initials]
	23rd		Relieved by the 2/4th Bn. South Lancashire Regt. on the night 22/23rd June 1918. - Battalion in Reserve (Divisional) taken over from the 2/4 Bn.	[initials]
CHATEAU de LA HAIE			South Lancashire Rgt. - "A" "B" "C" Companies and Headquarters in CHATEAU-DE-LA-HAIE; "D" Coy. in BEER TRENCH.	[initials]
	27th		Relieved by the 2/5 Bn. King's Own Rgt at the CHATEAU DE LA HAIE. Battalion in tents in wood at COUIN.	
COUIN	28th		Battalion carried out MUSKETRY on the RANGE. - Afternoon. Inspection of "A" Coy by the G.O.C. 170th Brigade	[initials]

1875 Wt. W593/826 1,000,000 4/15 J.B.C. & A. A.D.S.S./Forms/C. 2118.

Army Form C. 2118

Instructions regarding War Diaries and Intelligence Summaries are contained in F. S. Regs., Part II. and the Staff Manual respectively. Title Pages will be prepared in manuscript.

WAR DIARY
or
~~INTELLIGENCE SUMMARY~~

(Erase heading not required.)

Place	Date	Hour	Summary of Events and Information	Remarks and references to Appendices
COUIN June 29th			The Battalion relieved the 2/6th The King's (LIVERPOOL) Regt in the line on the night of 29/30th June.	
COMMECOURT	Feb 18		Line Quiet Day	

1875 Wt. W593/826 1,000,000 4/15 J.B.C. & A. A.D.S.S./Forms/C. 2118.

Instructions regarding War Diaries and Intelligence Summaries are contained in F. S. Regs., Part II. and the Staff Manual respectively. Title Pages will be prepared in manuscript.

WAR DIARY
or
~~INTELLIGENCE SUMMARY~~
(Erase heading not required.)

Army Form C. 2118

Place	Date	Hour	Summary of Events and Information	Remarks and references to Appendices
29.6.18			List of Awards:— 2nd. Lieut. E.A. Hollingrake – Bar to M.C.	
			27300 Cpl. A. Rolls. "C" Coy. M.M.	
			243402 Pte. C. Fletcher "C" Coy. M.M.	
			242929 Pte. C. Cooley "C" Coy. M.M.	
			242717 Sgt. A. Wray "C" Coy. M.M.	
			29395 C.S.M. J. Monaghan "C" " D.C.M.	
			242608 L/Cpl. J. Quigley. "C" D.C.M. (Birthday Honours)	
			DRAFTS:-	
			12.6.18 – 10.	
			19.6.18 – 13	
			20.6.18 – 10	
			24.6.18 – 43	

1875 Wt. W593/826 1,000,000 4/15 J.B.C. & A. A.D.S.S./Forms/C. 2118.

Army Form C. 2118

Instructions regarding War Diaries and Intelligence Summaries are contained in F. S. Regs., Part II. and the Staff Manual respectively. Title Pages will be prepared in manuscript.

WAR DIARY
or
INTELLIGENCE SUMMARY
(Erase heading not required.)

Place	Date	Hour	Summary of Events and Information	Remarks and references to Appendices
			Casualties:-	
			4.6.18 Killed – 1 Off. 2 O.R's	
			Missing 3 O.R's	
			Wounded 7 O.R's	
			5.6.18 " 3 O.R's	
			7.6.18. Killed 1 Off.	
			Wounded 2 Off. 3 O.R's	
			8.6.18. Killed 1 O.R.	
			Wounded 1 O.R.	
			13.6.18 " 1 O.R.	
			20.6.18. " 1 O.R.	
			22.6.18 Killed 1 O.R.	

1875 Wt. W593/826 1,000,000 4/15 J.B.C. & A. A.D.S.S./Forms/C. 2118.

SECRET.   Copy No. 11

Amendment No. 1 to 1/5th Battalion Loyal North Lancashire Regiment Order No. 56.

---

1. General Plan of Action. (Para. 12.) "B" Party for "L.7.c.15.40" read "L.7.c.37.70"
"D" Party for "L.7.c.37.70" read "L.7.c.30.40"

2. Liaison. (Para. 24.) For "Reserve Battalion Headquarters J.1.c.90.85. at 7 p.m." read "Left Brigade Headquarters [illegible].c.55.60. at 8 p.m."

3. Codenames. (Para. 25.) Add:-

Raiding Party Returned   SALOON.

4. Prisoners. (Para. 26.) All prisoners will be sent, under escort, to Headquarters of the Left Brigade in the Line - [illegible].c.55.60.

5. Battalion Representation. Captain T.H. Satterthwaite will represent the Battalion at the Left Brigade Headquarters in the Line.

Thomas Holt
Lieut.,
Act. Adjt.,
1/6/18.   1/5th Bn. L. N. Lancashire Regt.

Issued at 7-30 p.m. to all recipients of Order No. 56.

SECRET. Copy No...11....

1/5th Bn. Loyal North Lancashire Regiment
Order No. [illegible].

Reference Map [illegible].d.N.E. 1/[illegible].

Information. 1. A raid, with Artillery Support, will be carried out on the Enemy trenches on the night of the [illegible]/3rd June, [illegible].

Intention. 2. "C" Company, less 1 platoon, will carry out the raid. The object of the raid is to:-
(a) Obtain identification.
(b) Kill.
(c) Secure any documents or papers.
(d) Destroy dugouts.

Objective. 3. Enemy Front Line from L.7.c.[illegible]. to L7.c.[illegible]., and the two saps leading to our lines.

Composition of Raiding Party. 4.

"A" - O.C. Raid.	Captain F. Twaddle.	
Reserves	[illegible] Sections.	
Runners	4	
Signallers	[illegible]	
Stretcher Bearers	3	
"B" Right Blocking Party		1 Section.
"C" Left Blocking Party		1 Section.
"D" Left Flank Covering Party.		2 L.G. Sections.
"E" Right Assault Party		2nd Lieut. J.M. Bissett, 3 Sections & [illegible] men for demolition work.
"F" Left Assault Party		2nd Lieut. H.C. Mitchell, M.C., 3 Sections & [illegible] men for demolition work.

Forming up Line 5. For "A" L.7.c.45.[illegible].
For "B", "C", "E" & "F". L.7.c.[illegible].06. & L.7.c.[illegible].7[illegible].
For "D" L.7.c.7.7.
These parties will be in position by Zero - 15 minutes.

Action of Artillery. 6. Zero to Zero + 1 min. 18 Pdrs. On E.F.L. from K.12.d.[illegible].85. to L.7.c.65.10. E.S.L. from K.12.d.[illegible].[illegible]. to K.18.b.75.[illegible]. and on C.Ts. at about K.1[illegible].d. [illegible].[illegible].& K.1[illegible].d.75.40.
4.5s. on ROSSIGNOL WOOD & M.G.E's.
[illegible] T.M's. on ROSSIGNOL WOOD.

Zero + 1 min. to Zero + 45 mins. 18 Pdrs. On E.F.L. from K.12.d.7[illegible].[illegible]. to L.7.c.65.1[illegible]. lift on to E.S.L. from K.1[illegible].d.[illegible].65. to K.18.b.75.[illegible].
Remainder of Artillery as before.

Zero + 3 mins. to Zero + 45 mins. Heavy Artillery to assist with Counter Battery Work.
For full details of the action of the Artillery see Artillery Operation Orders.

Feint Barrage. 7. Zero to Zero + 15 mins. On Trenches in K.[illegible].c. & d. For further details see Artillery Operation Orders.

Machine Guns. 8. On E.S.L. in K.[illegible].d. On other targets as laid down in Operation Orders of O.C. 57th Div. M.G. Battalion.

Lewis Guns. 9. Arrangements have been made with the/Battalion in the line for their L.Gs. in RAILWAY TRENCH to fire into the East Corner of ROSSIGNOL WOOD during the raid.
[inserted above "Battalion": RARE]

Posts "C", "D" & "E". 10. Arrangements have been made with the Left Battalion in the line for the evacuation of Posts "C", "D" & "E" from 11 p.m. until the conclusionof the raid.

Assembly. 11. The Raiding Parties will embus at [illegible] CHURCH at [illegible]p.m. on Zero Day, and will debus at D.[illegible].b.[illegible]., from which point they will proceed to RAILWAY TRENCH

in the following order:-
"D","B", "C", "E" "F" "A" via the mule track, emergency mule track and HIGH STREET.
The prescribed intervals between Sections will be observed.
These parties will leave our lines at 11 p.m. and take up their respective positions on the Forming Up Line.

<u>General Plan of Action.</u> 12. At Zero hour the Artillery will put down an intense bombardment on the E.F.L. to be raided and on ~~other~~ other selected points.
From Zero to Zero plus 1 min. the raiding parties will advance close under the barrage.
At Zero plus 1 min. the bombardment on the E.F.L. will lift, and the action of the raiding parties will then be as follows:-
"B" Rush Forward to E.F.L. at L.7.c.[illegible].50. and establish a block at this point.
"C" Rush forward to E.F.L. at L.7.c.[illegible].35. and establish a block at this point.
"D" Move forward to top of ridge and open fire on E. Lines South of their position.
"E" Rush forward and capture or kill the garrison of the Enemy Post located at L.7.c.[illegible].40.
"F" Rush forward and capture or kill the garrison of the Enemy Post located at L.7.c.17.70.
The E.F.L. from L.7.c.[illegible].[illegible]. to L.7.c.3[illegible].35. will be cleared systematically and all dugouts demolished.
Prisoners captured will be sent back to O.C. Raid immediately under escort.
At Zero hour + 5 mins. the withdrawal will commence.
The Signal will be Green Very Lights fired in a series of ~~[illegible]~~. four
On return to our lines the raiders will pass along RAILWAY TRENCH, where the roll will be checked.
The raiders will then march back to the debussing point.

<u>RAID Headquarters.</u> 13. Will be at Post "D" - L.7.c.45.[illegible].

<u>Dress.</u> 14. All ranks taking part in the raid will blacken their faces and remove all marks of identification. A special identity label will be supplied to each man, and this label will be handed in on return to our lines.
Officers will be dressed like the men. Box Respirators will be worn at the Alert Position. Steel Helmets will be worn and will be coated with mud.

<u>Arms and Equipment.</u> 15. "A" - [illegible] reserve sections 3 bombs per man.
"B" - 4 men each with [illegible] bomb buckets holding [illegible] bombs per bucket.
"C" - ------------------do---------------------------
"D" - [illegible] bombs per man. 12 ammunition pans per Section.
"E" - 2 Sections - 3 bombs per man. (Each demolition
1 Section 6 bombs per man. man - [illegible] bombs, 3
"F" - [illegible] bombs per man. ('P' Bombs &
Each demolition man - [illegible] (demolition charge.
bombs, 3 'P' Bombs and
demolition charge.
All men excepting Nos. 1 & 2 per L.G. Section will carry rifles and bayonets and 15 rounds of S.A.A. in the pocket. All rifles will be loaded with 10 rounds, one of which will be in the breech. All bayonets and other bright articles will be painted a dark colour.

<u>Password.</u> 16. PETER.

<u>Forming Up Line.</u> 17. The I.O. will lay out the Forming Up Line prior to Zero hour.

Records. 18. List of Raiders will be made out by O.C. Raid and supplied to this Office.

Communications 19. The Battalion Signalling Officer will be responsible for establishing communication between Raid H.Q. – L.7.c.45.90. & Company Headquarters at K.3.d.7.1.

Zero Hour. 20. Zero hour will be notified later.

Medical. 21. All wounded will be evacuated through the R.A.P. at K.6.d.6.3. via Post "D". The Medical Officer will arrange for 2 dressers to be in attendance at the R. A. P.

Synchronization of Watches. 22. The Battalion Signalling Officer will be responsible for the synchronization of watches with a watch which will be forwarded by Divisional Headquarters at 5p.m. on Zero Day.

Reports. 23. O.C. Raid will arrange for all Officers & Section Commanders to report immediately on return to Battalion Headquarters for the compilation of the report of the raid.

Liaison. 24. An Artillery Officer will be present with O.C. Raid during the operations. He will meet O.C. Raid at Reserve Battalion Headquarters J.3.c.90.55. at 7 p.m. 2/6/18.

Code Names. 25. For telephonic use:-

Raid postponed 60 mins.		SOAP.
" " 24 hours.		RAZOR.
Much resistance.	Much	TOWEL.
Little resistance.	Little	SPONGE.
Retaliation - Heavy.		BATH.
" " Light.		BASIN.
Prisoners, with number.		BEARD.
M. Gs.		LATHER.
Casualties - Killed, with number		STROP.
" " Wounded " "		SHAMPOO.
" " Missing, " "		MANICURE.
NIL.		LOOFA.

Lieut.,
Act. Adjt.,
1/5th Bn. L. N. Lancashire Regt.

Issued at 8.30p.m. 1st June, 1918. Copies to:-

1. H.Q. 172nd Bde.
2. O.C. RIGHT Battalion in Line.
3. O.C. LEFT Battalion in Line.
4 - 7. O.C. RAID.
8. Signalling Officer.
9. Medical Officer.
10. War Diary.
11. File.
12. Spare.

War Diary

REPORT ON RAID 1/5TH BN. LOYAL NORTH
LANCASHIRE REGT. 3/4th JUNE,1918.

At [illegible]p.m. the raiding parties left COIGNEUX CHURCH and after debussing at SOUASTRE reached ST UT TRENCH at [illegible]p.m. All parties were in HERRING TRENCH by 10.30p.m. and in their respective positions at [illegible].45a.m.

The forming up line was laid out by the Intelligence Officer from "E" Post. The line from "C" Post was not laid owing to the fear of disturbing a reported enemy listening post previously reported at L.7.c.30.75. Prior to ZERO Hour a small patrol was sent out to this place which was found to be unoccupied.

The barrage fell at 12.50a.m. and was well placed. It did not seem to be so heavy as that of the previous night.

During the preliminary barrage our parties were able to approach within 25ˣ - 30ˣ of the E. F. L., and during the barrage, repeated cries were heard from wounded enemy.

When the barrage lifted our parties advanced and the enemy were found to be in large numbers, both in the E. F. L. and in front of the parapet.

"E" Party - The Right Assault Party - lost their Commander - 2nd Lieut. Wissett at the outset. The enemy held up the right section but the left section with the demolition party, succeeded in entering the E. F. L. and worked along the trench towards the post.
After proceeding 20ˣ they were met by a strong party of the enemy and came under heavy bomb fire.
Pte. COOLEY with a demolition charge climbed onto the parapet and threw the charge at the enemy, who gave no further trouble.
Another party of the enemy at about L.7.c.35.50 necessitated our party withdrawing from the E. F. L.

"F" Party under 2nd Lieut. Mitchell M.C., encountered the enemy in force in front of the parapet, and the enemy immediately threw a shower of stick bombs followed by hand grenades. A certain amount of loose wire was found in front of the post and in the face of the enemy resistance the raiding party failed to enter the E.F.L.

The Left Blocking Party - "C" Party - entered the enemy line but were driven out by greatly superior numbers and subsequently joined "F" Party.

The M. G. in the post at L.7.c.35.55 was very active as also were 2 Machine Guns in front of the Front Line on the Left.

In the Communication Trench leading from our "E" Post to E.F.L. were found [illegible] wires which are suspected to be alarm wires.

In response to our Artillery barrage the enemy put up Red Lights and from 1.15a.m. to 1.40a.m. several orange rockets were fired. The enemy artillery fire in reply was very slight.

At 1.[illegible]a.m. the withdrawal Signal Lights were fired and at 1.50a.m. all parties had returned to our lines.

Our Casualties were 3 Killed (including 2/Lieut. Wissett) and 7 O.Rs. wounded (including the Company Sergeant Major).

Judging by the numbers of the enemy, the resistance offer-~~kmm~~ ed and the stink barrage used against "F" Party it is conjectured that the enemy was fully prepared for the raid.

The accuracy of the barrage and the discharge of the demolition charge must have caused very heavy casualties to the enemy.

Signal Communication was maintained throughout between O.C. Raid and Headquarters of the Battalion in the Line.

C. Lloyd Sarford

Lieut-Col.,
4/6/18. Commdg. 1/5th Bn. L. N. Lancashire Regiment.

[illegible]. Copy No. ..11...

[illegible]th Bn. Loyal North Lancashire Regiment Order No. [illegible]

Reference:- Sheet [illegible]

1. The Battalion (less "C" Company) will relieve the [illegible]th Bn. L. N. Lancashire Regiment in BEER TRENCH and CHATEAU DE LA HAIE on the night [illegible]/[illegible]th June, [illegible].

2. Dispositions will be as follows:-
"A" Coy. [illegible]th Bn. L. N. L. Regt. will relieve "[illegible]" Coy. [illegible]/4th L. N. L. Regt. in the Left Sector, BEER TRENCH.
"D" Coy. [illegible]th Bn. L. N. L. Regt. will relieve "C" Coy. [illegible]th L. N. L. Regt. in the Right Sector, BEER TRENCH.
4 Lewis Gun Sections of "B" Company [illegible]th L. N. L. Regt. will relieve 4 Lewis Gun Sections of "A" Company [illegible]th L. N. L. Regt. in the Centre Sector, BEER TRENCH.
"B" Company [illegible]th L. N. L. Regt. (less Lewis Gun Sections) will relieve [illegible] Company [illegible]th L. N. L. Regt. in CHATEAU DE LA HAIE SWITCH.

3. Routes. Starting Point J.[illegible] b.[illegible] - J.[illegible] - J.[illegible] - E.[illegible].

4. Order of March. (a) "B" Company will pass starting point at [illegible] p.m. and will be met by guides at J.[illegible]
"A" Company will pass the starting point at [illegible] p.m.
"D" Company will pass the starting point at [illegible] p.m.
"A" & "D" Companies will be met by guides at [illegible].
(b) A distance of [illegible] between sections will be maintained.

5. Advance Parties consisting of:-

   1 Officer per Company.
   1 N.C.O. & [illegible] O.Rs. per Platoon.
   Sgt. Benjamin & [illegible] O.Rs. from Bn. H.Q.

will report at Battalion Headquarters at [illegible] p.m. to-day.

6. Baggage, etc. (a) All packs of men proceeding to the line will be handed into the Quartermaster's Stores at the following times:-

   Headquarters [illegible] p.m.
   "A" Company [illegible]-15 p.m.
   "B" Company [illegible] p.m.
   "D" Company [illegible] p.m.

(b) Officers' Valises, etc., not required in the trenches will be stacked at their Company Headquarters by [illegible] p.m. and the Transport Officer will arrange to have them collected and conveyed to the Quartermaster's Stores.
(c) Company Stores and Officers Mess Kits required in the trenches will be stacked at their Company Headquarters by [illegible] p.m. and the Transport Officer will arrange to have them collected and conveyed to the trenches.

7. All Trench Stores, Defence Schemes, etc., will be taken over on relief and receipts given, a copy of which must be forwarded to Battalion Headquarters by 10 a.m. on the [illegible]th inst.

8. All billets will be handed over scrupulously clean, and a certificate to that effect must reach this Office by [illegible] a.m. the [illegible]th inst.

9. Companies will report completion of relief, using the Code Word "COFFEE."

10. ACKNOWLEDGE.

[signature] 2nd Lieut.,
Act. Adjt.,
[illegible]th Bn. L. N. Lancashire Regt.

Issued at [illegible]-15 p.m. [illegible]/[illegible]/[illegible]. Copies to:-

1. Bde. H.Q.
2. O.C. [illegible]th L.N.L.Regt.
3. O.C. "A" Coy.
4. O.C. "B" Coy.
5. O.C. "C" Coy.
6. O.C. "D" Coy.
7. O.C. "H.Q." Coy.
8. Transport Officer.
9. Quartermaster.
11. War Diary.
12. File.

SECRET.

Copy No......9...

1/5th Battalion Loyal North Lancashire Regiment
Order No. 30

Reference Map, Sheet 57.D. N.E. 1/20:000.

1. (a) The Battalion will be relieved by the 2/4th Bn. South Lancs. Regt. in Reserve in the PURPLE SYSTEM on the night 22/23rd June, 1918.
(b) The Battalion will be in Divisional Reserve and will take over from the 2/4th Bn. South Lancs. Regt. "A", "B" & "C" Companies and Headquarters in CHATEAU-DE-LA-HAIE; "D" Company in BEER TRENCH.

2. Dispositions. The dispositions will be as follows:-
"A" Coy. 1/5th L.N.L. Regt. will be relieved by "C" Coy. 2/4th S.L. Regt. "B" Locality.
"C" Coy. 1/5th L.N.L. Regt. will be relieved by "D" Coy. 2/4th S.L. Regt. "C" Locality.
"B" Coy. 1/5th L.N.L. Regt. will be relieved by "A" Coy. 2/4th S.L. Regt. "E" Locality.
"D" Coy. 1/5th L.N.L.Regt. will be relieved by "B" Coy. 2/4th S.L. Regt. Right Sector BEER TRENCH.

3. Guides. Guides, as under, will meet Companies at the Rendezvous - HEBUTERNE - FONQUVILLIERS ROAD and MULE TRACK (E.27.c.9.3.) at 10 p.m. commencing with "D" Company at intervals of ½ hour, followed by "C", "A" & "B" Companies and Headquarters:-
1 Guide per Post.
1 Guide per Company Headquarters.
1 Guide per Battalion Headquarters.

4. Routes:- (a) From the rendezvous, the Guides will lead the Companies of the 2/4th S. Lancs. Regt., ~~Guides will~~ rendezvous at ST. MARTINS LANE & GUINNESS TRENCH.
(b) The route for Companies of the 1/5th L. N. L. Regt. to the rendezvous (E.27.c.9.3.), where they will be met by guides from their respective Companies, will be the above reversed.
(c) A distance of 50 yards between Sections and 100 yards between Platoons will be maintained.

5. Advanced Parties. The following Advanced Parties will report at Battalion Headquarters at 1 p.m., and proceed to take over:-
Lieut. Dixon & 1 Other Rank for Battalion Headquarters.
1 Other Rank for Company Headquarters.
1 Sergt. & 1 Other Rank per Platoon.
"A", "B" & "C" Companies and Battalion Headquarters will report at the Headquarters 2/4th Bn. South Lancs. Regt. at the CHATEAU-DE-LA-HAIE, and "D" Company to O.C. BEER TRENCH.

6. Trench Stores. (a) All Trench Stores, Maps, etc., will be handed over to the incoming Unit, and receipts obtained, a copy of which will be forwarded to this Office, in duplicate, by 9 a.m. on the 23rd inst.
(b) All Trench Stores, etc., will be taken over from the 2/4th Bn. South Lancs. Regt. and receipts given, a copy of which must reach this Office, in duplicate, by 9 a.m. on the 23rd inst.

7. Baggage. (a) All Company Stores, Officers Mess Kits, etc., of "A", "B" & "C" Companies and Headquarters will be stacked at the dump at the NOTICE BOARD S. of the IRON GATE on the MULE TRACK by 9 p.m.
(b) The Transport Officer of the 2/4th S. Lancs. Regt. will arrange to have the above baggage conveyed to CHATEAU-DE-LA-HAIE by 10-30 p.m.

8. Cleanliness. All dugouts, trenches and shelters will be handed over scrupulously clean. A certificate to this effect to reach this Office, in duplicate, by 9 a.m. on the 23rd inst.

9. Completion of Relief. Will be reported as follows:-

PURPLE SYSTEM	Code Word	"TOWEL."
CHATEAU-DE-LA-HAIE	" "	"RAZOR."

10. ACKNOWLEDGE.

Capt & Adjt

P.T.O.

Issued at 9 a.m. 22nd Junes 1918. Copies to:-

1. H.Q. Bde. (Advcd.)
2. O.C. 2/4th Bn. S. Lancs. Regt.
3. O.CM "A" Coy.
4. O.C. "B" Coy.
5. O.C. "C" Coy.
6. O.C. "D" Coy.
7. Transport Officer.
8. Quartermaster.
9. War Diary.
10. File.
11. R.S.M.
12.

SECRET. Copy No. 11

1/5th Bn. Loyal North Lancashire Regiment
Order No. 32.

28/8/18.

Issued at 11 p.m. 28/8/18.

Reference:- Map Sheet 57 d. 1/20,000.

Copies to:-
7. O.C. Personnel with Bn.H.Q.
8. Quartermaster.
9. Transport Officer.
10. O.C. /6th Bn.K.L.Regt.
11. War Diary.
12. File.

1. The Battalion will relieve the /6th Bn. The King's (Liverpool) Regt. in the line, Left Bn. of the Left Brigade Sector.

2. Dispositions. Dispositions will be as follows:-

"A" Coy. 1/5th L.N.L.Regt. will relieve "D" Coy. /6th K.L.Regt. in the Left Sector.
"D" Coy. " will relieve "C" Coy. /6th K.L.Regt. in the Right Sector.
"B" Coy. " will relieve "B" Coy. /6th K.L.Regt. in Support.
"C" Coy. " will relieve "A" Coy. /6th K.L.Regt. in Reserve.

3. Guides. The following guides of the /6th Bn. The King's (L'pool) Regt. will meet "A", "D", "B" Coys. and personnel of Bn.H.Q. at junctn. of ALLSOPP C.T. and FONQUEVILLERS Road (E.26.c.90.70) at 9.45 p.m.
Guides for "C" Company will be at junctn. of MULE TRACK and FONQUEVILLERS Road at E.26.d.30.10. at 10.15 p.m.
There will be 2 guides per Platoon and 3 for Personnel with Bn. Headquarters.

4. (a) Order of March. Companies will pass the starting point D.26.d. 35.90. at 7 p.m. in the following order:-
"A", "D", "B" Coys., Personnel with Bn.H.Q. and "C" Company.
(b) A distance of 50x between Sections and 100x between Platoons will be maintained.
(c) Dress. Battle Order.

5. Route. Starting Point - D.27.d.70.00.-D.28.c.00.30.-D.29.c.85.35- J.6.b.30.95.-E.26.d.30.10.-E.27.d.60.79.-E.28.c.10.70.

6. Advance Parties. The following Advance Parties will proceed and take over:-
1 N.C.O. & 2 Signallers for Personnel with Bn. H.Q.
1 Officer per Company.
1 N.C.O. per Platoon.
They will parade at the Battalion Orderly Room at 9.45 a.m. on the 29th inst., and will report at the Battalion H.Q. of the /6th Bn. The King's (L'pool) Regt. in SALMON TR. at 11 a.m.

7. Baggage.
(a) All Valises and mens' packs will be stacked near the Battalion Ordy. Room by 2 p.m. on the 29th inst.
The Transport Officer will arrange to have them collected and conveyed to the Quartermaster's Stores, where they will be stored.
(b) All Company Stores and Officers' Mess Kits, required in the trenches, will be stacked near the Bn. Orderly Room by 6 p.m. on the 29th inst.
The Transport Officer will arrange to have them collected and conveyed to the Battalion Ration Dump situated at E.28.c.80.30. by 11 p.m. After unloading he will convey the baggage of the /6th Bn. The King's (L'pool) Regt., to ROSSIGNOL FARM.

8. Stores, &c.
(a) All tents and stores will be handed over to the /7th Bn. The King's (L'pool) Regt. and receipts obtained. Copies of receipts, in duplicate, must reach this Office by 9 a.m. on the 30th inst.
(b) All Trench Stores, &c., will be taken over on relief and receipts given. Copies of receipts, in duplicate, must reach this Office by 9 a.m. on the 30th inst.

9. Cleanliness. The Company Lines, &c., will be handed over scrupulously clean, and a certificate obtained to that effect, a copy of which must reach this Office by 9 a.m. on the 30th inst.

10. Surplus Personnel. Surplus Personnel in accordance with App. VI Column I of Battalion Organization, will proceed to MARIEUX in the afternoon on the 29th inst.

11. ACKNOWLEDGE.

[signature] Captn. & Adjt.,
1/5th Bn. Loyal North Lancashire Regiment.

P. T. O.

[illegible]

Copy No.

Amendment to 1/5 Bn Loyal
North Lancs Regiment Order No 30.

25/6/18

Para 1 (b) Delete "D" Company in BEER TR"
and substitute "Four Lewis Guns and nucleus
teams of "D" Company in centre sub sector BEER
TR and remainder of Company to CHATEAU
DE LA HAIE".

A. Runnacre [signature] Capt & Adjutant
1/5 Bn L. N. Lancs Reg.

Issued at 9 a.m. 25/6/18.
Copies to all recipients of Order No 30.

[initials]

[illegible]

SECRET.

Vol 36

Confidential

War of Diary

1/5th Battalion Royal North Lancashire Regiment

Period 1st July 1917 to 31st July 1918.

Volume 18.

Instructions regarding War Diaries and Intelligence Summaries are contained in F. S. Regs., Part II. and the Staff Manual respectively. Title Pages will be prepared in manuscript.

WAR DIARY

~~or~~

~~INTELLIGENCE SUMMARY~~

(Erase heading not required.)

Army Form C. 2118

Place	Date 1918.	Hour	Summary of Events and Information	Remarks and references to Appendices
LEFT SECTOR LEFT DIVISIONAL FRONT - GOMMECOURT	July 1		Trenches. Quiet day. At night relieved by N.Z. Division. Marched to SOUASTRE + embussed for VAUCHELLES	[illegible]
VAUCHELLES	2		Camp. Rest + cleaning up. Reconnaissance	[illegible]
	3		" " " "	[illegible]
	4		" Training	[illegible]
	5		" "	[illegible]
	6		" "	[illegible]
	7		" Sunday. Church Parade	[illegible]
	8		" Training	[illegible]
	9		" "	[illegible]
	10		" "	[illegible]
	11		" " 1 company working party	[illegible]
	12		" "	[illegible]
	13		" "	[illegible]
	14		" Sunday. Church Parade	[illegible]

1875 Wt. W593/826 1,000,000 4/15 J.B.C. & A. A.D.S.S./Forms/C. 2118.

Army Form C. 2118.

WAR DIARY
or
~~INTELLIGENCE SUMMARY.~~
(Erase heading not required.)

Instructions regarding War Diaries and Intelligence Summaries are contained in F. S. Regs., Part II. and the Staff Manual respectively. Title pages will be prepared in manuscript.

Place	Date 1918	Hour	Summary of Events and Information	Remarks and references to Appendices
VAUCHELLES	JULY 15		Camp Training	J
	16		" " & Brigade Parade for farewell speech by Brig General F. G. Guggisberg B.G.C. 170th Infantry Brigade	J
	17		" Training - Brigade Operation	J
	18		" Training	J
	19		" " & Battalion Sports	J
	20		" " 2 Companies - Working party	J
	21		" Sunday. Divisional Sports.	J
	22		" Training & do.	J
	23		" Inspection by Brig General G. F. Boyd CMG., DSO. DCM., BGC 170th Infantry Brigade ~~& Training~~.	J
	24		" Training	J
	25		" do.	J
	26		" do. Brigade & Divisional Contests for A.R.A. Competition	J
	27		" do. 1 Company Working Party	J

AMENDMENT TO REPORT ON RAID 1/[illegible]TH BN. LOYAL NORTH LANCASHIRE REGIMENT [illegible] June, 1916.

Our casualties were 3 Killed (including [illegible]/Lieut. Wissett), 7 O.Rs. wounded (including the Company Sergeant Major) and 3 O.Rs. Missing.

Lieut-Col.,

4/6/16. Commdg. 1/[illegible]th Bn. L. N. Lancashire Regt.

Army Form C. 2118.

Instructions regarding War Diaries and Intelligence Summaries are contained in F. S. Regs., Part II. and the Staff Manual respectively. Title pages will be prepared in manuscript.

WAR DIARY

or

~~INTELLIGENCE SUMMARY~~.

(Erase heading not required.)

Place	Date 1918	Hour	Summary of Events and Information	Remarks and references to Appendices
VAUCHELLES	JULY 28		Camp. Sunday. Brigade Church Parade + Brigade Sports	[illegible]
VAUCHELLES	29		moved by march route to LE SOUICH	[illegible]
LE SOUICH	30		moved by march route to HAUTEVILLE	[illegible]
HAUTVILLE	31		moved by march route to Camp near ETRUN	[illegible]

A5834 Wt. W4973/M687 750,000 8/16 D. D. & L. Ltd. Forms/C.2118/13.

Ex 21

Addenda to Battn Order No 33

Para I. add (c)

The Battalion will be in Corps Reserve and will be in readiness to move at 1 hour's notice between 9 PM and 9 AM and at 2 hours notice between 9 AM and 9 PM.

[illegible signature]

Capt & Adjt
1/5 L.N.L. Regt

Secret — Copy No. 9

1/5 Bn Loyal North Lancs Regt
Order No. 33.

Ref trench [illegible] 5 [illegible] 1/20,000

1 (a) The Battalion will be relieved by the [illegible] [illegible] [illegible] [illegible] [illegible] [illegible] [illegible] Wellington Regt on the night 1st/2nd [illegible]

(b) On completion of relief the Battalion will be [illegible] of VAUCHELLES and will proceed by [illegible] from SOUASTRE CHURCH D 22 [illegible]

2 Relief will be as follows:–

"A" Coy 1/5 L N L Regt LEFT FRONT SECTOR will be relieved by [illegible] Coy [illegible] Regt.

2 Platoons "D" Coy 1/5 L N L Regt RIGHT FRONT SECTOR will be relieved by 2 platoons [illegible] Company [illegible] Wellington Regt.

2 Platoons D Coy 1/5 L N L Regt RIGHT FRONT SECTOR will be relieved by [illegible] platoons [illegible] Wellington Regt

"B" Coy 1/5 L N L Regt SUPPORT will be relieved by 6th Coy [illegible] Regt.

"C" Coy 1/5 L N L Regt RESERVE will be relieved by [illegible] Company [illegible] Wellington Regt.

3 Guides – [illegible] guides per platoon of "A" "B" & "D" Companies will report to Lieut DEAN at [illegible] at 8.30 P.M. They will proceed to [illegible] at ALLSOPP'S TR & FONQUEVILLERS [illegible] ROAD (E. 25 a. 15 70) and meet the platoons of the incoming unit at 9.30 P.M.

2 Guides per platoon of C Company [illegible] at E [illegible] [illegible] at 9.30 P.M. and meet [illegible] of the Wellington Regt.

[illegible] will be in possession of [illegible] with the [illegible] of [illegible] and the platoon, company and [illegible] that [illegible] [illegible]

4 (a) [illegible] [illegible] to E. 25 a. 15 70 MULE TRACK (E. 27 d. 60 70) – E. 26 [illegible] – E. 26 [illegible] – D. [illegible] 40 60 – D. 22 [illegible] where they will be met by Lieut FORSHAW who will allot them [illegible]

(b) 2/Lieut FORSHAW will meet the [illegible] 1/6th [illegible] at D. 22 [illegible] 20 10 and [illegible] with the [illegible] for the [illegible] at [illegible] P.M.

5 Baggage

All Company [illegible] stores [illegible] of "A" "B" and "D" and Headquarters will be dumped at the junction of TRAMLINE and HIGH ST by 5.30 PM.

"C" Company will dump their stores at the Bn H.Q. [illegible] by 10 P.M.

6 All Trench Stores maps [illegible] will be handed over to the relieving units receipts [illegible] in duplicate and 1 copy to be forwarded to this office by 9 a.m. the 2nd inst.

7 Cleanliness

All billets will be [illegible] certificate [illegible] will be forwarded to this office by 9 a.m. the 2nd instant.

8 Completion of relief will be reported using the code words:

"A" Company — ADAM

"B" " — BENJAMIN

"C" " — CHARLIE

"D" " — DAVID

9 Companies will report [illegible] the location of their Company H.Q.

10 Acknowledge.

[illegible] Capt & Adjt

1/5 L.N.L. Regt.

Issued at 8.30 AM 1/7/18.

Copies to

1 Headquarters 17[illegible] Inf Bde
2 [illegible] Regt
3 1 Wellington Regt
4 [illegible] Wellington Regt
5 – 8 All Companies
9 Lieut [illegible]
10 Quartermaster
11 [illegible]
12 File
13 Spare

Lieut Dean

S E C R E T Copy. No. 10

1/5th Battalion Loyal North Lancs. Regt.

ORDER No. 36.

Reference Map, LENS 11, 1.100,000

1. The Battalion will move by march route to HAUTEVILLE to-day 30th inst.

2. The Battalion will be formed up in Column of route, facing East and in the following order, Bn. Headquarters, "A", "B", "C" and "D" Company and transport, with the head of the column at a point Road Junction 4.E.45.69 by 11.20 a.m.

3. (a) Route. INVERGNY- SUS. St.LEGER - X Roads. ½ mile N. of R. in SUS. St. LEGER - GRAND RULLECOURT- AVESNES-LE-COMTE - thence to billets.
(b). Dress. Battle Order.

4. Baggage.
(a). Officers' valises and company stores will be stacked at the Quartermaster's stores by 9.30 a.m.
(b). Men's packs will be stacked near the Quartermaster's Stores by 9.30 a.m. by companies.

5. O. C. "D" Companu will detail an officer to march in rear of the Battalion to collect all N.C.Os. and men who fall out, and march them as a party to the destination.

6. Distances. A distance of 100 yards between companies and its transport will be maintained, and 200 yards between Battalions.

7. Lieut. Wyles will report to Brigade Headquarters at Starting Point (Road Junction 4.E.50.64). He will be mounted. The Transport will arrange to supply a horse.

8. Baggage wagons will march with No. 2 Company Divisional Train and will join that unit as it passes the Starting Point (4.E.50.64)

9. Billeting party. 2nd Lieut. Grose, 4 C.Q.M.Sgts. and Sgt.Willets for Bn. Headquarters will reportto the Staff Captain at the TOWN Majors at HAUTEVILLE at 11 a.m. to arrange Billets for the battalion.

10. Cleanliness. All billets will be left scrupulously clean and in a sanitary conditions and certificates will be handed in to this Office by 6 p.m. to-day, 30th inst.

11. Companies will report when present in Billets, giving the location of their Company Headquarters.

12. Acknowledge.

[signature]
Capt. & Adjt.
1/5th Bn. L. N. Lancashire Regt.

COPIES to :-

1- 4. All Companies.
5. Headquarter Coy.
6. Brigade.
7. Transport Officer.
8. Quartermaster.
9. Lieut. Grose.
10. ~~Commanding Officer.~~ War Diary.
11. File.

SECRET. Copy No. 

1/4th Bn. L. N. Lancashire Regiment.

Map Reference, LENS 11. 1.100,000

ORDER No. 37.

1. The Battalion will move to ETRUN by march route, 31st inst.

2. (a). The Battalion will be formed up in column of route at a point G.6.38.31, at 1. 38 p.m. in the following order :- Bn. Headquarters "B", "C", "D", and "A" Company and Transport.

(b). A distance of 100x will be maintained between Companies and transport, and 200x between Battalions.

3. Baggage. Officers' valises and Company Stores will be stacked near the Quartermaster's Stores by 12 noon.

4. Dress:- Marching Order, (steel helmets carried on the packs).

5. Billeting party. A Billeting Party, consisting of 2nd Lieut. Grese, 4 C.Q.M.Sgts., and Sgt. Willets for Bn. Headquarters will report at the Battalion Orderly Room at 11 a.m. to-morrow the 31st inst., for the purpose of taking over billets. On arrival at destination they will report to Y Huts near E. in ETRUN and take over from opposite number of 171st Brigade.

6. Cleanliness. All billets will be left in a clean and sanitary condition, and certificates to that effect will be forwarded to this Office by 7 p.m. to-morrow, 31st inst.

7 Acknowledge.

Capt. & Adjt.
1/4th Bn. L. N. Lancashire Regt.

COPIES TO :-

1. O. C. "A" Coy.
2. O. C. "B" Coy.
3. O. C. "C" Coy.
4. O. C. "D" Coy.
5. O. C. H. Q. Coy.
6. Transport Officer.
+ 7. Quartermaster.
8. 170th Infantry Brigade.
9. R. S. M.
10. Commanding Officer.
11. File.
12 War Diary

30/7/1[illegible].

16

CONFIDENTIAL

VR 37

War Diary

—"—

1/5th L. N. Lancashire Regt.

August 1918.

—"—

170/57

Army Form C. 2118.

Instructions regarding War Diaries and Intelligence Summaries are contained in F. S. Regs., Part II. and the Staff Manual respectively. Title pages will be prepared in manuscript.

WAR DIARY
or
~~INTELLIGENCE SUMMARY.~~
(Erase heading not required.)

Place	Date	Hour	Summary of Events and Information	Remarks and references to Appendices
ETRUN	1-8-18		Battalion relieved the 5th CANADIAN CAVALRY in the line in the FEUCHY SECTOR. 'B' Company repulsed a raid on them, capturing one wounded prisoner & killing one of the enemy. Lt. Maclagan killed going up the line. Lt Dell, 2nd Lts BENJAMIN & BUTTERFIELD gassed & evacuated.	
FEUCHY SECTOR	2-8-18		A quiet day in the line, enemy artillery being very quiet. No movement observed behind his line. Our patrols	
"	3-8-18		Enemy artillery fairly active on our front. Our patrols saw nothing of the enemy.	
"	4-8-18		A quiet day, except for intermittent shelling of the enemy front line by our artillery. Our patrols active.	
"	5-8-18		Suspicious noises heard in wire on 'B' Company's front in early morning, but a strong patrol which was sent out failed to discover any signs of the enemy. Much individual movement behind the enemy lines, men being seen by our observers in small parties throughout the day. Our artillery active against E.F.L.	
"	6-8-18		Enemy fired about 70 gas shells on our front line between 1-2 a.m. Harassing fire throughout the day on the enemy support lines.	
"	7-8-18		Harassing fire by artillery on enemy support lines all day. Increased artillery activity on our front & support line. Battalion relieved by 2/4th L. N. Lancs, & went into reserve at ANZIN-ST-AUBIN.	

A5834 Wt. W4973/M687 750,000 8/16 D. D. & L. Ltd. Forms/C.2118/13.

Army Form C. 2118.

Instructions regarding War Diaries and Intelligence Summaries are contained in F. S. Regs., Part II. and the Staff Manual respectively. Title pages will be prepared in manuscript.

WAR DIARY
or
INTELLIGENCE SUMMARY.

(Erase heading not required.)

Place	Date	Hour	Summary of Events and Information	Remarks and references to Appendices
ANZIN-ST AUBIN	8-8-18		BATTALION arrived at ANZIN-ST-AUBIN between 2-4 a.m. No parade during day. Company Scouts sent out to reconnoitre route to be followed to reserve position in event of an attack.	
"	9-8-18		A Company on range, D Company baths, B & C Coys route march of 6 miles. C Coy proceeded to ARRAS to work under the 502 Field Coy R.E.	
"	10-8-18		B Coy to baths, A & D Coy route march. Battalion ceremonial under the C.O. at 12 noon.	
"	11.8.18		Training	
"	12.8.18		Sunday	
	13.8.18		Training. 'B' Company Special training for projected operation	
	14.8.18		Training	
	15.8.18		Relieved the 7/5 "The King's Own" as Batt. in Support	
BLANGY LINE etc.	16.8.18		In Trenches. Quiet day	
	17.8.18		do. do.	
	18.8.18		Moved into forward trenches on evening of 18/19th and at 1 am. 'B' & 'D' Companies attacked the Enemy Trenches just South of the River SCARPE on a frontage of 600x.	

A5834 Wt. W4973/M687 750,000 8/16 D. D. & L. Ltd. Forms/C.2118/13.

Instructions regarding War Diaries and Intelligence Summaries are contained in F. S. Regs., Part II. and the Staff Manual respectively. Title pages will be prepared in manuscript.

WAR DIARY
or
~~INTELLIGENCE SUMMARY.~~
(Erase heading not required.)

Army Form C. 2118.

Place	Date 1918	Hour	Summary of Events and Information	Remarks and references to Appendices
FEUCHY	Aug 18/19		ICELAND & IONIAN trenches were captured & consolidated, and MURRAY TRENCH was secured by 2.30 am.	
	19		Numerous counterattacks were repulsed during the day. At 10.30 pm we occupied & garrisoned INDIAN TRENCH.	
	20		At 8.30 am the Enemy strongly attacked INDIAN TR. and at the third attempt secured a footing in the trench. Our garrison was eventually forced to withdraw to MURRAY TR. Subsequent counterattacks on MURRAY, ICELAND & IONIAN were successfully dealt with. At 4 pm the Enemy with increased Artillery heavily bombarded our trenches and this bombardment ceased at 6 pm. At 9 pm, under orders our troops were withdrawn to the original line. This withdrawal was completed successfully by 11 pm. Our Casualties during the whole operation were –	

Army Form C. 2118.

Instructions regarding War Diaries and Intelligence Summaries are contained in F. S. Regs., Part II. and the Staff Manual respectively. Title pages will be prepared in manuscript.

WAR DIARY
or
~~INTELLIGENCE SUMMARY.~~
(Erase heading not required.)

Place	Date 1918	Hour	Summary of Events and Information	Remarks and references to Appendices
FEUCHY	August 20		Killed 5 Other Ranks.	
			Wounded 2/LTs WYLES + LONG.	
			24 Other Ranks.	
			The Battalion moved to ~~ANZIN~~ ARRAS as Reserve Battalion.	[illegible]
ARRAS	21		Resting + Baths. At 7 pm Battalion moved to ANZIN.	[illegible]
ANZIN	22		Rest. C.O.s parade to express Congratulations of Corps Commander, Divisional + Brigade Commanders.	[illegible]

A5834 Wt. W4973/M687 750,000 8/16 D. D. & L. Ltd. Forms/C.2118/13.

Army Form C. 2118.

Instructions regarding War Diaries and Intelligence Summaries are contained in F. S. Regs., Part II. and the Staff Manual respectively. Title pages will be prepared in manuscript.

WAR DIARY
or
~~INTELLIGENCE SUMMARY.~~
(Erase heading not required.)

Place	Date	Hour	Summary of Events and Information	Remarks and references to Appendices
ARRAS	20-8-18		Battalion relieved in line FEUCHY SECTOR. Returned to billets in Arras	
ARRAS	21-8-18		Battalion moved from ARRAS to billets at ANZIN.	
ANZIN	22-8-18		Battalion proceeded by route march to WANQUETIN	
WANQUETIN	23-8-18		Battalion moved to SUS-ST. LEGER, and went into billets.	
SUS-ST-LEGER	24-8-18		Remained for one day at SUS-ST. LEGER prior to proceeding up the line	
SUS-ST. LEGER	25-8-18		March continued to BAILLEULMONT. Battalion billetted there for one night	
BAILLEULMONT	26-8-18		March continued to HENDECOURT-lez-RANSART. Bivouacked in trenches	
HENDECOURT-lez-RANSART	27-8-18		Battalion proceeded to NEUVILLE VITASSE, and slept in the open.	
NEUVILLE-VITASSE.	28-8-18		Battalion moved into line, and acted as "mopper-up" to 172 Brigade who made an attack in front of HENDECOURT and RIENCOURT. Subsequently the Battalion took up positions ready to make an attack on RIENCOURT the following day.	
RIENCOURT Sector	29-8-18		Battalion moved forward in close support to the 2/5 R.O.R.L.R. who attacked and took RIENCOURT.	

D. D. & L., London, E.C.
(10340. Wt W5300/P713 750,000 3/18 E 2688 Forms/C/2118/16.

Instructions regarding War Diaries and Intelligence Summaries are contained in F. S. Regs., Part II. and the Staff Manual respectively. Title pages will be prepared in manuscript.

WAR DIARY
or
~~INTELLIGENCE~~ SUMMARY.
(Erase heading not required.)

Army Form C. 2118.

Place	Date	Hour	Summary of Events and Information	Remarks and references to Appendices
RIENCOURT Sector	30-8-18		Positions taken up by the Battalion to guard the western outskirts of RIENCOURT, which had been retaken from the 2/5 K.O.R.L.R.	
RIENCOURT Sector	31-8-18		Battalion relieved by the 8th Irish (the King's) and came into support.	

		Officers	O.R.
Battalion Strength	1-8-18	38	912
	31-8-18	38	902
Casualties		8	97

D. D. & L., London, E.C.
(10340) Wt W5300/P713 750,000 3/18 E 2688 Forms C/2118/16.

WAR DIARY

1/5th. Loyal North Lancs. Regt.

Sept. 1918.

Confidential

War of Diary

1/5th Battalion Loyal North Lancashire Regt.

Period 1st September to 30th September 1918

Volume 20.

Army Form C. 2118.

WAR DIARY

~~or~~

~~INTELLIGENCE SUMMARY.~~

(Erase heading not required.)

Instructions regarding War Diaries and Intelligence Summaries are contained in F. S. Regs., Part II. and the Staff Manual respectively. Title pages will be prepared in manuscript.

Place	Date	Hour	Summary of Events and Information	Remarks and references to Appendices
RIENCOURT SECTOR	1-9-18		Battalion took over from 2/6 K.L.R. the positions in CORSE TRENCH and CRUX TRENCH, ready to move forward to support the 171 Inf. Brigade. Capture of RIENCOURT by 171 Inf Brigade (6 p.m.). 2 Lt Dean wounded gassed.	
"	2-9-18		At 5 a.m. the Battalion took up positions in MORDEN, TERRIER, BULLDOG, and STARFISH TRENCHES. Attack on enemy position by CANADIAN CORPS and XVII Corps began at 5.0 a.m very satisfactory, the enemy being eventually pushed back to the CANAL DU NORD. One company of the Battalion went forward and cleared the trenches forward of the DROCOURT – QUEANT LINE. Liaison posts were established forward with the 2/4 S LANCS Regt. 2/Lt LEES wounded (shell shock)	
"	3-9-18		Battalion moved back to the HINDENBURG Support Line near TUNNEL TRENCH (S.W. of FONTAINE-LES-CROISILLES)	
HINDENBURG SUPPORT LINE	4-9-18		Refitting of companies	
	5-9-18		Brig Gen BOYD C.M.G., D.S.O., D.C.M., left the Brigade to take command of 46th DIVISION. Training	

A5834 Wt. W4973/M687 750,000 8/16 D. D. & L. Ltd. Forms/C.2118/13.

Army Form C. 2118.

WAR DIARY
or
~~INTELLIGENCE SUMMARY.~~
(Erase heading not required.)

Instructions regarding War Diaries and Intelligence Summaries are contained in F. S. Regs., Part II. and the Staff Manual respectively. Title pages will be prepared in manuscript.

Place	Date	Hour	Summary of Events and Information	Remarks and references to Appendices
HINDENBURG SUPPORT LINE	6-9-18		Training by Companies	
— " —	7-9-18		Battalion moved up into reserve north of QUEANT	
PROCOURT-QUEANT LINE	8-9-18		Reconnoitring of forward area by all Officers	
	9-9-18		Relieved IRISH GUARDS in MOEUVRES Sector - Front Line	
MOEUVRES	10-9-18		Throughout day, resisting Enemy bombing attacks. Enemy Artillery fairly quiet.	
	11-9-18		Again enemy active with bombing attacks right up to 6-15 pm when the Battalion attacked the village of MOEUVRES under cover of Artillery barrage. Attack successful and line established following day approx just east of the CANAL DU NORD	
	12		Enemy bombing counterattack repulsed. At 6 pm heavy T M barrage put down on our new line and	

A5834 Wt. W4973/M687 750,000 8/16 D. D. & L. Ltd. Forms/C.2118/13.

Army Form C. 2118.

Instructions regarding War Diaries and Intelligence Summaries are contained in F. S. Regs., Part II. and the Staff Manual respectively. Title pages will be prepared in manuscript.

WAR DIARY
or
~~INTELLIGENCE SUMMARY.~~
(Erase heading not required.)

Place	Date	Hour	Summary of Events and Information	Remarks and references to Appendices
MOEUVRES			Enemy infantry attacks in conjunction dealt with. At 9 pm Enemy succeeded in filtering men into MOEUVRES on the left of the Batt boundary and enveloped our left Company. After 2 hours fighting the Company succeeded (after failing to get touch with flank Company) in fighting its way through the village & in taking up a defensive position west of the village. At dawn after reorganising the Company the Company Commander cleared the village of the enemy and re-established our new line.	
	13		Enemy fairly quiet. Small bombing attacks dealt with successfully. At night ~~out~~ relieved by 1/5 The King's Own the Batt moving into reserve in the HINDENBURG LINE	

A5834 Wt. W4973/M687 750,000 8/16 D. D. & L. Ltd. Forms/C.2118/13.

Instructions regarding War Diaries and Intelligence Summaries are contained in F. S. Regs., Part II. and the Staff Manual respectively. Title pages will be prepared in manuscript.

WAR DIARY

or

~~INTELLIGENCE SUMMARY~~.

(Erase heading not required.)

Army Form C. 2118.

Place	Date	Hour	Summary of Events and Information	Remarks and references to Appendices
MOEUVRES RESERVE	14		In Reserve	
"	15			
"	16		Relieved at night by R S FUSILIERS – 52nd Div – and proceeded to bivouac in vicinity of BULLECOURT.	
BULLECOURT	17		Resting	
	18		Marched to BOYELLES entrained for SAULTY-LABRIERE and marched to billets at SAULTY	
SAULTY	19		Training + reorganisation	
	20		Training + Baths	
	21		Training	
	22		"	
	23		"	
	24		"	
	25		At night marched to SAULTY STATION entrained, + detrained at VRAUCOURT. Marched to NOREUIL + arrived at bivouac ground at 5-30 am.	

A5834 Wt. W4973/M687 750,000 8/16 D. D. & L. Ltd. Forms/C.2118/13.

Instructions regarding War Diaries and Intelligence Summaries are contained in F. S. Regs., Part II. and the Staff Manual respectively. Title pages will be prepared in manuscript.

WAR DIARY

or

~~INTELLIGENCE SUMMARY~~.

(Erase heading not required.)

Army Form C. 2118.

Place	Date 1918	Hour	Summary of Events and Information	Remarks and references to Appendices
NOREUIL	SEPT 26		Resting at NOREUIL. ~~Reconnaissance~~	
	27	AM. 4.30	Marched from NOREUIL as part of Reserve Brigade via QUEANT, PRONVILLE & HINDENBURG LINE and reached Sunken road E 29 a (57c N.E.) at midnight. Bivouacked here.	
E 29 a	28	8 am	Followed up the attack via ANNEUX and took up dispositions in line F 23 c 1.4. F 28 central F 29 c 0.0 (57c N.E.) with Batt H.Q. at F 28 a 7.2.	
F 28 a 7.2	29		Withdrew to bivouac area F 25 b & spent night there.	
F 25 b	30		Moved forward at 4.50 am. awaited orders in F 23 b until 5 pm when Batt. relieved 1/7th K.L.R. in PROVILLE sector.	
~~PROVILLE~~			Strength of Battalion 1st Sept. 1918. Officers 36, O.Rs. 922 30th " " 35, 805	

Ey 10/18

G. J. Gordon
Lieut Col
Cmdg. 1/5th L. N. Lancs Regt

A5834 Wt. W4973/M687 750,000 8/16 D. D. & L. Ltd. Forms/C.2118/13.

On His Majesty's Service.

170/57

1/5th L N Lancs

October 1918.

Vol 39

Confidential

War Diary

of

1/5th Bn Loyal North Lancashire Regt.

Period 1st October to 31st October 1918.

Volume 21.

Instructions regarding War Diaries and Intelligence Summaries are contained in F. S. Regs., Part II. and the Staff Manual respectively. Title pages will be prepared in manuscript.

WAR DIARY
or
~~INTELLIGENCE SUMMARY.~~
(Erase heading not required.)

Army Form C. 2118.

Place	Date 1918	Hour	Summary of Events and Information	Remarks and references to Appendices
	Oct.			
PROVILLE	1	1744	Attacked from PROVILLE, objective being trench through A 15 c, + A 21 b (57c N.W.) Attack unsuccessful. Prisoners secured 21. Casualties 7 Officers (Killed Lt G B COOK, Lt THORNLEY, 2/Lt WALLIS; wounded Capt MALLETT, 2/Lt MITCHELL, Lt DELL, Wounded & missing 2/Lt FORSHAW). Other Ranks 23 killed, 110 wounded, 18 missing, 3 wounded & missing	"A" Narrative Operations Oct 1st. R6.
	2		Heavy shelling + T.M. bombardment. Frequent patrols out in an endeavour to get touch with Batt. on left (2/4th Loyal N. Lancs), who had been successful with their attack made by one Company. At night relieved by 1/5 The King's Own (R.L.) Regt. Batt taking up position in Brigade Reserve on CANAL BANK F 30 a + F 29 d. (57c N.E.)	R6
	3		Same position.	R6
	3 & 4	0430	B + D Cos attached to 1/5th The King's Own (R.L.) Regt to assist in defence of PROVILLE. Orders issued for reconnaissance (See App B)	"B"
			At night 4/5 Batt relieved by 1 Royal MUNSTER Fusiliers, Batt moving to bivouac ground F 21 d.	R6.

A5834 Wt. W4973/M687 750,000 8/16 D. D. & L. Ltd. Forms/C.2118/13.

Instructions regarding War Diaries and Intelligence Summaries are contained in F. S. Regs., Part II. and the Staff Manual respectively. Title pages will be prepared in manuscript.

WAR DIARY
or
~~INTELLIGENCE SUMMARY.~~
(Erase heading not required.)

Army Form C. 2118.

Place	Date 1918	Hour	Summary of Events and Information	Remarks and references to Appendices
F21d	Oct 5		Bivouacs – Refitting & Resting.	HB
	6		Sunday – Refitting & Resting. Voluntary C. of E. Service. Received preliminary orders regarding the role of the Batt. in an attack to take place on the 8th Oct.	HB
	7		Reconnoitred area of attack in morning. In afternoon Batt. moved forward to assembly position and before	HB
	8		Zero hour got into position on Forming up line – See special report on Operations.	(C)
G.3 & 4 57b N.W.			At night relieved by 1/5 The King's Own (R.L.) Regt.	HB
G 8 & 9	9		Batt. in Support. In afternoon Batt. moved back to area F21	HB
F 21 57c N.E.	10		Morn cleaning up & refitting. In afternoon Batt. marched to area D29c (57C N.E.)	HB

A5834 Wt. W4973/M687 750,000 8/16 D. D. & L. Ltd. Forms/C.2118/13.

Instructions regarding War Diaries and Intelligence Summaries are contained in F. S. Regs., Part II. and the Staff Manual respectively. Title pages will be prepared in manuscript.

WAR DIARY
or
INTELLIGENCE SUMMARY.
(Erase heading not required.)

Army Form C. 2118.

Place	Date 1918	Hour	Summary of Events and Information	Remarks and references to Appendices
Sheet 57CNE D29c.	Oct. 11		Training under Company arrangements.	R.L.
—"—	12		Battalion marched to HERMIES (Ref. Map 57CNE J34a) and entrained there at 17-30 hrs en route for CALONNE-RICOUART.	R.L.
CALONNE-RICOUART (Ref. Map LENS 11. F80.80)	13		Battalion arrived by train at LAPUGNOY at 08-30 hrs and marched to billets at CALONNE-RICOUART. Refitting of companies.	R.L.
—"—	14		Battalion moved by route march to FOSSE (Ref. Map Bethune (Combined Sheet) R21b and R22a), and entered billets there.	R.L.
FOSSE {Ref. Map BETHUNE (combined sheet). R21b + R22a}	15		Reconnaissance by C.O. and Company Commanders of the positions to be taken over by the Battalion when the Brigade moves into the line. Training under Company arrangements. Address to the battalion by the C.O.	R.L.
FOSSE	16		Training by Companies. Tactical scheme for one Platoon of each Company, & topography class under C.O. for Platoon Commanders.	R.L.
—"—	17		Battalion moved by route march to FROMELLES (Ref. Map Bethune (Combined Sheet) N23a) and entered billets. At 13.45 hrs battalion left FROMELLES and marched to RADINGHEM (O9c) and entered billets there.	R.L.

A6945 Wt. W11422/M1160 350,000 12/16 D. D. & L. Forms/C./2118/14.

Instructions regarding War Diaries and Intelligence Summaries are contained in F. S. Regs., Part II. and the Staff Manual respectively. Title pages will be prepared in manuscript.

WAR DIARY
or
INTELLIGENCE SUMMARY.
(*Erase heading not required.*)

Army Form C. 2118.

Place	Date	Hour	Summary of Events and Information	Remarks and references to Appendices
RADINGHAM	Oct 18		Battalion moved by route march to LE CANTELEU (Ref Map Sheet 36 P36c) and entered billets there	P6.
LE CANTELEU	19		Battalion marched to HELLEMMES, taking a route round the southern boundaries of LILLE, no troops being allowed in the latter town. Battalion entered billets at HELLEMMES.	P6.
HELLEMMES (Sheet 36 R12b4d)	20		Battalion moved by route march to LE GRAND MARAIS (Ref Map Sheet 37 M4c) and entered billets there.	P6.
LE GRAND MARAIS	21		Battalion marched to TEMPLEUVE and took over billets from the 13th WEST RIDING'S (59th Division). The battalion became support battalion of the 170 Infantry Brigade the other two battns being in front line.	P6.
TEMPLEUVE (Sheet 37 H 33b)	22		Battalion parade in battle order. Lewis Gun instruction. Battn. under 30 mins notice to move forward in support.	
— " —	23		Company training. Lewis Gun instructions. Reconnaissance by C.O. & Adjutant of line to be taken over	

D. D. & L., London, E.C.
(10340. Wt W5300/P713 750,000 3/18 E 2688 Forms/C/2118/16.

Instructions regarding War Diaries and Intelligence Summaries are contained in F. S. Regs., Part II. and the Staff Manual respectively. Title pages will be prepared in manuscript.

WAR DIARY
or
INTELLIGENCE SUMMARY.
(Erase heading not required.)

Army Form C. 2118.

Place	Date	Hour	Summary of Events and Information	Remarks and references to Appendices
TEMPLEUVE (Sheet 37 H32b)	Oct 24.		Battalion relieved the 2/5 Bn. K.O.R.L. Regt. in the front line. Relief completed by 19-30 hrs. 'C' (Right) 'A' (Centre) and 'D' (Left) Companies in the front line, with 'B' Coy. in reserve. Intermittent hostile artillery fire throughout the relief. Right Coy in touch with a post of 172 Inf. Brigade at O 2 d 9.4. Left Coy in touch with a post of the Somerset Light Infantry (59th Div) at I 26 c 8.2. Battn. frontage extended along R. ESCAUT from I 26 central to O 3 a. 0.0.	Appendix K
Sheet 37 H 36 c 75.75.	25.		Heavy bombardment of PONT-A-CHIN (I 32) at frequent intervals. Several heavy shells in neighbourhood of B.H.Q. (H 36 c). Our artillery not very active. Inf. bridges which had been constructed by the R.E. at I 32 a 9.1, I 26 c 8.4, I 32 a 8.3 were all found to be broken. During the night R.E.s did not complete repair of the bridge at I 26 c 8.4	
— " —	26		Increased activity on part of our artillery. Enemy artillery very active against PONT-A-CHIN in retaliation for which our field guns and 4.5 hows. fired on the [illegible] and [illegible] at PARADIS (I 33 a). Enemy planes brought down one of our artillery planes in the vicinity of N.S. Patrol sent out across river to examine the road from I 32 d 4.9 to I 33 c. 1.9. Nothing seen of the enemy. B Coy relieved A Coy in front line	Appendix L
— " —	27		Hostile batteries engaged and retaliatory shoots made throughout the day, especially on PARADIS (I 32 a). Enemy artillery very active, PONT-A-CHIN being heavily shelled. Bridge at I 26 c 8.4 repaired by R.E. A patrol crossed the river at I 26 c 8.4 and met an enemy patrol, the enemy suffering casualties. A second patrol crossed the river at I 32 a 9.1, but saw nothing of the enemy	Appendix M & M1
— " —	28		Enemy artillery again active against our positions. Retaliatory shoots carried out by our artillery. Battalion was relieved in front line by 2/5 Bn. K.O.R.L. Regt. and moved back into reserve at TEMPLEUVE	Appendix N

D. D. & L., London, E.C.
(10340. Wt W5300/P713 750,000 3/18 E 2688 Forms C/2118/16.

Instructions regarding War Diaries and Intelligence Summaries are contained in F. S. Regs., Part II. and the Staff Manual respectively. Title pages will be prepared in manuscript.

WAR DIARY
or
INTELLIGENCE SUMMARY.
(Erase heading not required.)

Army Form C. 2118.

Place	Date	Hour	Summary of Events and Information	Remarks and references to Appendices
TEMPLEUVE	Oct 29		Refitting of Companies. Training under Company arrangements. Instructions [illegible] by the Battalion [illegible] sent to Brigade (see Appendix D) for use by the relieving [illegible] (4th)	[illegible] Appendix D
—"—	30		Training for 3 hours under Company arrangements. Presentation by Brigade Commander of parchments awarded to men of the battalion for gallantry during recent operations. Riding classes for officers started.	[illegible]
—"—	31		Battalion marched to RUE FRANCHE (Sheet 37 M11c) and took over billets vacated by 1st Bn. London Irish Regt., the latter replacing the battalion at TEMPLEUVE	Appendix [illegible] "E"

		Officers	ORs
Strength of Battalion on	1-10-18	34	778
"	31-10-18	35	667
Killed in action		3	44
Wounded		6	156
Wounded and missing		1	9
Missing		—	11

G. P. [illegible] Lt Col
Cd. 1/5th LN LR
3/11/18

D. D. & L., London, E.C.
(10340. Wt W5300/P713 750,000 3/18 E 2688 Forms/C/2118/16.

SECRET.

'D'

War Diary

Copy No. 19.

170TH INF. BDE. ORDER NO. 159.

11th Octr. 1918.

Reference Shts:- 57C.N.E.) 1-20,000.
57C.N.W.)
LENS.) 1-100,000.
HAZEBROUCK.)

1. 170th Inf. Bde. Group (less portion of transport which has already proceeded by road) will move by tactical trains to the MARLES-LES-MINES Area on Octr. 12th, and will be transferred to I Corps, Fifth Army.

2. March to entraining stations and entrainment will be carried out in accordance with the attached Tables 'A' and 'B'. Table 'C' shows detail of troops and transport to proceed by Train No. 5.

3. On arrival at LAPUGNOY (detraining station) units will proceed to billots as follows:-

Bde. H.Q.	MARLES - LES - MINES.
2/4th L.N.L.R.... ...	
170th L.T.M.B.... ...	
502nd Fld. Coy., R.E.....	
3/2nd (W.L.) Fld. Ambce.	
No. 2 Coy., 57th Div. Train.	
2/5th K.O.R.L. Rogt.....	LOZINGHEM.
1/5th L.N.L. Rogt......	CALONNE - RICOUART.

Units will march to billets from the detraining station in the order of their serial Nos. in Tables 'A' & 'B'.

4. (a) Quartermasters of battalions and 1 Officer from each other unit proceeding by train No. 5 will report to the Staff Captain at FREMICOURT STATION at 14.00 hours Octr. 12th.

(b) One officer from each unit proceeding by train No. 4 will report to the Bde. Major at HERMIES STATION at 15.00 hrs. Octr. 12th to assist in entrainment.

These officers will know the entraining strengths of their unit.

(c) The above officers will be required to assist in detraining at LAPUGNOY.

5. No detrainment will take place until definite orders have been given to that effect.

6. Intervals of 100 yds. between Coys. and 100 yds. between transport of units will be maintained during all marches.

7. Arrival in billets in the new area and location of new H.Q. will be reported to Bde. H.Q.

8. Bde. H.Q. will close at D.29.c.8.8 at 12.30 hrs. Octr. 12th. and will be on No. 5 train, re-opening at MARLES-LES-MINES on completion of move.

9. ACKNOWLEDGE.

[signature]
Captain,
Brigade Major,
170th Infantry Brigade.

Issued through Sigs.
at 17.30 hours. 11/10/18.

COPIES TO-
1-2. 2/5th K.O.R.L.R. 7-8. 170th L.T.M.B. 13. 57th Div. 'G'.
3-4. 2/4th L.N.L.R. 9-10. 502nd Fld. Coy. R.E. 14. do. 'Q'.
5-6. 1/5th L.N.L.R. 11-12. 3/2nd (W.L.) F.A. 15. Brigadier.
16. Bde. Major. 17. Staff Capt. 18. Bde. Sigs. Offr. 19. W.D. 20. File.

Train No 4

Bat[illegible] markers ready to move off

[illegible] ——— [illegible] to [illegible] at 12.00 to [illegible]

[illegible] (note [illegible] strengths)

Repeat 5

Train No 5

Transport [illegible] march off 11.30
route ———

[illegible] Staff [illegible] leave 14.00
note [illegible] ~~strengths~~

Synchronize 9.15 Am.

D

Copy No. 4

S E C R E T. 1/5th Bn. Loyal North Lancashire Regt.

O R D E R No. 49.

Ref. Sheets, 57c. N.E. - 1/20,000.
57c. N.W. - 1/20,000.
LENS - 1/100,000

---

1. The Battalion will move by march route to HERMIES STATION, where ~~they~~ it will entrain. ~~They~~ It will detrain at LAPUGNY, and will march to billets in the Area of CALONNE - RICOUART.

2. STARTING POINT J.5.b.05,80.

3. Order of March.
(a). Battalion Headquarters, "A", "B", "C" and "D" Companies. The head of the column will be ready to pass the Starting Point at 12.55.
(b). A distance of 100x between Companies ~~[illegible]~~ will be maintained.

4. Dress. Marching Order (Steel helmets and blankets carried on the packs).

5. Route.
Brigade Starting Point Road junction J.5.b.5.8. - ~~[illegible]~~ - Track J.6.a.7.1. - DEMICOURT - HERMIES - J.30.a.3.3. - ~~[illegible]~~ - ~~[illegible]~~ ~~K.[illegible]~~. J29 central - J35 a 01

6. Transport.
(a). The following transport will be ready to move off at 10.55, and will pass Starting Point Road Junction J.4.b.3.1 at 11.25, and will entrain at FREMICOURT Stn.

1 G.S. Wagon
2 Cookers.
1 Watercart.
1 Mess Cart.
4 riders.

(b). Route. LOUVERVAL - BEUGNY - FREMICOURT.

7. (a). R.Q.M.S. Rigby will report to the Staff Captain at FREMICOURT Stn. at 14.00.
(b). 2nd Lieut. Cook will report to the Brigade Major at HERMIES Stn. at 15.00 to assist in entrainment. He will know the entraining strength. No detrainment will take place until orders have been given to that effect.

8. Baggage.
Officers' kits will be stacked at the Quartermaster's Stores by 10.00. The Mess Cart will be loaded by 10.30 a.m.

9. Cleanliness. The Area occupied by the Battalion will be left in a clean and sanitary condition. Certificates to that effect will be rendered to this office by 12.30.

10. On arrival in billets Company Commanders will report when settled down, and give the location of their Company Headquarters.

11. (a) Time of entrainment for Battalion, 15.15. Time of arrival 20.20

(b). Transport entrain 14.15. Time of arrival 21.30.

12. Rations for consumption on the 13th instant will be issued at HERMIES Stn. prior to entraining.

13. ACKNOWLEDGE.

G.P. Gordon
~~Capt. & Adjt.~~ Lt. Col
Cmdg 1/5th Bn. L. N. Lancashire Regt.

ISSUED at 07.00

Copies to :- 1 - 4. All Coys.
5. Commanding Officer.
6. R.Q.M.S.
7. File.
8. 170th Inf. Bde.

D

TABLE "A" for personnel moving by Train No. 4.

SERIAL NO.	UNIT.	FROM.	TO.	STARTING POINT.	TIME PASSING S.P.	ROUTE TO STATION.
1.	Part of 170th Bde. H.Q.	D.29.c.	HERMIES STA:	Rd. junc. J.5.b. 3.4.	13.00.	Track to J.6.a. 7.1 -DEMICOURT-HERMIES J.30.a. 3.3-J.~~30.b.2.4-J.30.c.8.3-K.31.a.0.3.~~ J35 a 01
2.	1/5th L.N.L.	do.	do.	do.	13.03.	do.
3.	2/5th K.O.RL.	do.	do.	do.	13.12.	do.
4.	2/4th L.N.L. (less 1 Coy.)	do.	do.	do.	13.21.	do.
5.	502nd Fld.Co.	do.	do.	do.	13.27.	do.
6.	3/2nd (W.L.) Fld.Ambce.	do.	do.	do.	13.35.	do.

NOTE - The above train will convey PERSONNEL ONLY. Time of entrainment - 15.15. Time of arrival at LAPUGNOY - 20.20.

TABLE "B" for personnel moving by Train No. 5.

SERIAL NO.	UNIT.	TO.	STARTING PT.	TIME PASSING S.P.	ROUTE.	REMARKS.
1.	170th Bde.H.Q. (less portion travelling by Train No.5)	FREMICOURT STA:	Rd. junc. J.4.b.3.1.	11.15.	LOUVERVAL-BEUGNY - FREMICOURT	-
2.	1 Coy.2/4th L.N.L.R.	do.	do.	11.20.	do.	Loading & unloading party
3.	1/5th L.N.L.R. (T'pt. only)	do.	do.	11.25.	do.	
4.	2/5th K.O.R.L. (T'pt. only)	do.	do.	11.30.	do.	
5.	2/4th L.N.L.R. (T'pt. only).	do.	do.	11.35.	do.	
6.	170th L.T.M.B.	do.	do.	11.40.	do.	
7.	502nd Fld.Coy. R.E.(T'pt.only)	do.	do.	11.45.	do.	
8.	3/2nd (W.L.)Fld. Ambce.(T'pt.only)	do.	do.	11.50.	do.	

NOTE - This train will convey transport and such personnel as is laid down in Table 'C'.
Time of entrainment - 14.15. Time of arrival at LAPUGNOY- 21.20.

::::::::::

TABLE 'C'. Detail of transport proceeding by Train No.5.

UNIT.	PERSONNEL Offrs.	O.Rs.	HORSES.	4-WHEELED VEHICLES.	2-WHEELED VEHICLES.
Bde. H.Q.					
1 G.S. & 1 L.G.S.	6	14	7	-	-
wagon.	-	4	4	2	-
Bde. Sig. Secn. (L.G.S. wagon).	1	27	9	1	-
Battns. (each).	1	-	-	-	-
2 cookers.	-	2	4	2	-
1 water cart.	-	2	2	-	1
1 baggage wagon.	-	2	2	1	-
1 mess cart.	-	1	1	-	1
4 riders.	-	4	4	-	-
1 L.G.S.	-	1	2	1	-
502nd Fld.Coy.,R.E.	1	-	-	-	-
1 L.G.S. wagon.	-	1	2	1	-
1 mess cart.	-	1	1	-	1
4 riders.	-	4	4	-	
3/2nd (W.L.) Fld.A.	1	-	-	-	-
1 G.S.Wagon.	-	2	2	1	-
1 L.G.S.Wagon.	-	1	2	1	-
1 mess cart.	-	1	1	-	1
3 riders.	-	3	3	-	-
170th L.T.M.B.	4	50	-	-	-
1 Coy. 2/4th L.N.L. (loading and unloading party).	4	100.	-	-	-

Copy No....

E.

1/5th Bn. Loyal North Lancashire Regiment.

ORDER NO. 50.

Ref. BETHUNE, Combined Sheet, 1:40,000.

1. Routine Order No.565 of to-day is cancelled, and the following substituted:-
   170th Infantry Brigade Group will move to the FOSSE - BOUT - DEVILLE Area to-morrow, 14th inst.

2. Billeting Area will be allotted by the Staff Captain. Arrangements to be made later. Lieut. GROSE and the usual billeting parties will be prepared to move early to-morrow.

3. Halt will be made for dinner at 11.50 hours, the march being resumed at 13.30 hours. During this halt, the road will be kept clear. Troops will not halt in villages.

4. The Battalion will follow the 2/4th Bn. L. N. Lancs. Regt. A distance of 500^x between Battalions, 100^x between other units, companies, and the Battalion and its Transport will be maintained on the march.

5. Location of Transport and Company Headquarters will be reported to Battalion Headquarters on arrival.

6. The Battalion will march in the following order:-
   Battalion Headquarters.
   "B" Company.
   "C" Company.
   "D" Company.
   "A" Company.

   The head of the column will pass the starting point namely:- CHURCH N.E. corner of CALONNE-RICOUART on MARLES -les-MINE Road at 08.15. hrs.

7. Route:- CHOCQUES - CHAUXL'ABBAYE - W,14.d.4.6. - HINGES - Q.28.d.9.-. - Q.30.b.5.8. - R.31.d.1 7.

8. Baggage. Officers' Kits to be stacked at the Quartermaster's Stores by 07.15. hrs. Mess Kit will be packed by 07.45. hrs.

9. ACKNOWLEDGE.

Issued at 10.15 p.m. 13/10/18.

[signature]
Captn. & Adjt.,
1/5th Bn. Loyal N. Lancashire Regt.

Copies to:-
1 - 4. All Coys.
5. Commanding Officer.
6. 2nd Lieut. P. Grose.
7. Quartermaster & Transport Officer.
8. 170th Infantry Brigade.
9. File.
10. R. S. M.

SECRET.

Copy No....3

170TH INF. BDE. ORDER NO.163.

24.10.18.

1. 1/5th L.N.L.R. will relieve 2/5th K.O.R.L.R. in the front line tonight.
   On relief 2/5th K.O.R.L.R. will move into Reserve at TEMPLEUVE.
   H.Q. 1/5th L.N.L.R. will be established at H.36.c.75.75. on relief.

2. All arrangements for relief will be made between Commanding Officers concerned.

3. Completion of relief will be wired to Bde. H.Q. by the Code Words "RATIONS ARRIVED".

4. ACKNOWLEDGE. done

Issued at 1045 hrs.

24.10.18.

Captain.
for Brigade Major.
170th Infantry Brigade.

COPIES TO:-

1. 2/5th K.O.R.L.Regt.
2. 2/4th L.N.L. Regt.
3. 1/5th L.N.L. Regt.
4. 170th L.T.M.Batty.
5. 502nd Fld.Coy.R.E.
6. "C" Coy.57 Bn.M.G.C.
7. 171st Inf. Bde.
8. 177th Inf. Bde.
9. 57th Div. "G".
10. Bde. Signal Offr.
11. Offr. I/C Aux. Stretcher Bearers.
12. 2/3rd Wessex Fld.Amb.
13. War Diary.
14. File.

SECRET.

On completion of relief of 2/5th K.O.R.L.R. by 1/5th L.N.L.R., the latterwill form the advance guard in case of enemy withdrawal as laid down in 170th Inf. Bde. Order 162 dated 22.10.18.

Lt.Col. G.J.P. GOODWIN, D.S.O., R.E. Commdg., 1/5th L.N.L.Regt. will be the Advance Guard Commander.

Captain.
Brigade Major.
170th Infantry Brigade.

Issued at 1045 hrs.
24.10.18.
To :- All recipients of
170th Inf. Bde. Order 162.

K

B.M. 3549.

Date 23.10.18.

170TH I.

O.C. 2/5th K.O.R.L. Regt.
O.C. 2/4th L.N.L. Regt.
O.C. 1/5th L.N.L. Regt.

1. Tactical situation permitting, 1/5th L.N.L. Regt. will relieve 2/5th K.O.R.L. Regt. in the line tomorrow, Oct. 24th.

On relief 2/5th K.O.R.L. Regt. will move into Reserve.

2. It is considered that the present Bn. H.Q. at RAMEGNIES is unsuitable and is too much on the extreme left of the line.

O.C. 1/5th L.N.L. Regt. will therefore have a reconnaissance carried out with a view to finding a H.Q. in a more central position and more suitable for that of a Battn. holding the line on what is for the present a stable front.

The vicinity of I.36.c. is sugested.

Captain.
Brigade Major.
170th Infantry Brigade.

23.10.18.

N

Copy No....3

170TH INF. BDE. ORDER NO.166.

27.10.18.

1. 2/5th K.O.R.L. Regt. will relieve 1/5th L.N.L. Regt. in the line tomorrow, Oct. 28th.
On relief 1/5th L.N.L. Regt. will move into Reserve at TEMPLEUVE.

2. All arrangements for relief will be made between Commanding Officers concerned.

3. Completion of relief will be wired to Bde. H.Q. by the Code Word "CONCRETE".

4. ACKNOWLEDGE. (Done [illegible] 27/10/18)

[signature]

Captain.
Brigade Major.
170th Infantry Brigade.

Issued at 1845 hrs.
27.10.18.

COPIES TO:-
1. 2/5th K.O.R.L.R.
2. 2/4th L.N.L.R.
3. 1/5th L.N.L.R.
4. 170th L.T.M.B.
5. 502 Fld.Coy.R.E.
6. "C" Coy.57 Bn.M.G.C.
7. 286 Bde. R.F.A.
8. 172nd Inf.Bde.
9. 177th Inf.Bde.
10. 57th Div. "G".
11. Brigadier.
12. Brigade Major.
13. Bde. Signal Offr.
14. War Diary.
15. File.

OC "A" Company
OC "B" Company
OC "C" Company
OC "D" Company
Bde HQ
War Diary

—·—

1. It is possible that the enemy may attempt to establish a bridge-head in the vicinity of RAMEGNIES-CHIN and PONT-A-CHIN to secure his position on the River. Preparations are to be made to resist such an attempt.
2. The main line of resistance of the out post system will be the MAIN Road, through O.2.a and b, I.32.a & c. I.26.c including the village of PONT-A-CHIN and the Southern portion of RAMEGNIES-CHIN
3. Companies will prepare posts on this LINE tonight as follows:–
"D" Company from Northern boundary to I.32.a.0.6 Road junction inclusive.
"A" Company from I.32.a.0.6 Rd. junction exclusive to I.32.c.6.4.
"C" Company I.32.c.6.4 to

[illegible] boundary

[illegible] flags [illegible]

[illegible] marking of [illegible]

[illegible] of trench at the side

of the road.

A. [illegible] posts, as far as

possible [illegible] R.B. & L.G.

posts [illegible] to

[illegible] roads [illegible]

towards the [illegible]. Every

post must be reconnoitred

before dark and [illegible]

[illegible] by night

[illegible]

[illegible] should be

[illegible] at once [illegible]

[illegible]

These posts are to be used

[illegible] in case the

posts at present held are

driven in.

[signature illegible]

26/10/18 [illegible] Capt. [illegible]

1

Copy No 6

SECRET.

1/5 Bn Loyal N. Lancs Rgt
Order No

B Company will relieve A Company tonight. Company Commanders will make all arrangements for relief and O.C. B Coy will reconnoitre the front before 17.30 hrs. Actual time when relief is to be completed will be wired to all companies from Battalion Headquarters. Code word CAMBRAI being used.

26.10.18. [illegible] Capt.
Issued at 14.15 hrs 1/5 L.N.L. Rgt.
Copies to: 1-4 All companies.
5. Bde H.Q.
6 File

M

O.C. D Coy   R 10.

A
B
C } For Information

Bde HQ

Party of R E [illegible] start work on the repairing of [illegible] 2 Camp bridges at E.0651 & [illegible] 7392 a 9.1 respectively about 1600 [illegible] today. [illegible] of R E repairing party [illegible] at HQ of D Coy.

O.C. D & A Coys will arrange for that there is a L.G. post on the WEST BANK of the river at each of these points to cover the working parties and that as soon as the bridges are sufficiently repaired [illegible] each has to [illegible] across to the EASTERN bank until the bridges are completed. These posts should remain on the EASTERN bank, until [illegible] they will be withdrawn to the WESTERN bank.

[illegible] Capt & Adjt
1/5 L N L Regt

26-10-18

"A" Form (In pads of 100).

MESSAGES AND SIGNALS.

No. of Message..................

Prefix..........Code..........m.	Words.	Charge.	This message is on a/c of:	Recd. at..........m.
Office of Origin and Service Instructions.	Sent		..........Service.	Date..........
M.I	At..........m.		COPY	From..........
	To..........		(Signature of "Franking Officer.")	
	By..........			By..........

TO { GUKI

Sender's Number.	Day of Month.	In reply to Number.	AAA
* C 20	28		

A	patrol	was	sent
over	the	river	by
the	bridge	at	I 26 c 8 6
at	22.30	27th	aaa.
Enemy	post	encountered	immediately
which	was	shortly	reinforced
up	to	estimated	strength
of	50	aaa	after
considerable	firing	on	both
sides	enemy	fired	Very
light (2	red lights)	which	was
followed	by	the	discharge
of	light	Minenwerfer	shells
which	fell	along	the
canal	bank aaa	To	avoid
being	cut	off	patrol
withdrew	about	01.00	aaa.

From			
Place			
Time			

The above may be forwarded as now corrected. (Z)

Censor. Signature of Addressor or person authorised to telegraph in his name.

* This line should be erased if not required.

(J8065.) Wt. W12952/M1294. 187,500 Pads. 1/17 McC. & Co., Ltd. (E. 818.)

MESSAGES AND SIGNALS. No. of Message..................

Prefix.............Code.................m. | Words. | Charge.

Office of Origin and Service Instructions.

Sent
At.....................m.
To.........................
By.........................

This message is on a/c of:
................................*Service.*
....
(Signature of "Franking Officer.")

Recd. at.............m.
Date.......................
From......................
By.........................

TO | Page 2

Sender's Number.	Day of Month.	In reply to Number.	AAA
C 30	28		

Second	patrol	crossed	river
by	bridge	I32a 9.1	at
01.30	and	moved	100
yards	south	eastwards	along
river	bank	aaa	returned
03.45	no	enemy	seen
aaa	Two	enemy	trench
mortars	reported	at	I33c 05 95
aaa	MG	flash	spotted
on	edge	of wood	at
I27c 1.6	aaa	String	of
3 red	lights	sent	up
several	times	during	night
from	about	I33a 8 3	

From HOK
Place (Signed) G.P. Goodman [illegible]
Time 03.45

The above may be forwarded as now corrected. (Z)

Censor. Signature of Addressor or person authorised to telegraph in his name.

* This line should be erased if not required.

(18065.) Ws. W12952/M1294. 187,500 Pads. 1/17 McC. & Co., Ltd. (E. 818.)

"N"

Copy No.

Secret 1/5 Bn Loyal N. Lancs Rgt
Order No 58

Ref Map Sheet 34 1/40,000

1. The Battalion will be relieved tonight by the 2/5 Bn K.O.R.L. Rgt, and on completion of relief will move into RESERVE at TEMPLEUVE

2 Guides.

One guide per platoon and one guide per Company HQ will meet relieving Companies and guide them to their stations as follows:-

1/5 L.N.L. Rgt Guides from	Meet 2/5 K.O.R.L Rgt	At	At	Dispositions
A Coy	B Coy	FARM W. END of RUMEZ H.29.d.2.2	16.30	Support
B Coy	D Coy	Road Junct. O.1.a.9.1.	16.45	Centre
C Coy	C Coy	-do-	16.30	Right
D Coy	A Coy	Entrance to CHATEAU J.25.d.3.9	16.55	Left

2

3. Tools & S.O.S. Signals will be handed over to relieving companies at Company Headquarters, and receipts obtained.

4. The Transport Officer will collect:–

12 boxes S.A.A.
2 boxes S.O.S.

from Battalion Headquarters this evening.

5. Billeting

Lieut Grose will be at TEMPLEUVE by 15 hrs to take over billets and arrange for companies to be met at TEMPLEUVE CHURCH (H.33. a.6.3.)

6. Companies will march to their billets after relief at not less than 50x distance between platoons.

7. Relief will be reported to present Battalion HQrs. using the Code Word

3

7 (Contd)
"COMPLETE" and will report their arrival in Billets at New Battalion HQrs. at which location will be made known to Companies by Lieut Gross

8. Acknowledge

28/10/18

Capt & Adjt.
1/5th Bn L. N. Lanc Regt.

Copies to.-
1. Bde HQ
2. OC A Coy
3. OC B Coy
4. OC C Coy
5. OC HQ Coy
6. OC D Coy
7. QM & T.O
8. File
9. War Diary

	Off	OR	Signallers etc	
A	4	71	+	4
B	3	90	+	4
C				
	3	96	+	3
D	4	78	+	4
Total	14 =	336	+	15

Bn HQr

[illegible]

SECRET. Q 1/5th Bn. Loyal North Lancashire Regiment Copy No...10
Order No. 58.

Ref. Map: Sheet 36. BELGIUM & FRANCE.

1. The Battalion will be ready to march in Battle Order, at 15.00 hrs. to-morrow the 31st inst. The exact time will be notified later.

2. Starting Point. Cross Roads H.32.a.7.1.

3. Order of March. Headquarters, "A", "B", "C", "D" Companies and Transport.
Companies will march at 100^{x} intervals.

4. Baggage, &c. Blankets and Packs will be stacked under Company arrangements at the Quartermaster's Stores by 08.50 hrs.

5. Lieut. GROSE and 2 other ranks per company will proceed with this lorry. One other rank per company and Headquarters, under the directions of Lieut. GROSE will take over billets from the 1st Bn. London Irish Regt., at RUE FRANCHE (M.11.c.9.9.) and will meet the Battalion on arrival at RUE FRANCHE.
Remainder of billeting party will proceed on lorry with kits and blankets to HELLEMMES, where billets will be arranged for the night 1st/2nd November.
After arranging billets for the night Oct. 31st/ 1st Nov., Lieut. GROSE will proceed to HELLEMMES by the lorry on its second journey.

6. Cleanliness. Billets and Horse Lines will be left in a clean and sanitary condition.
Certificates to this effect will be forwarded to this Office by 3 p.m. 31st inst.

7. It will be taken as a standing order, that Companies will report to Battalion Headquarters immediately on arrival, their arrival in New Billets, location of their Headquarters and the names and numbers of any March Casualties.

8. Officers' Kits will be stacked at the Quartermaster's Stores at 09.30 hrs.
All Limbers are to be packed by 14.00 hrs.

9. ACKNOWLEDGE.

Captain & Adjt.,
30/10/18. 1/5th Bn. Loyal North Lancashire Regiment.

Issued at hrs. Copies to:-

1. Bde. H.Q.
2. O.C. "A" Company.
3. O.C. "B" Company.
4. O.C. "C" Company.
5. O.C. "D" Company.
6. O.C. "H.Q" Company.
7. Quartermaster.
8. Transport Officer.
9. Lieut. Grose.
10. War Diary.
11. File.
12. Commanding Officer.

War Diary

F

Copy No.

S E C R E T. 1/5th Bn. Loyal North Lancashire Regt.

ORDER No. 51.

Ref. BETHUNE. Combined Sheet, 1/40,000.

1. The Battalion will march to-morrow to FROMELLES.

2. Order of March. Battalion Headquarters, "C", "D", "A" and "B" Coys. The head of the column will be immediately West of Road Junction R.29.a.[illegible].5. at 09.15 hours.

3. Route. M.1[illegible].d.6.7. - M.[illegible].d.9.2. - M.1[illegible].d.4.[illegible]. - N.[illegible].c.7.[illegible].- N.16.b.6.[illegible]. - N.[illegible]3.a.2.2., thence to billets.

4. Intervals. The Battalion will follow Brigade Headquarters at a distance of 100x. 100x interval will be kept on the march between Companies ~~and~~ Transport, and between rear of "B" Company and Transport A distance of 10x will be kept between Companies when the Battalion is formed up.

5. Billeting Party. 2nd Lieut. F. Grose and usual Billeting party will meet the Staff Captain at N.[illegible].d.[illegible].5. at 10.30 hours. These parties will meet the Battalion on arrival.

6. Baggage. Blankets packed as usual will be ready for loading on a lorry on the main road outside Battalion Headquarters at [illegible].15 hours. The packs of the band will also be carried on this lorry.
Officers' valises will be packed by 08.30 hours.
Mess Equipment by 08.50 hours.

7. Dinners will be served on arrival.

8. ACKNOWLEDGE.

Issued at 23.35 hrs
16.10.18

Capt. & Adjt.,
1/5th Bn. L. N. Lancs. Regt.

Copies to :- 1 - 4. All Coys.
5. O.C. "H.Q." Coy.
6. Commanding Officer.
7. 17 th Inf. Bde.
8. Transport Officer.
9. Quartermaster.
10. War Diary.
11. File.

K

SECRET. 1/5th Bn. Loyal North Lancashire Regiment. Copy No. 11...

Order No. 58.

Ref. Map: Sheet 37.

forwarded by K.C.

1. The Battalion will relieve the 2/5th Bn. L. O. R. L. Regt., in the FRONT LINE to-night.

2. Dispositions. "C", "A" and "D" Companies will take over the dispositions in that order from Right to Left of the corresponding Companies of the 2/5th Bn. K.O.R.L.Regt.
"B" Company will be in Support in H. 31.c.central.

3. Guides. One guide per platoon and one guide per Company H. Q. will meet "C", "A" and "D" Companies at corner of Road at H.d.1. . at 17.00 hrs.

4. Starting Point. H. 33.b.4.3.

5. Starting Point will be passed by "B" Company at 15.30 hours, Bn. H. Q. at 15.40 hours, "C" Company at 15.45 hours, "A" Company at 15.55 hrs. and "D" Company at 16. 5 hours.

6. Route. "C", "A" and "D" Companies - H.33.b.4.1. - HUREZ - [illegible]-THUN.
Bn. H. Q. and "B" Company - H.33.b.4.1. - H. 3.d.0.3. - MOUILLY - H.36.c. .0.70.

7. Distances. 50x between Platoons and 200x between Companies.

8. Lewis Guns and Ammunition will be carried by Lewis Gun Sections.

9. Battalion Headquarters on completion of move will be at H.36.c.75.75. R.A.P. will be situated at Battalion Headquarters.

10. Lieut. GHOSE will be at Battalion Headquarters, 2/5th Bn.K.O.R.L.Regt. (H.36.a.b.1.1.) at 17.45 hours, and remain until Relief is reported completed by O.C., 2/5th Bn. K.O.R.L.Regt., when he will report at Battalion Headquarters.

11. Rations. A water cart will be taken to "D" Company Headquarters (H.36. d.3. .) where rations for "A", "C" and "D" Companies will be dumped. One Cooker and rations for Battalion Headquarters and "B" Company will be taken to Battalion Headquarters (H.36.c.75.75).

12. Packs & Baggage. To be stacked by arrangement with Major SEWARD by 14.30 hours.

13. S.A.A. Reserve. 12 boxes of S.A.A. will be taken by the Transport Officer to Battalion Headquarters. The Transport Officer will also remove the S.A.A. at HUMEZ (handed over by 2/5th Bn. K.O.R L.Regt.) to Battalion Headquarters.

14. Completion of relief will be reported at once to Battalion Headquarters using Code Word "[illegible]".

15. ACKNOWLEDGE.

Captn. & Adjt.,
1/5th Bn. Loyal North Lancashire Regt.

Issued at 12.30 hours, 31.10/18.

Copies to :-
1. Bde. H. Q.
2. O.C. "A" Company.
3. O.C. "B" Company
4. O.C. "C" Company.
5. O.C. "D" Company.
6. O.C. "H.Q." Company.
7. Quartermaster.
8. Transport Officer.
9. 2/5th Bn. K.O.R.L.Regt.
10. File.
11. War Diary.
12. R.S.M.
13. Spare.

War Diary

SECRET.

HEADQUARTERS.
No. B.M.2535.
Date 21.10.18.
170TH INF. BDE.

170th Inf.Bde. Group will move to TEMPLEUVE area today as follows aaa Starting Point Rd. Junction M.5.d.7.0. aaa Units will pass Starting Point as follows aaa Bde.H.Q. 14.00 hrs. aaa 2/5th K.O.R.L.R. 14.10 hrs. aaa 2/4th L.N.L.R. 14.25 hrs. aaa 1/5th L.N.L.R. 14.40 hrs. aaa 170th L.T.M.B. 15.05 hrs. aaa "C" Coy. 57 Bn. M.G.C. 15.10 hrs. aaa No.2 Coy. 57 Divl. Train 15.20 hrs. aaa 502nd Fld.Coy.R.E. 15.30 hrs. aaa Route via ESTAFFLERS aaa Packs will be dumped at TEMPLEUVE aaa Bde. H.Q. will close at WILLEMS at 14.00 hrs. and will reopen at TEMPLEUVE on completion of move aaa TEMPLEUVE will be temporary H.Q. until further orders.

Issued at 1200 hrs.

21.10.18.

Captain.
Brigade Major.
170th Infantry Brigade.

COPIES TO;-

2/5th K.O.R.L.R.	"C" Coy. 57 Bn. M.G.C.
2/4th L.N.L.R.	502nd Fld.Coy. R.E.
1/5th L.N.L.R.	No.2 Coy. 57 Divl.Train.
170th L.T.M.B.	2/3rd Wessex Fld.Amb.

O.C. 2/5th K.O.R.L. Regt.
O.C. 2/4th L.N.L. Regt.
O.C. 1/5th L.N.L. Regt.
O.C. 170th L.T.M.Batty.
O.C. "C" Coy. 57th Bn.M.G.C.

HEADQUARTERS.
No. B.M.2532.
Date 20.10.18.
170TH INF. BDE.

Following from 57th Div :-

BEGINS. "G.B.537 20th aaa Sittuation 1200 as follows aaa Leading troops of 8th K.L.R. (Van guard Bn.) of 171st Inf. Bde. in H.12.b. & d. aaa Patrols being sent out to N.17.b., 7 10.b. & 4.d. to get touch with 74th & 59th Divs. respectively aaa 2nd and 3rd Bns. 171 Inf. Bde. moving to BLANDAIN and LES EMPIRES respectively aaa M.G. fire being encountered by 8th K.L.R. aaa BLANDAIN heavily shelled from 0900 to 1130 with 77 mm, 10.5 and 15 cm VERT BOIS also shelled and shelling still continueing aaa 2 Secns of our artillery coming into action just West og BLANDAIN aaa 74th Div. are reported at MARQUAIN which is stated to be vacated by enemy butroad to West of ORCQ heavily wired and strongly held by M.Gs." ENDS.

[signature]
Captain.
Brigade Major.
170th Infantry Brigade.

SECRET.

HEADQUARTERS.
No. B.M.2531.
Date 20.10.18.
170TH INF. BDE.

170th Inf.Bde. will probably relieve 178th Inf.Bde. (Right Bde. of 59th Div.) in the line tomorrow aaa Bn. Commanders and O.C. "C" Coy. M.G. Bn. will report at Bde. H.Q. WILLEMS at 09.30 hrs. tomorrow before proceeding with the Brigadier to H.Q. 178th Inf.Bde. at TEMPLEUVE aaa Addsd 3 Bns. "C" Coy. M.G.Bn. reptd. L.T.M.B.

Recd. 23.45

Captain.
Brigade Major.
170th Infantry Brigade.

20.10.18.

Issued at 2045 hrs.
20.10.18.

SECRET.

Copy No. 7.

H

1/5th Battalion Loyal North Lancashire Regt.

ORDER No. 53.

Ref. Sheets, 36 & 37. 1/40,000

1. The Battalion will march to Area, M.3, 4, 9 and 10 to-day. Starting Point, X Roads R.7.a.2.0. The Battalion will probably be required to move further.

2. The Battalion will march in the following order, Bn. Headquarters A, B, C and D. Coys.

3. Head of Column will be at Starting Point at 08.30 hours.

4. Route. R.1, central - ANNAPPES - R. 17.b.6.1. - M. 13.b.0.6. - M. 14.a.0.1. - M. 15.b.5.0. - M. 10.b.0.5.

5. Baggage. Officers' Kits will be packed in G.S. Wagon at 07.45 hours. Mess Cart to be packed by 08.15 hours. The Transport Officer will arrange to carry the packs of the Band.

6. ACKNOWLEDGE.

Issued at 06.00 hours.
20th October, 1918.

Capt. & Adjt.
1/5th Bn. L. N. Lancashire Regt.

Copies :-

1 - 4. All Coys.
5. H.Q. Coy.
6. 170th Inf. Bde.
7. C. O.
8. File.
9. Quartermaster.
10. Transport Officer.
11. War Diary.

SECRET. 1/5th Bn. Loyal North Lancashire Regiment.
Order No.50.(a)

Ref. Map: Sheet 36, BELGIUM & FRANCE.

1. The Battalion will move to Area P.2.a. & c. to-morrow.
Starting Point:- O.15.a.8.7.

2. Order of March:- Bn. H.Qrs., "D", "A", "B" and "C" Companies.
Head of Column will be at Starting Point at 09.15 hrs.

3. Route:- VERT - BALLOT - P.1.d.3.9.

4. Lieut. GROSE and the usual Billeting Party will be at MAIN Road near Battalion Headquarters at 08.15 hours.

5. Officers' Kits, etc., will be packed on G.S. Wagons by 08.30 hrs. and Mess Cart by 90.15 hrs.

6. Intervals on March as this morning.

7. The Battalion will probably move further forward during the day at short notice.

8. ACKNOWLEDGE.

Captn. & Adjt.,
17/10/18. 1/5th Bn. Loyal North Lancashire Regiment.

Copies to:-
1 - 5. All Companies.
6. Q.M. & T.O.
7. Lieut. Grose.
8. File.
9. War Diary.
10. Commanding Officer.

6

SECRET. 1/5th Bn. Loyal North Lancashire Regiment Copy No. 10

Order No. [illegible].

Ref. Map: Belgium & France Sheet 36.

1. The Battalion will march to HELLEMMES Q.1[illegible] and R.7 to-morrow the 17th inst.

2. Starting Point on MAIN ROAD 300x EAST of Battalion Headquarters.

3. Order of March:- Battalion Headquarters, "A", "B", "C" and "D" Companies. The Battalion will be drawn up in File on the WEST SIDE of MAIN STREET facing EAST at 05.05 hours. Right of Headquarters Company at the Starting Point.

4. Intervals. 5x between Companies and distances between Companies on the march 100x.

5. Route:- P.6.b.4.7. - Bridge at P.6.a.[illegible].3. - Road on East Bank of CANAL to P.[illegible].c.1.4. - P.1[illegible].a.5.[illegible] - P.1[illegible].d.[illegible].4. - Road along railway to Q.[illegible].b.[illegible].7 - Q.[illegible].a.[illegible].[illegible]. - R.7.b.[illegible].[illegible].

6. LIEUT P. CROSE and the usual Billeting Party will be ready to move off at 7.15a.m., and will be mounted on cycles.

7. Baggage &c. Officers' Kits will be packed on G. S. Wagon by 7.45a.m. Mess Cart will be packed by 7.55 a.m.
Blankets will be carried on the pack, and Steel Helmets will be worn by all ranks.
The Transport Officer will arrange to carry the packs of the Band.

8. Cleanliness. Billets will be left in a clean and sanitary condition.

9. ACKNOWLEDGE.

[signature]

Captn. & Adjt.,
1/5th Bn. Loyal North Lancashire Regiment.

Issued at [illegible].15 hours. 1[illegible]/10/1[illegible].
Copies to All Coys.
Transport Officer.
Quartermaster.
R. S. M.

OC HQ Coy

1/5th Bn. Loyal North Lancashire Regiment.

A M E N D M E N T.

Reference Order No. 55, dated 24/10/16, para. 3, for "H" after road, read "I".

Capt. & Adjt.,
1/5th Bn. Loyal North Lancs. Regt.

To all recipients of Battalion Order No. 55.

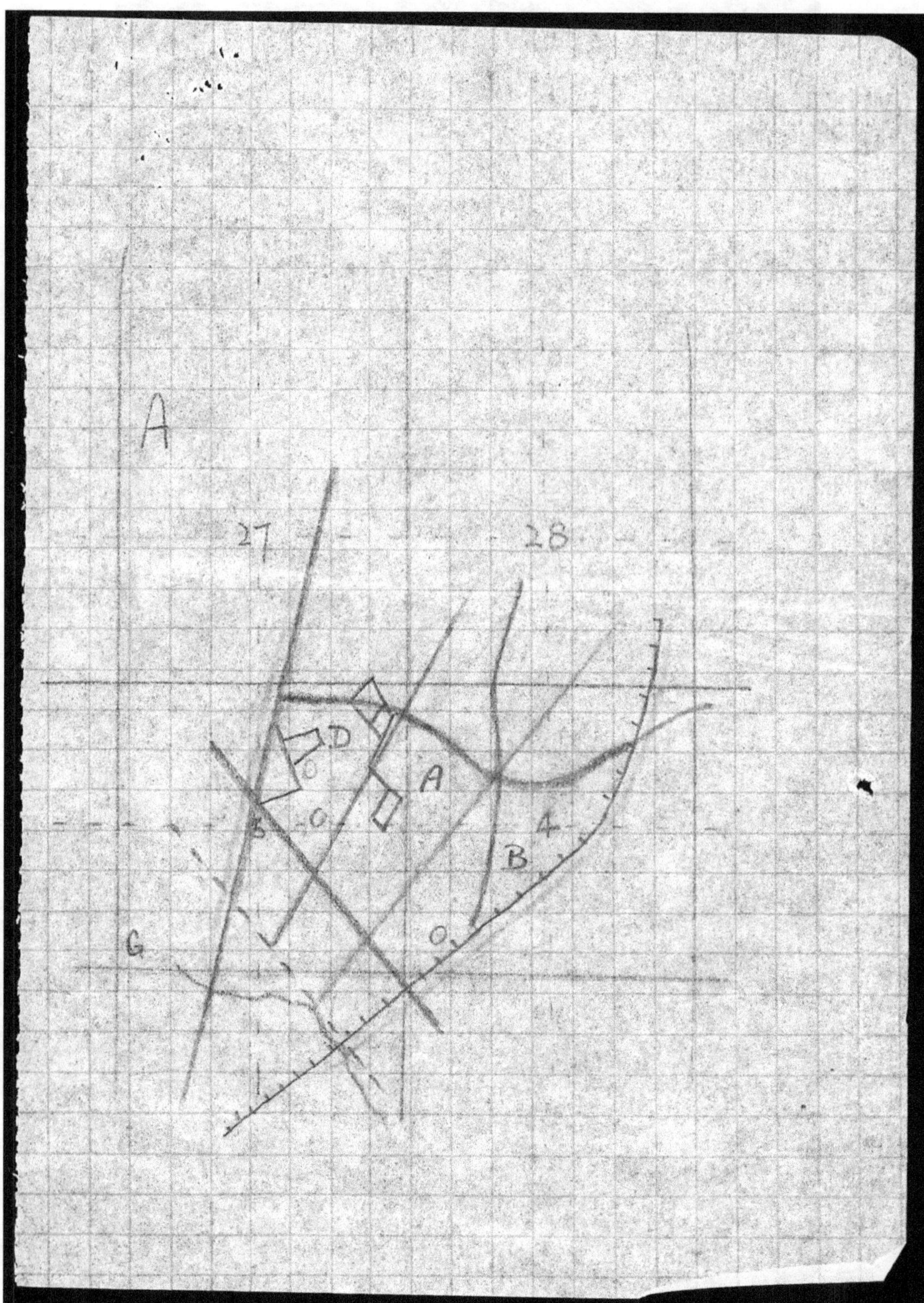

A
27
28
D
A
4
B
G

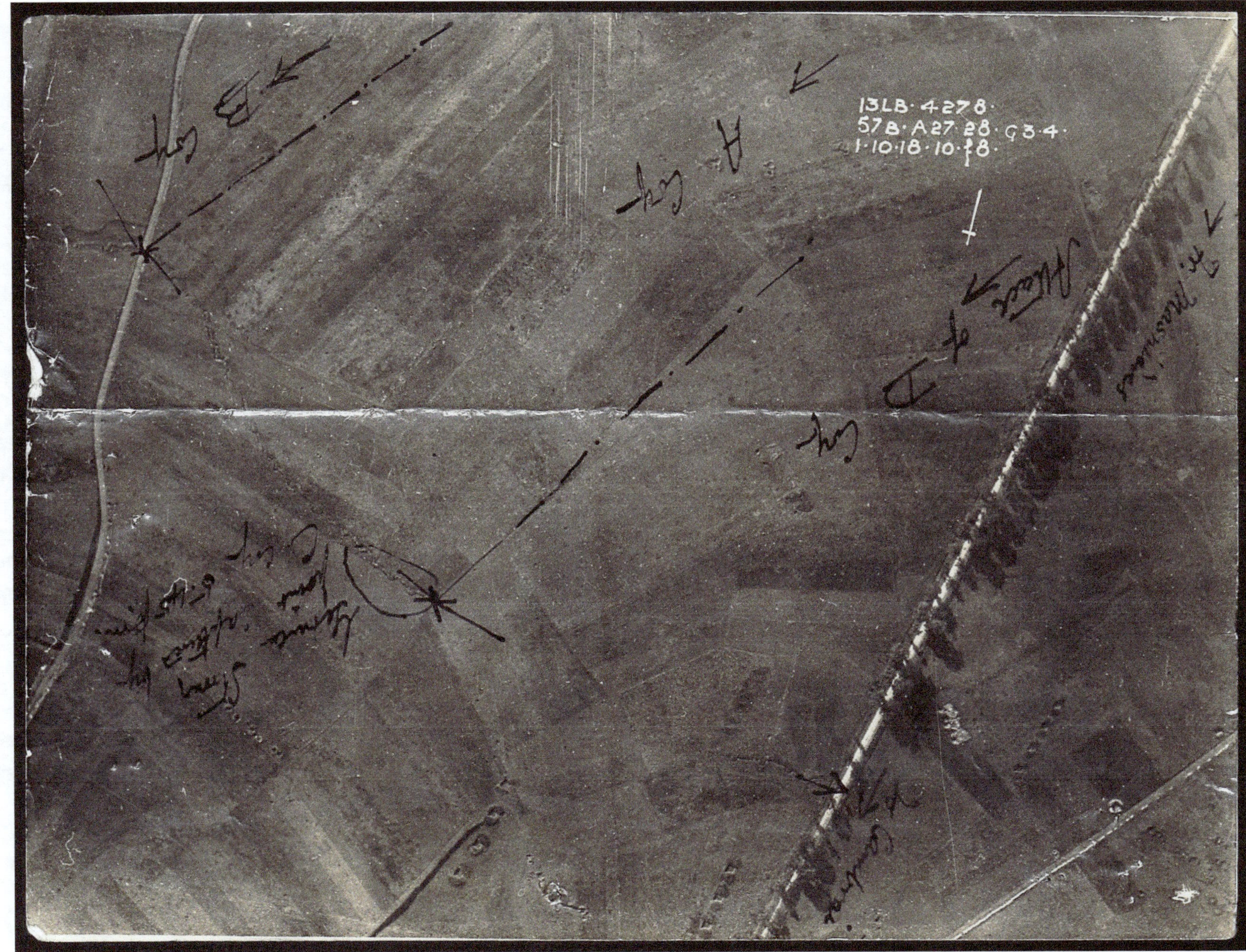
13LB·4278·
57B·A27·28·G3·4·
1·10·18·10·18·
B Coy
A Coy

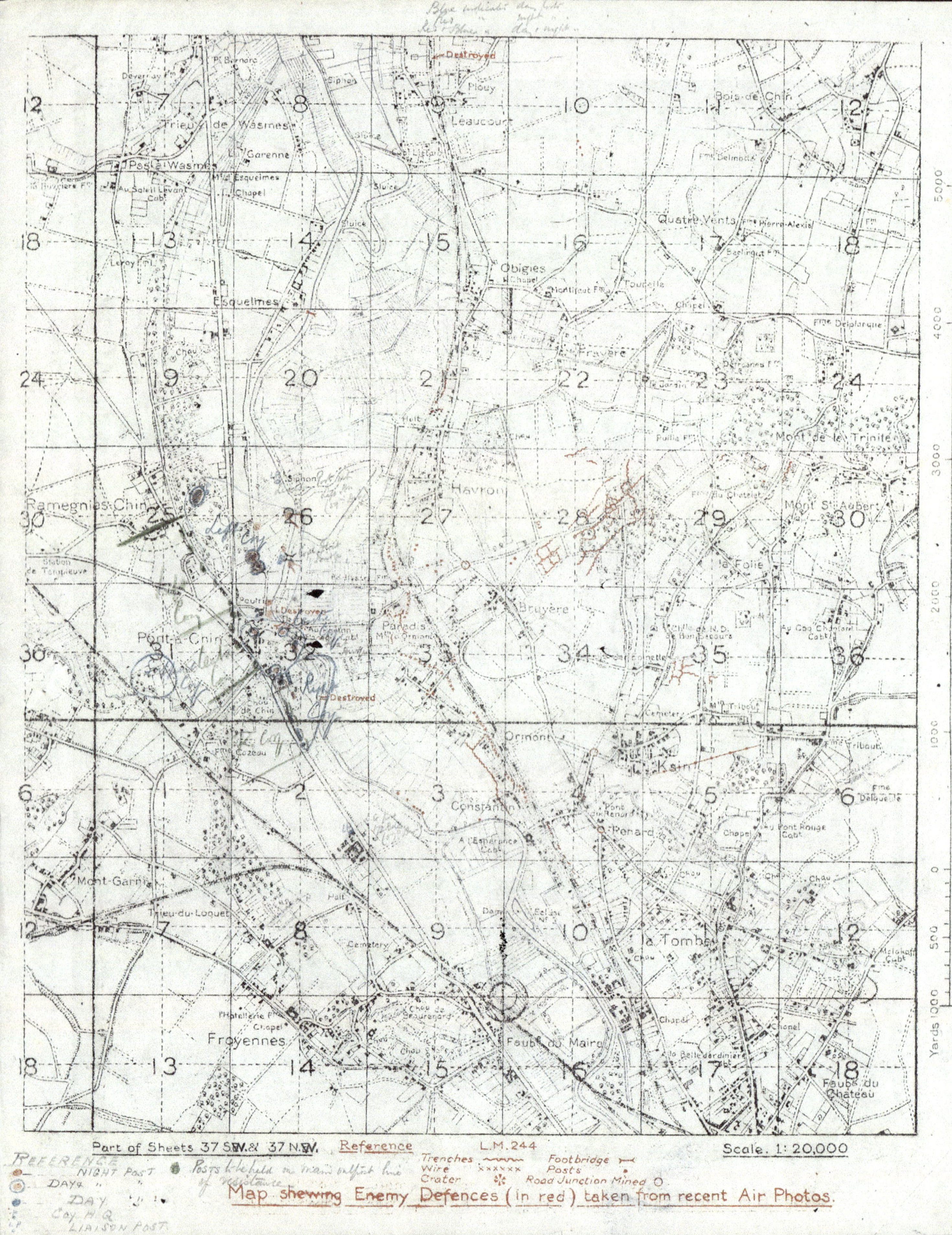

Part of Sheets 37 S.W. & 37 N.W.
Reference
L.M. 244
Trenches
Wire
Crater
Footbridge
Posts
Road Junction Mined
Scale. 1: 20,000
Map shewing Enemy Defences (in red) taken from recent Air Photos.
REFERENCE
NIGHT POST
DAY
Coy. H.Q.
LIAISON POST
Trieu de Wasmes
Leaucourt
Bois-de-Chin
Quatre Vents
Obigies
Esquelmes
Fravère
Mont de la Trinité
Havron
Ramegnies Chin
Mont St Aubert
la Folie
Bruyère
Pont-à-Chin
Paradis
Orinont
Ksin
Constantin
Penard
Mont-Garni
Trieu-du-Loquet
la Tombe
Froyennes
Faubᵍ du Maire
Faubᵍ du Château
Destroyed
Yards 1000

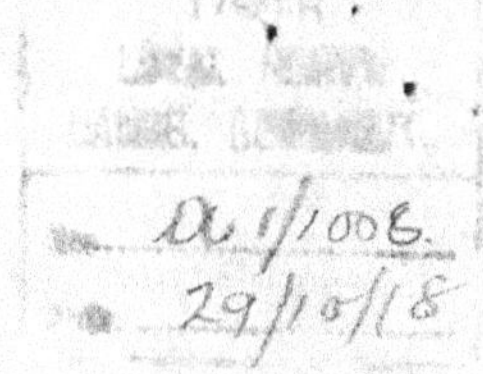

SECRET.

Headquarters,
170th Infantry Brigade.

In accordance with your verbal orders I attach a trace showing the dispositions of my Battalion when relieved in the Line yesterday by the 2/5 K.O.R.L.Regt.

The posts held by day are shown in blue, by night in Red; those in the outpost Line of Resistance in Green. The posts shown East of the river at the two existing bridges were manned on the night of the 27th/28th. This was actually not done on the night of relief, as in the case of the left Company the approaches were being sniped, and of the Centre Company it was rather too light when relief took place for the post to be moved over the bridge.

SCHEME.

By day the Outpost Line is held, generally speaking, by Sentry Groups, with Lewis Guns in inconspicuous positions, the Rifle Sections being rested in buildings or dug-outs, close by.

By night the Rifle Sections are pushed up to strengthen the Outpost Line on the River Bank.

Movement by day is almost entirely forbidden. By night inter--communication is kept up by half/hourly patrols to flank posts of adjacent Battalions, and all the Battalion Front Line posts.

Each Company has a counter-attack Company in Reserve, close to Company Headquarters.

Every Section has an allotted post on the Outpost Main Line of Resistance.

All posts are entrenched, or behind walls of houses prepared for defence.

The approaches to the River Bank are few, and with the except--ions given below the ground between them mostly marshy and difficult of approach.

Extensive wire entanglement would, therefore, be rather a disadvantage than otherwise. One short belt has been put down be--tween the stream and the road about I.32.a.4.2.

In front of the Right Flank the ground is open and passable but wire entanglement would, I think, instantly disclose the fact that the road is held, and would have disastrous results.

The Company in support in I.31.c., less one Platoon is avail--able to reinforce any of the three Companies in the Front Line.

One Platoon remains at I.31.c.80.75, with a Lewis Gun in a building with a good field of fire to cover the approach from the East towards the woods in I.31.c.

G J Gordon
Lieut-Col.,
Comdg 1/5th Bn. L. N. L. Regt.

29/10/18.

'A'

1/5th Bn. L. N. Lancashire Regiment.

OPERATIONS, 1/2 October, 1918.

REF. MAP. 1/20,000. 57b. N.W.

PREAMBLE.

On the morning of the 1st October, the Battalion dispositions were as shewn on attached tracing "A", with Battalion Hd. Qrs. on the Canal Bank at F.24.a.1.5. (57c. N.E.).

On returning from the line I found a message awaiting me at Battn Hd. Qrs. at 13.15 to attend at Brigade H.Q. at once to receive in--structions regarding the attack. Written orders were immediately sent to the Company Commanders notifying them of impending attack and the objective of the Battalion, and to meet me for detailed orders at Battalion Hd. Qrs. at 15.00.

ORDERS.

I received details of the attack from the G.O.C., 170th Inf. Bde. personally at 14.00. These details were subsequently received in writing at 15.59. (G.69, issued at 15.25.). I then met Company Com--manders, M. G. Officer, Liaison Officer, L. T.M. Officer, O.C. "A" Coy 2/5th The King's Own R.L.Regt. at Battalion Headquarters, explained the situation, gave each verbal instructions as to the role of his command in the attack with a tracing - copy attached "B", showing the boundaries of advance and objective of each Company.

The plan was as follows :-

"B" Coy, which was holding posts on the N. & E. of PROVILLE, was to hold its position during the attack, and to be available for support at any point desired, or to repel counter-attack on either flank. Ten minutes before ZERO HOUR posts were to withdraw into dug-outs & cellars in their immediate vicinity to avoid possible casualties from our own barrage. The posts were to be re-occupied as soon as the barrage moved forward.

"A" Coy. were to move from the trenches occupied 10 minutes before Zero hour.

"C" Coy. at ZERO homr and "D" Coy. as soon as "C" Coy was clear of the trench.

"A" Coy. was to clear PROVILLE on the North. "C" and "D" Coys. on the South.

"A" and "C" Coys. to deploy as soon as they were clear of the village in two waves, 25x apart.

"D" Coy - 3 platoons in the same formation, with one platoon 100x in rear of second wave, in Artillery formation, with the object of deal--ing with M.G.Nests or other points of resistance anticipated on this flank.

Special L.T.M.

1 Section to bombard the known M.G.positions in road at A.21.a.3.5., at 17.35 with 20 rounds, and to remain in reserve for action after the development of the attack.

1 Section to move forward 100x in rear of "A" Coy. on left flank.

M. Gs.

2 Sections "C" Coy, M.G.Battalion to advance, after the area had been cleared, along Sunken Road A.20.b.5.0. to fork roads at A.21.a.1.4. and to operate, if possible, from this point.

1 Section to advance subsequently to extreme right of objective and to take up positions to guard this flank.

Guns of the remaining sections to be emplaced in the most suitable positions in the objective about A.21 Central, after reconnaissance by M.G.Commander.

"A" Coy. 2/5th The King's Own (R.L.) Regt. to occupy the trench in A.20.a. b. d. as soon as vacated by "A" "C" and "D" Coys, 1/5th L.N.L. Regt and to hold this as a main line of resistance in the event of counter-attack.

Special attention was to be paid to the following points :-

(A). Assembly was to be made not less than 200x W. of starting barrage line, and after deployment, the leading wave to advance as closely as possible behind the creeping barrage, and the objective, when taken, to be consolidated in posts of not less than 2 sections.

(B). Contact was to be immediately obtained and kept throughout between Companies and with troops on the flanks.

(C). Posts would be established at all roads leading E. and N. from the objective, and a post was to be established by the right flank Company in the trench - 20x - 30x Eastwards from the road junction at A.22.a.1.0.

(D). 2 Flares per Platoon were to be carried and 1 flare per platoon was to be fired at 7.15 p.m. to shew its position.

I opened Battle Headquarters at S. end of PROVILLE A.20.b.3.2. at 17.25.

A telephone line was through to Brigade H.Q. at 17.30 but was almost immediately disconnected and was not re-established until 19.10.

~~The barrage~~

NARRATIVE.

The barrage opened at ZERO hour - 17.44. A message was received almost immediately from the Right Company Commander that our shrapnel were bursting short. From my position at Battle H. Q. this did not appear to be the case on the right flank but on the N.side of the village, where L.T.M.carrying party and the left Company were assembling shell fire considerably disorganised movement, and Officers reported later that some of our own shells fellhere, and the damage done to the CHATEAU on the west face I think bears out the reports.

O.C. "A" Coy, 2/5 The K.O. (R.L.) Regt. reported his Coy. in posit-ion from A.20.a.30.90. to A.20.d.40.90 at 18.00.

Heavy hostile shell fire opened at about 17.52 and O.C. Right Coy. was wounded at about this time while assembling his Company near Battle Headquarters. The following message received at 18.50 from the right Company was the first notification of progress :-

"Held up with M.G.fire. Both Officers wounded & casualties "pretty heavy. C.S.M.HASLAM"

and at 19.50 I had a message from O.C."A" Coy. 2/5 The K.O.(R.L.) Regt. that some men of the left Company had fallen back behind the village.

O.C. Centre Coy. was wounded and brought back to Battle H.Q. at 18.30 (approx). He reported the capture of a M.G.Position at fork roads A.29.a.2.4. with 40 prisoners but that the group which had effected the capture was subsequently surrounded and he thought a number of the prisoners had escaped.

I reported the situation to Brigade H.Q. at 19.55 (vide my I.D.O.2).

The information regarding the position of E. M.G.posts which were causing casualties was obtained from the C.S.M. Right Company through H. Q. Runners.

At 20.30 only two Officers remained with the three attacking Coys. and the men who had not become casualties had fallen back to the trench occupied by "A" Coy. 2/5 The King's Own (R.L.) Regt. with the exception of (a) 3 platoons of Right Coy. occupying the trench running from A.20.d. 8.7. to A.21.c.1.6. and (b) 1 Platoon of the Centre Coy at 20.b.5.0.

To clear up the situation on the right I sent for the C.S.M.of the right Coy. He reported that his men were being enfiladed by a M.G. which was apparently in position about A.21.c.25.55 and was being fired on at intervals by other M.Gs.at uncertain distances to the N., S.E., and E.

I then gave orders for all the stragglers to be reorganised by Companies in the trench in A.20.a. and b. with "A" Coy. 2/5 The K.O. on the Left and withdrew the exposed portion of the right Coy. to the trench from A.20.d.4.8 to A.20.d.7.7.

At 23.50 I received a message from O.C. "A" Coy 2/4 L.N.L.Regt stating that at 19.15 he had taken his objective and instructions were received at 08.00 (2/4/18) to get in touch with the post established by 155th Bde at A.20.d.2.2. This was done immediately by patrolling the road from A.20.d.7.7. to A.20.d.65.90 and this patrol was maintained until my Battalion was relieved on the night of the 2nd/3rd Oct.

At 2000 (1/10/18) an Officer's patrol was sent out from the post at A.20,b.3.9, with orders to proceed along the South side of the River and get in touch with "A" Coy, 2/4 L. N. L. Regt. This patrol reported that Enemy movement was heard in houses at A.15.b.5.9. Subsequently the patrol came under heavy M.G.fire from about A.21.a.6.9., and was compelled to return to our lines.

At 18.15 (2/10/18) a patrol proceeded Eastwards from our post at A.20.b.3.9. along south bank of River ESCAUT in order to gain touch with patrol of 2/4 L.N.L.Regt. operating on north bank of river.

Owing to heavy shell and minnenwerfer fire on area A.15.c.1.4. approx. patrol could not proced beyond this point. The patrol re--turned to our lines by a route about 100x South of river.

No Enemy was seen.

During the operations 21 prisoners were captured of whom 1 was killed and one wounded by the Escort in an endeavour to escape.

Our Casualties were :-

	Officers.	O.Rs.
KILLED....................................	2.	23.
WOUNDED..................................	5.	110.
MISSING...................................	-	18.
WOUNDED & MISSING.......................	1	3

[illegible signature] Lt Col
Comd 1/5 L.N.L.R

4/X/18

At 20,00 (1/1/18) and

'B'

O. C. "   " Coy.

While in Reserve, the Battalion will be pre ared to counter--attack on any part of the front held by the Brigade. It is therefore of the utmost importance that Officers and N.C.Os. should know inti--mately the shortest way to the Canal and River Crossings, and all forward routes.

O.C. "B" Coy and O.C. "C" Coy. will make reconaissances with a view to being ordered to counter-attack on the front at present held by the 8/4 L.N.L.Regt.,

O.C. "A" Coy., and O.C. "D" Coy. will make reconaissances with a view to being ordered to counter-attack on the front at present held by the 2/5 K.O.R.L.Regt.

Officers Commanding "A and "C" Coys after ascertaining from the Battalions in front the exact location of their Main Line of Resistance, are to-day reconnoitering as follows :-

O.C."A" Coy. is reconnoitering the crossings of Canal and River ESCAUT between the Lock at F.24.a. 4.0., inclusive, and crossing at F.23.d.95.75.

O.C. "C" Coy is reconnoitering crossings of Canal and River ESCAUT between Lock at F.24.a.4.0. exclusive and the line of breastwork at A.14 d.2.5. inclusive.

G.J.P. Goodman
Lieut-Col.
Commdg. (MAID) Bn. L.N.L.Regt.

4/10/18.

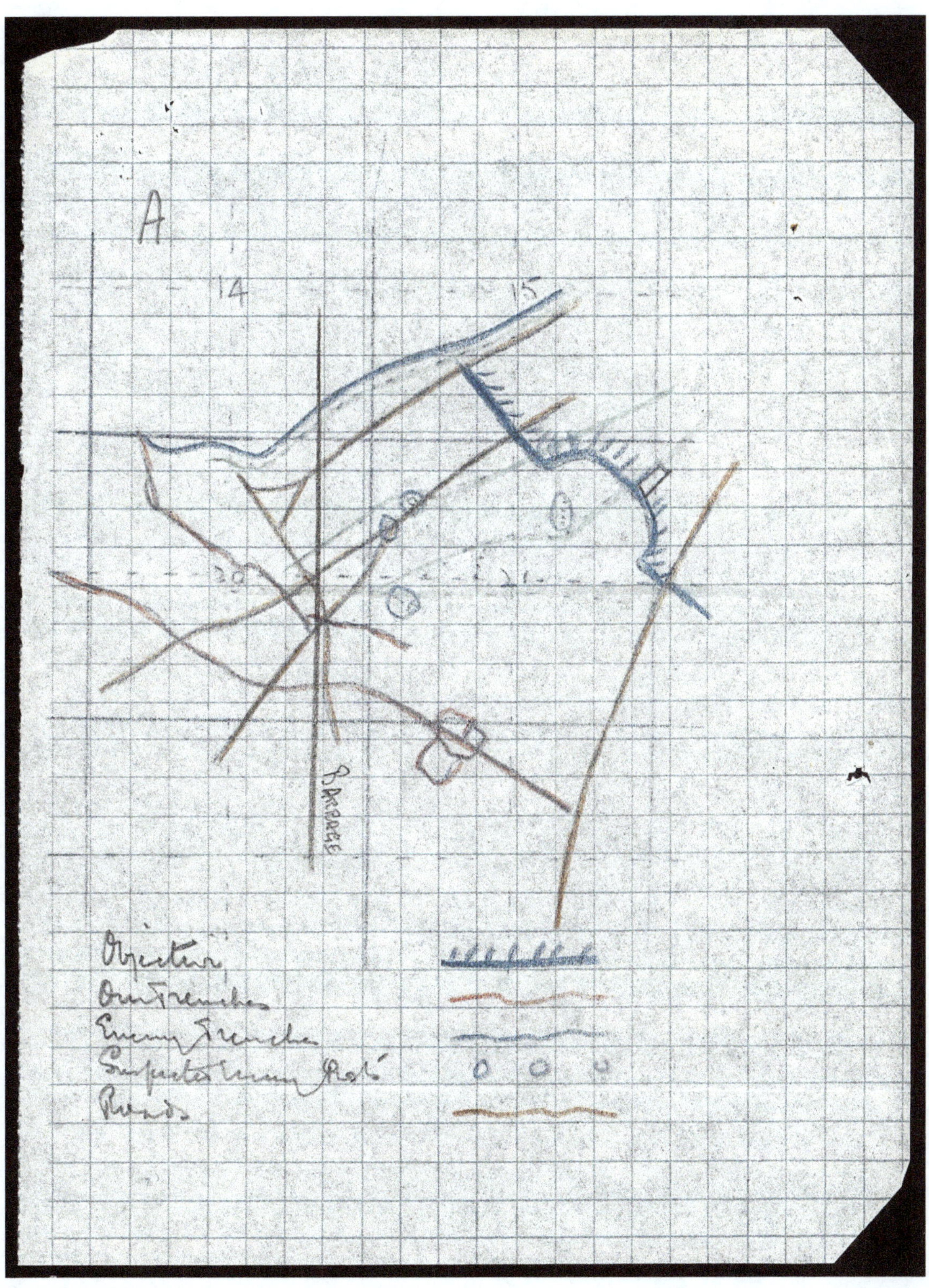
A
14
15
20
21
BARRAGE
Objective
Our Trenches
Enemy Trenches
Suspected Enemy Posts
Roads

1/5th Loyal Noth Lancs. Regiment.
OPERATIONS 7th-8th October, 1918.

Ref. Map.
57c. N.E.1/20,000
57b. N.W. 1/20,000

6/10/18.

The Battalion was located in bivouacs South of FONTAINE NOTRE DAME - F. 21.c.3.0.

I received orders at 1500 to report at Headquarters of 170th Infantry Brigade, and was given verbal details as to the role of my Battalion in an attack to take place South and East of CAMBRAI on the early morning of the 8th October. On return to Camp I called a conference of Company Commanders and arranged to leave Camp with them at 0650 the following morning to reconnoitr the area.

7/10/18.

The area was reconnoitred by Company Commanders, Intelligence Officer, Signalling Officer and myself and forward roads by the Transport Officer.

I issued orders for the attack to Company Commanders, Signall-ing Officer, M. G. Officer, L.T.M.Officer at 1200.

The plan was as follows :-

The Battalion would leave Camp at 1800 in Column of route with platoons at 100x intervals; 2 companies to cross the Canal by the Bridge at L.19.c.7.2; 2 Companies by the Bridge at L.6.c.3.2.

The Battalion would rendezvous East & West of FLAT FARM (G.7. d. 6.1.) at which point tools (20 shovels and 16 picks per Coy) and 2 Cookers with hot tea would meet the Companies.

After dark the Companies were to move forward independently with guides to hollow roads and trenches (previously selected) in G.8.d., G.9.c., and G.14.b.

Battalion Headquarters would be opened at the same time in the Quarry at G.9.a.0.6.

Plan of Attack - vide Tracing "A".

Companies would leave last named Assembly positions and form up :-

"B" Company on RIGHT.
"A" Company in CENTRE.
"D" Company on LEFT.

to be in position bhind forming up linex at 0330 to move forward as close as possible under ARtillery Barrage opening at 0430. "C" Company in Reserve in dugouts at G.9.a.4.8.

L.T.M.Battery. 1 Section to follow immediately in rear of Right Company.

1 Section immediately in rear of Left Company.

1 Section in reserve with Reserve Company.

M. Gs.

2 Sections to get into position about G.4.c.6.4., as soon as this was cleared by Infantry and one of these sections, when the right flank was gained, to consolidate close to Railway on Right flank of the Objective.

2 guns to gain crossing of road and trench in G.4.a.6.3. on a point close behind from which to enfilade the Sunken Road in A.28.c

2 guns to move forward to left flank to guard that flank and to sweep the ground in A.28.a. and c.

If the Infantry Attack were held up, the guns were to be employed in posts occupied prior to the Attack by the 2nd Div. in Squares G.3.b. & d. and G.4.c. to break down opposition.

Tanks.

One Tank was placed at my disposal, and its Commander reported to me at 1700, when I gave the following orders.

To be on forming up line one hour before ZERO on the West side of the railway immediately in front of Right Company.

To move forward close under the barrage and leave the Railway at G.4.c.55.35, moving Northward along the road, destroying M.G. nests known to exist close to this road.

To cross the objective trench at G.4.a.6.3, move along the objective Eastwards to right flank.

If all the objective gained it would cross railway at right flank and join the tanks East of the railway.

If the attack of my Battalion was held up on the left, it would return to assist it on that side.

One Company 2/5 K.O.R.L.Regt, was placed under my orders and reported to me at 2345 (7/10/18). I held in reserve in trenches at G.14.b.8.6.

3

N A R R A T I V E.

All arrangements were carried out according to plan up to ZERO hour.

Between the period of assembly and this hour there was heavy Enemy Artillery fire over our area without casualties

8/10/18.

At Zero-30 minutes posts of the 2nd South Staffs. Regt holding the existing line in G.3.b. & d. and G.4.c. were withdrawn round the flanks of my Battalion.

The barrage opened punctually and appears to have been perfectly regulated throughout.

The left flank Company reached its objective and commenced to dig in at 0530.

On the right the Tank had collapsed in a cellar at G.4.c.5550 owing to darkness it had been unable to keep its direction or to destroy several M.G.nests in its immediate neighbourhood, and was out of action at 0550.

The right Flank Company in advancing from the Signal Box at G.4.c.55.40 came under very heavy M.G.fire from its immediate front and suffered heavily. This report was received about 0620, and being anxious as to the security at all costs of this flank and to keep in touch with the 63rd Div. in its advance up the East side of the Railway I immediately sent forward my Reserve Company (a) (C) to work up the East side of the Railway as far as possible out of view (b) to gain the right flank of my objective and to keep touch with the Right Flank Company.

The Right Flank Company Commander had meanwhile anticipated my orders for a flanking movement from the East, had caputured the posts in his immediate front and was in his objective at 0640, with his L.T.M.B.Section in Support.

This Company was in touch with the HAWKE Battalion on the Right but had lost touch with my Centre Company and was feeling along the trench to the West.

On the Reserve Company reaching the objective ~~they~~ it passed through the Right Flank Company and occupied the trench for a short distance beyond (i.e; to the West of it).

Meanwhile no news had come in of the Centre Company, and at 06.15 I had sent out a patrol from my Reserve Company to find out the situation.

News was brought back that the whole of this Company was held up by M.G.Fire apparently coming from the trench and road in A.28 a. & c. and from houses in A.27.b.6.4. 2 Machine Guns had by this time been established on the left flank, and opened fire on the last named Target.

I directed the Commander of the Company of the 2/5th K.O.R.L. Regt. to send 2 platoons at once up the CAMBRIA MAIN ROAD to come under the Orders of my left flank Company Commander. I ordered the latter Officer to extend his right in order to get touch with the Centre Company and to employ the King's Own in holding the left flank as he vacated it. This he was however unable to do as although the right of his Company had dug themselves into posts in comparative darkness all movement between the end of the trench between G.3.b.3.9. and G.4.a.0.8., was now impossible owing to the fire from the aforementioned places in front. He accordingly left his Company in position and kept backin support the two platoons of the K.O.R.L.Regt. in a more or less concealed position about G.3.b.6.

At about 08.00 I found that a few men of the Centre Company had reached their objective about G.4.a.3.6. and that my Reserve (C) Company was in the trench between it and the Right Flank Coy.

From this time all forward movement in G.3.b. and G.4.a. was attended by heavy loss by M.G.Fire apparently coming from A.27.b.&d. and A.28.a. & c.

An Artillery Liaison Officer managed to direct artillery fire on these targets and the M.G.fire from the ground to the N.W. and W. of my position then greatly diminished. I was still unable to close the gap between the left and centre of the objective owing to a strongly held post centred about G.3.b. 95.75. covering with M.Gs. all the ground in G.3.b. and enfilading the trench held by the Centre Company.

I ordered the Reserve (C) Company to attack this post with a strong bombing party but in spite of several attempts this party was driven back by M.G.fire from the post without being able yet within ~~in~~ bombing range.

At 1600 I gave orders for 2 sections L.T.M.B. to move under cover of the road ~~to~~ G.4.c.65.75. (the road up to this point being in a half cutting and hidden from the west) and at 1740 to project 60 shells on the enemy post. The troops occupying the trench east of this post to be withdrawn 200x along the trench from the post and the 2 right platoons of the Left Flank Company to swing back at right angles to form a defensive flank, the 2 platoons of the 2/5 The King's Own (R.L.) Regt to be held in readiness at about G.3.b.6.4., these movements to be carried out by 1735; the L.T.M.B officer having projected his 60 rounds was to fire a very light; at this signal the Reserve Company was to leave the trench - 2 platoons on either side of it - and assault the post from the East; the 2 platoons of the 2/5 The King's Own (R.L.) Regt. to charge simultaneously from the S.W.

The plan worked successfully and the post was carried. 11 prisoners were captured and 2 heavy and 3 light M.Gs. The remainder of the garrison fled, and were fired on by L.Gs. It appears from the statements of prisoners captured at this post that the garrison consisted of 3 officers and 24 or 28 other ranks, the survivors of a complete M.G. Company

The Reserve Company then occupied the gap and the line was organised throughout on posts of 2 sections.

The Company of 2/5 The King's Own (R.L.) Regt. was moved into the posts in G.3.b. and d. and G.4.c. and an additional section of M.Gs. which had a short time previously been sent up to my assistance, was emplaced in suitable positions in this defensive line.

The position thus reorganised was taken over without incident and without hostile interference by the 2/5 The King's Own (R.L.) Regt by 0130 (6/10/18).

PRISONERS.

1 wounded and 1 unwounded Officers and 125 other Ranks (20 wounded) passed through my Headquarters. A party of 64 were taken over from an escort of my Battalion by an Officer of the 2nd Division (I believe Capt. Harrison, M.C., G.S.O.3).

I can therefore account for 191 prisoners. The Right Flank

Company Commander assures me that he sent back at least one other large part which joined another party under an escort of the 63rd Division. Advantage had necessarily to be taken of this means of disposing of prisoners captured in view of the opposition met with and ~~the~~ losses sustained by my Battalion and the long dis--stance over which prisoners had to be escorted. Escorts report that in two cases receipts for prisoners were refused by the A.P.M 63rd Divition.

About 52 dead Germans were seen on the morning of the 9/10/18 on the ground captured. About two thirds of these had I think been killed by rifle or M.G.fire.

CAPTURED WAR MATERIAL.

26 Light and 8 Heavy M.Gs. and 1 Minnenwerfer were brought back to salvage (Receipt attached). It was not possible to get back all. The numbers estimated captured are :-

32 Light M.G.
12 Heavy M.G.
1 Minnenwerfer.

A large quantity of rifles and ammunition was left in the area but could not be collected.

S U M M A R Y.

I believe that the objective would have been gained three hours after daylight if the Tank had not gone out of action, be--fore doing any effective work, and that its chances of successful operation would have been greatly increased had ZERO hour been in daylight.

G.H. Gordon
Lt. Col.,
Comdg. 1/5th Bn. L. N. Lancashire Regt.

10/10/18.

One Copy to each Company.

O.C. 2/5th K.O.R.L. Regt.
O.C. 2/4th L.N.L. Regt.
O.C. 1/5th L.N.L. Regt. (6)
O.C. 170th L.T.M. Batty.
:::::::::::::

War Diary

On conclusion of the period of recent fighting, which extended from 27th September to 9th October, I want to thank all ranks of the Brigade for their splendid and successful work.

The operations were extremely arduous and threw a very great strain upon Officers and men, yet all ranks were equal to the numerous tasks required of them.

The crossing of the ESCAUT CANAL by 2/5th K.O.R.L. Regt. on 28th October without artillery support and in face of very heavy machine gun fire was a magnificent performance, which had a marked effect on the success of subsequent operations.

The attack by this Battalion on 4th October near PROVILLE was very gallantly carried out and produced very useful results.

In addition, this Battalion was largely responsible for repelling a heavy counter attack at ANNEUX on 27th September.

2/4th L.N.L. Regt. were set a difficult task on 28th October in attacking the MARCOING Line unsupported by artillery, yet throughout the day the Battalion never gave up attempts to gain ground in face of heavy machine gun fire.

Much excellent work was done also when this Battalion was in the line North of the CANAL DE ST.QUENTIN.

1/5th L.N.L.Regt. was called upon to carry out two attacks, both of great difficulty. It was no fault of any Officer, N.C.O. or man of the Battalion that the attack near PROVILLE on 1st October was unsuccessful.

The task of forming a defensive flank for the 3rd Army in the great attack of 8th October was entrusted to 1/5th L.N.L. Regt. How well the task was carried out is now a matter of common knowledge.

In this attack 'B' Company of this Battalion, whose duty it was to secure the right flank of the objectiv although held up at first, fought their way forward, and completed their task, causing the enemy heavy losses and capturing a number of machine guns.

Throughout the operations all ranks of L.T.M. Battery particularly distinguished themselves. Again and again they assisted in overcoming strong points and pockets of the enemy, which without their help could not have been successfully dealt with. The efficiency and fighting spirit of the Battery is much above the average.

We now have a short period before us in which to prepare for further active operations. Let us all set to work at once so that we may be prepared to carry out whatever task is set us when we reach our new area further North.

A.W. Rawsrice(?)

Brigadier General.
Commanding, 170th Infantry Brigade.

11th Oct, 1918.

Confidential

War Diary

of

1/5th Bn Loyal North Lancashire Regt

Period. 1st November to 30th November 1918

Volume 22

Instructions regarding War Diaries and Intelligence Summaries are contained in F. S. Regs., Part II. and the Staff Manual respectively. Title pages will be prepared in manuscript.

WAR DIARY
or
INTELLIGENCE SUMMARY.
(Erase heading not required.)

Army Form C. 2118.

Place	Date	Hour	Summary of Events and Information	Remarks and references to Appendices
RUE FRANCHE (Sheet 37 M.11.b.c.)	Nov 1		Battalion moved by route march to HELLEMMES & entered billets there	Appendix A
HELLEMMES	2		Refitting & cleaning up by companies. C.O. & Company Commanders attended lecture by Corps Commander.	[illegible]
— " —	3		Riding class for Officers re-commenced. Battalion Church Parade in conjunction with 2/4 L.N.L. Regt. Companies formed up according to new organisation & inspected by C.O.	[illegible]
— " —	4		Training by Companies. Lewis Gun classes for Officers & Section Commanders started	[illegible]
— " —	5		Company training in billets owing to bad weather	[illegible]
— " —	6		Company training. Lecture for Officers on "Discipline and Co-operation between Artillery & Infantry".	[illegible]
— " —	7		Company training	[illegible]
— " —	8		Company training. Battalion played 1st MUNSTERS ~~2/4 L.N.L.R.~~ in Division Football League. Result – Draw 2–2	[illegible]

D. D. & L., London, E.C.
(10340. Wt W5300/P713 750,000 3/18 E 2688 Forms C/2118/16.

Instructions regarding War Diaries and Intelligence Summaries are contained in F. S. Regs., Part II. and the Staff Manual respectively. Title pages will be prepared in manuscript.

WAR DIARY
or
INTELLIGENCE SUMMARY.
(Erase heading not required.)

Army Form C. 2118.

Place	Date	Hour	Summary of Events and Information	Remarks and references to Appendices
HELLEMMES	9		Brigade Parade in practice for inspection by Divisional Commander.	PB Appendix B
"	10		Battalion Church parade. Battalion defeated 2/6 K.L.R. in Divisional Football League by 7 goals to 1.	PB
"	11		Inspection of 170 Brigade by Divisional Commander. News received that armistice with Germany came into effect from 11 hours.	PB Appendix C
"	12		Battalion practice in 'Attack'. B C and D Companies attacked A Company. New draft of 107 men arrived.	PB
"	13		Company training. B.H.Q. football team defeated by Brigade H.Q. by 3 goals to 0.	PB
"	14		Battalion practice in 'Advanced Guards' and 'Outposts'.	PB Appendix C
"	15		Inspection of Companies and Billets by C.O.	PB
"	16		Battalion route march.	PB
"	17		Battalion Church Parade.	PB

D. D. & L., London, E.C.
(10340) Wt W5300/P713 750,000 3/18 E 2688 Forms C/2118/16.

Instructions regarding War Diaries and Intelligence Summaries are contained in F. S. Regs., Part II. and the Staff Manual respectively. Title pages will be prepared in manuscript.

WAR DIARY
or
INTELLIGENCE SUMMARY.
(*Erase heading not required.*)

Army Form C. 2118.

Place	Date	Hour	Summary of Events and Information	Remarks and references to Appendices
HELLEMMES	18		Company training. Commencement of inter-platoon football competition.	PB
— " —	19		Company training.	PB
— " —	20		Battalion route march. Lecture to Officers and N.C.O's on "Demobilisation". 1/8 Kings defeated the battalion in Football League by 4 goals to 1.	PB
— " —	21		Company training and competitions.	PB
— " —	22		Company training and competitions. 2/4 S. Lancs Regt. defeated the battalion in Divisional Football League by 4 goals to 2	PB
— " —	23		Battalion route march	PB
— " —	24		Battalion Church parade. Battalion cross-country run won by 'D' Company	PB
— " —	25		Company training. B Company won Best Shooting Section competition. Football match between Officers of the Battalion & Officers of 57th M.G. Batt. drawn 2 – 2.	PB
— " —	26		Company training. Best Shooting Sight competition won by Headquarters Company	PB

D. D. & L., London, E.C.
(10340, Wt W5300/P713 750,000 3/18 E 2688 FormsC/2118/16.

Army Form C. 2118.

WAR DIARY
or
INTELLIGENCE SUMMARY.
(Erase heading not required.)

Instructions regarding War Diaries and Intelligence Summaries are contained in F. S. Regs., Part II. and the Staff Manual respectively. Title pages will be prepared in manuscript.

Place	Date	Hour	Summary of Events and Information	Remarks and references to Appendices
HELLEMMES	Nov. 27		Battalion route march through LILLE. Battalion drew with 57th M.G. Batt. in Divisional Football League, each side scoring 2 goals	PG
"	28.		Battalion ceremonial drill. Company training	PG
"	29		B.H.Q. details defeated Transport by 3 goals to 0 in the final of the inter-platoon football competition. Lecture on 'INDIA and the War' by Sir Francis Younghusband	PG
"	30		Company Training	PG

D. D. & L., London, E.C.
(10340, Wt W5300/P713 750,000 3/18 E 2688 Forms C/2118/16.

SECRET. A 1/5th Bn. Loyal North Lancashire Regiment Copy No...9
Order No. 60.

Ref. Maps: Sheets 36 & 37. BELGIUM & FRANCE. 1/40,000.

1. The Battalion will march to-morrow the 1st Nov., to HELLEMMES Area.

2. Starting Point. M.17.b.0.9.

3. Order of March:- Battalion Headquarters, "B","C","D","A" Companies and Transport.
Head of Column ready to march off at 11.05 hrs., facing South.
Remainder of Battalion will be formed up along WILLEMS - SIN Rd. at 50^x intervals between Companies.
Transport will join Column direct from Transport Lines.
The Battalion will follow Brigade Headquarters at a distance of 500^x.
100^x will be kept between Companies and between Head of Transport and "A" Company.
50^x interval between every 12 vehicles.

4. Route. SIN - CHERENG - BOIS BLANC (R.15.a.)

5. Baggage. G.S. Wagons and Mess Cart will be packed by 09.45 hours.
Ammunition beyond 120 rounds per man, Bombs, S.O.S. Signals, etc., will not be carried by the men on the march, but are to be packed on Limbers by 09.00 hours.

6. Dress. Soft Caps will be worn. Steel Helmets will be carried on Right Shoulders.

7. ACKNOWLEDGE.

[signature]

Captn. & Adjt.,
31/10/18. 1/5th Bn. Loyal North Lancashire Regiment.

Issued at 20.30 hours. Copies to:-

1. Bde. H.Q.
2. O.C. "A" Company.
3. O.C. "B" Company.
4. O.C. "C" Company.
5. O.C. "D" Company.
6. O.C. "H.Q" Company.
7. Quartermaster.
8. Transport Officer
9. War Diary.
10. File.

B

Copy No. 8....

1/5th Bn. Loyal North Lancashire Regiment
Order No. 81.

<u>Ref. Sheet 36. 1/40,000.</u>

1. A Brigade parade will be held at 1000 hours to-morrow November 9th., in practice for the Divisional Commanders inspection on November 11th.

2. The parade ground will be at R.15.c.8.9. and Battalions will be formed up in Mass facing the LILLE - TOURNAI ROAD, 2/5th Bn. K.O.R. L. Regt. on the right, 2/4th Bn. L.N.Lancs. Regt. in the centre, 1/5th Bn. L.N. Lancs. Regt. on the left.

3. The Battalion will parade in the RUE SALEMBIER facing West in the order "A", "B", "C", "D", "H.Q", ready to move off at 0840 hrs. On this parade 1 marker will report at the Battalion Orderly Room at 08.30 hours.

4. <u>Dress:-</u>
<u>Officers</u> - SAM BROWNE, Steel Helmets, Ankle Boots and puttees will be worn by Dismounted officers. Sticks will not be carried.
<u>Other Ranks</u>- Marching Order. Steel Helmets will be worn. Company Commanders will not be mounted.

5. Companies and Platoons will not be sized or equalised.

6. Battalion Headquarters will form up in rear of the Companies. Company Headquarters will form a separate unit under command of the C. S. M. in rear of each company.

7. On completion of the Inspection Units will march past in Column of Platoons.

8. 1 marker per Company (including H.Q. Company) will report at the Battalion Orderly Room at 0800 hours.

9. (a) Stretchers will not be carried.
(b) Lewis Guns will not be carried.
(c) No.30 Rifle Grenade Dischargers will not be carried on the rifle.

10. Officers Commanding Companies will render to the Battalion Orderly Room by 0800 hours a Return showing the number of files in the strongest platoon.

C. [illegible]
Lieut.,
Act. Adjt.,
1/5th Bn. Loyal North Lancashire Regiment.

Issued at 1715 hours 8/11/18. Copies to:-

1. O.C. "A" Company.
2. O.C. "B" Company.
3. O.C. "C" Company.
4. O.C. "D" Company.
5. O.C. "H.Q" Company.
6. 2nd in Command.
7. File.
8. War Diary.

B 1

1/5th Bn. Loyal North Lancashire Regiment
Order No.62.

Copy No. 3

Ref. Sheet 36 1:40,000.

1. The Divisional Commander will inspect 170th Inf. Bde. at R.15.c.8.8. at 1030 hours to-morrow the 11th November.
The Battalion will parade as strong as possible.

2. The Battalion will be formed up in Mass facing the LILLE -TOURNAI ROAD with double distances (14 paces) between platoons, in the order 2/5th Bn. K.O.R.L. Regt., 2/4th Bn. L. N. Lancs. Regt., 1/5th Bn. Loyal N. Lancashire Regt., 170th L. T. M. Btty.
Company Headquarters will form a separate Unit, under the Command of the C.S.M., in rear of each Company.
Battalion Headquarters will form up in line in rear of the Centre Company of the Battalion.
The Band will be on the right of Battalion Headquarters.
Transport will be in rear of the Battalion, formed up as already arranged by the Staff Captain.
Cookers and Cooks will not parade.
Lewis Guns will be packed in the Company Limbers.

3. The Battalion will parade in the RUE FERDINAND MATTHIAS (outside the Battalion Orderly Room) facing West in the order "A","B","C","D", "H.Q" ready to move off at 0850 hours. On this parade 1 marker per Company will report at the Battalion Orderly Room at 0840 hours.

4. Dress:- Officers. Sam Browne belts, Steel Helmets, Sticks will not be carried. Dismounted Officers will wear puttees.
Officers will not wear Box Respirators.
Company Commanders will not wear spurs.
Other Ranks. Marching Order. Steel Helmets.

5. Companies and Platoons will not be sized or equalised.

6. On completion of the Inspection the Brigade will march past by platoons at 14 paces distance.

7. 1 Marker per platoon and Company Headquarters will report at the Battalion Orderly Room at 0800 hours.

8. Officers Commanding Companies will render to the Battalion Orderly Room by 0800 hours ~~a-xxxxxx~~
(i) A parade State.
(ii). A return showing the number of files in the strongest platoon.

C Brereton
Lieut.,
Act. Adjt.,
1/5th Bn. Loyal North Lancashire Regiment.

Issued at 2000 hours 10/11/18. Copies to:-

1. O.C. "A" Company.
2. O.C. "B" Company.
3. O.C. "C" Company.
4. O.C. "D" Company.
5. O.C. "H.Q" Company.
6. Commanding Officer.
7. File.
8. War Diary.

'C'

1/5th Bn. Loyal North Lancashire Regiment Copy No...

Order No. 63.

---

1. The Battalion will march to LES TOUQUETS R.9.a.

2. Order of March:- H.Q., "B","C","D","A" Companies. 25x between Companies.

3. Route:- Track along Southern edge of Football Field from H.7.a.5.9. to R.8.b.8.9.

4. The Battalion will be formed up in the RUE FERDINAND MATTHIAS ready to march off at 0845 hours.

5. (a) On arrival at LES TOUQUETS, "B" and "C" Companies will form an Advance Guard to the remainder of the Battalion.
The advance will be on a frontage limited on the North by line running through R.3.b.3.6. - R.4. central - R.5.c.0.4. - R.5.c.9.3. and on the South by the Main Road R.9.a.4.8. - R.9.b.1.4. - R.10.a.7.0. - R.11.c.1.2. to Railway Crossing at R.17.a.80.95.
(b) The ground to be cleared in front of the main body will be divided by the track from R.3.c.9.6. to R.4.c.8.0. thence by an imaginary line to R.11.d.1.8.
"B" Company will advance on the Right and "C"Company on the Left of this line.
(c) The Main Body will remain at R.3.d.0.8. until the ground is reported clear up to the Main N.S. Road through R.4.c. and R.10.a. Main Body will then move to R.4.c.8.0. and when "B" and "C" Companies Scouts have reached the Main N.S. Road through R.5.d. - R.11.b., a, d, c. Main Body will move to CHATEAU DE BRIGODA.
When the Scouts have reached the last named road "B" and "C" Companies will stand fast and in reporting to Headquarters will send back guides to take up "D" and "A" Company and Platoon Commanders to reconnoitre. After reconnaissance Officers Commanding "D" and "A" Companies will receive orders to take up an Outpost Line for a Main Line of Resistance extending approx. along the line R.5.c.9.3. to Railway Crossing ar R.11.c.8.9. In doing so they will pass through"B" and "C" Companies which will be withdrawn to, and await further orders at, R.4.c.8.0. arrival at this point being reported to Battalion Headquarters CHATEAU DE BRIGODA.
O.C. will be at the head of the Main Body until its arrival at CHATEAU DE BRIGODA where H.Q. will be established.

6. ACKNOWLEDGE.

Lieut.,
Act. Adjt.,
1/5th Bn. Loyal N. Lancashire Regiment.

Confidential

War Diary

of

1/5th Battn Loyal North Lancashire Rgt.

Period 1st December to 31st December 1918

Volume 23

VII 41

Army Form C. 2118.

WAR DIARY
or
~~INTELLIGENCE SUMMARY.~~
(Erase heading not required.)

Instructions regarding War Diaries and Intelligence Summaries are contained in F. S. Regs., Part II. and the Staff Manual respectively. Title pages will be prepared in manuscript.

Place	Date	Hour	Summary of Events and Information	Remarks and references to Appendices
	DEC			
HELLEMMES	1		Battalion moved by route march to BOIS D'EPINOY (Sheet LENS 11. 1 L. 80 ?) and billetted in the wood in old German ammunition huts.	PB appendix A
BOIS D'EPINOY	2		Battalion marched to AGNEZ-LES-DUISANS and entered billets there.	PB appendix B
AGNEZ-LES DUISANS (LENS 11 3H 90.65)	3		Battalion resting and cleaning up.	PB
— " —	4		Company training	PB
— " —	5		Company training: Battalion ceremonial drill. Battalion defeated by 2/4 L.N.L. Regt by 3 goals to 0	PB
— " —	6		Training under Company arrangements	PB
— " —	7		Inspection of kits and billets by C.O. Company training	PB

D. D. & L., London, E.C.
(10340) Wt W5300/P713 750,000 3/18 E 2688 Forms/C/2118/16.

Instructions regarding War Diaries and Intelligence Summaries are contained in F. S. Regs., Part II. and the Staff Manual respectively. Title pages will be prepared in manuscript.

WAR DIARY
or
~~INTELLIGENCE SUMMARY~~.
(Erase heading not required.)

Army Form C. 2118.

Place	Date	Hour	Summary of Events and Information	Remarks and references to Appendices
AGNEZ-LES-DUISANS	Dec 8		Battalion Church parade.	RB
"	9		Training under Company arrangements. Battalion Officers' Football Team defeated by Officers of 57th M.G. Batn by 1 goal to 0	RB
	10		Company training. Commencement of Brigade Inter-Platoon Football Competition	RB
"	11		Company training	RB
"	12		Battalion route march. Battalion defeated by 9th K.L.R. in the Football League by 2 goals to 0.	RB
"	13		Company Training	RB
	14		Company training. Battalion defeated 2/4th N. Lancs Regt. in the Football League by 2 goals to 0.	RB

D. D. & L., London, E.C.
(10340. Wt W5300/P713 750,000 3/18 E 2688 Forms C/2118/16.

Instructions regarding War Diaries and Intelligence Summaries are contained in F. S. Regs., Part II. and the Staff Manual respectively. Title pages will be prepared in manuscript.

WAR DIARY
or
~~INTELLIGENCE SUMMARY.~~
(Erase heading not required.)

Army Form C. 2118.

Place	Date	Hour	Summary of Events and Information	Remarks and references to Appendices
AGNEZ-LES-DUISANS.	DEC 15		Battalion Church parade.	PB [?]
"	16		Company training. Arrival of Battalion Colours. Battalion defeated 2/5 K.O.R.L.R. by 3 goals to 2. Officers Football Team (6 a side) defeated by 8th IRISH by 5 goals to 0.	PB [?]
"	17		Colours presented to Battalion	PB [?]
"	18		Company training. Battalion defeated 286 Battery, R.F.A., in Football Competition by 5 goals to 0.	PB [?]
"	19		Battalion route march.	PB [?]
"	20		Company training	PB [?]
"	21		Billet + Kit Inspection	[illegible]
"	22		Battalion Church Parade	[illegible]
	23		Company Training + Salvage	[illegible]
	24		do do	[illegible]
	25		Christmas Day	[illegible]
	26		Boxing Day – Route march	

D. D. & L., London, E.C.
(10340) Wt W5300/P713 750,000 3/18 E 2688 Forms C/2118/16.

Instructions regarding War Diaries and Intelligence Summaries are contained in F. S. Regs., Part II. and the Staff Manual respectively. Title pages will be prepared in manuscript.

WAR DIARY

or

~~INTELLIGENCE SUMMARY.~~

(Erase heading not required.)

Army Form C. 2118.

Place	Date 1918	Hour	Summary of Events and Information	Remarks and references to Appendices
AGNEZ-LES DUISANS	Dec. 27		Salvage + Company Training	[illegible]
	28		do do	[illegible]
	29		Battalion Church Parade	[illegible]
	30		Salvage + Company Training	[illegible]
	31		do do	[illegible]
			Strength of Battalion 1/12/18 - 43 Offrs. 778. O.Rs.	
			do 31/12/18 - 43. Offrs. 811. O.Rs.	
			F.W. Seward Major Comdg. 1/5 Loyal North Lancs Regt	

D. D. & L., London, E.C.
(10340. Wt W5300/P713 750,000 3/18 E 2688 FormsC/2118/16.

SECRET. 1/5th Bn. Loyal North Lancashire Regiment Copy No. 12
Order No. 1.

APP A

Ref. Sheet 36, 1/40,000.
TOURNAI 5.)
HAZEBROUCK 5A.) 1/100,000.
LENS 11.)

1. MOVE. The Battalion will march to-morrow December 1st. 1918 with the 170th Infantry Brigade, to the CAMPHIN - CARVIN Area.

2. STARTING POINT. Level Crossing R.7.d.5.5.

3. ORDER OF MARCH. H.Q., "A", "B", "C" and "D" Company.
100x distance will be maintained between Companies, between the rear Company and Transport and 50x distance between sections of 12 vehicles. 500x distance will be maintained between the head of the Battalion and the 2/4th Bn. L. N. Lancs. Regt.

4. Head of the Column will pass the starting point at 0845 hours.

5. Route:- LEZENNES - RONCHIN - LESQUIN - VENDEVILLE - TEMPLEMARS - SECLIN - CAMPHIN.

6. There will be a halt for Dinner from 1150 to 1300 hours.

7. Dress:- Fighting order. Steel helmets will be carried.

8. Officers' Kits. Officers' Kits will be stacked at the Quartermaster's Stores by 0745 hours.
Officers' Mess gear will be outside Battalion Headquarters ready for packing on the Mess Cart at 0810 hours. Headquarters Officers' Mess gear will be ready at the Headquarters Mess at 0830 hours.

9. Blankets. Blankets will be stacked by 0700 hours in accordance with the instructions issued by the Quartermaster.

10. Lieut. Crase and the usual Billeting Party will proceed by a Motor Lorry in advance.

11. Billets. All Billets will be handed over scrupulously clean and a certificate to that effect handed in to the Battalion Orderly Room by 0800 hours. The Asst. Adjutant will obtain a similar certificate from the Town Major after the departure of the Battalion.

12. ACKNOWLEDGE.

[signature]
Captn. & Adjt.,
1/5th Bn. Loyal North Lancashire Regiment.

Issued at 1200 hours 30/11/18. Copies to:-

1. Bde. H.Q.
2. O.C. "A" Company.
3. O.C. "B" Company.
4. O.C. "C" Company.
5. O.C. "D" Company.
6. O.C. "H.Q" Company.
7. Quartermaster.
8. Transport Officer.
9. Commanding Officer.
10. R. S. M.
11. File.
12. War Diary.

War Diary

Lt. Grose

App. B Copy No 9

Secret.

1/5 Bn. Loyal N. Lancs Regt

Order 2

Ref. Map Sheet 11 LENS 1/100,000

1. The Battalion will march to AGNES-LEZ-DUISANS tomorrow [illegible]
2. Starting Point. CARVIN Rd WEST END of present billets.
3. Order of March. H.Qrs. A, B, C, D Companies
4. Head of Column will pass the Starting point at 0745 hours.
   Same distances as on todays march will be maintained.
5. Route X Rds immediately E. of X in VACHEUX - ESTEVELLES - LENS - CROSS Rds 1/4 mile WEST of THELUS - NEUVILLE ST. VAAST - MAROEUIL - ETRUN thence to billets AGNES-LEZ-DUISANS.
6. DINNERS. There will be a halt for dinner from 1150 hours to 1500 hours.
7. Dress. As today, but blankets will be carried over packs.
8. Baggage. All officers kits will be at Q.M. Stores by 0700 hours. One loading party per company will be detailed to be at the Q.M. Stores at 0700 hours.
   The Officers Mess Cart will be packed at Bn H.Q. Mess by 0730 hours.
9. Quartermaster and billeting party will be prepared to leave in advance under arrangements to be notified later.
10. Acknowledge.

Signed. G. [illegible] Capt.
Adjt. 1/5 Bn. L. N. Lancs Regt

Issued at 2000 hours. 1/12/18. Copies to:-

1. Bde H.Q.
2. H.Q. Coy
3. A Company
4. B Company
5. C Company
6. D Company
7. Transport Officer
8. Quartermaster
9. War Diary
10. File.

2/Lt Gosse, for information & for War Diary

Instructions regarding War Diaries and Intelligence Summaries are contained in F. S. Regs., Part II. and the Staff Manual respectively. Title pages will be prepared in manuscript.

WAR DIARY
or
~~INTELLIGENCE SUMMARY.~~
(Erase heading not required.)

Army Form C. 2118.

Place	Date 1919	Hour	Summary of Events and Information	Remarks and references to Appendices
AGNEZ-LES-DUISANS	Jan			42
	1		Salvage work & Camp improvements.	
	2			
	3			
	4			
	5		Sunday	
	6		Salvage work & Camp improvements	
	7			
	8			
	9			
	10			
	11			
	12		Sunday	
	13		Salvage work & Camp improvements	
	14			
	15			
	16			
	17			
	18			
	19		Sunday	

[illegible signature] Lt Col
Comdg. 1/5 L N Lancs Regt

D. D. & L., London, E.C.
(10340. Wt W5310/P713 750,000 3/16 E 2688 Forms C/2118/16.

Instructions regarding War Diaries and Intelligence Summaries are contained in F. S. Regs., Part II. and the Staff Manual respectively. Title pages will be prepared in manuscript.

WAR DIARY
or
~~INTELLIGENCE~~ SUMMARY.
(Erase heading not required.)

Army Form C. 2118.

Place	Date 1919	Hour	Summary of Events and Information	Remarks and references to Appendices
AGNEZ LES DUISANS	JAN 20		Salvage & Camp Improvements (3 officers & 12 OR demobilised)	[initials]
	21		Salvage & Camp Improvements. 2 tons.	[initials]
	22		Salvage & Camp Improvements 3 tons	[initials]
	23		Salvage & Camp Improvements 2 tons. Route March	[initials]
	24		Salvage & Camp Improvements. Collected [illegible] 13 OR demobilised	[initials]
	25		Salvage & Camp Improvements 1 ton. 1 officer 16 OR demobilised	[initials]
	26		Sunday. Church Parade. Band Concert. 1 officer & 18 OR demobilised.	[initials]
	27		Consecration & Presentation of Colours to 1/5 LNL – 1/4 LNL – 1/5 KO RLR [illegible] Education & Salvage – 18 OR demobilised.	[initials]
	28		Education & Salvage. Football match v 2/6 KLR 2 officers 24 OR demobilised. Concert given by 2/6 R L Regt	[initials]

[signature] Comdg 1/5 Loyal N Lancs

D. D. & L., London, E.C. (10340. Wt.W5300/P713 750,000 3/18 E 2688 Forms C/2118/16.

Instructions regarding War Diaries and Intelligence Summaries are contained in F. S. Regs., Part II. and the Staff Manual respectively. Title pages will be prepared in manuscript.

WAR DIARY
or
INTELLIGENCE SUMMARY.
(*Erase heading not required.*)

Army Form C. 2118.

Place	Date 1919	Hour	Summary of Events and Information	Remarks and references to Appendices
AGNEZ LES DUISANS	JAN 29		Education & Salvage Football Match v 4/4 RLR we won 3-0 — Our Concert Party - "The Loyals" gave a concert to Bde HQ	[signature]
	30		Education & Salvage - 1½ tons - The "Loyals" gave a concert to 2/6 KL Regt	[signature]
	31		Education & Salvage - ½ ton - Electric light installed in the Camp 12 OR demobilised.	[signature]
			From 24-1-19 - to 31-1-19. 12 tons of sleepers were salved for use in camps Total salvage from 21 - 31/1/19 - 22 tons Demobilisation for month officers 11 - OR 185 — Ration strength 1/2/19. 460	[signature]

[signature] Major
Comdg
Cmd. 1/5 Loyal N. Lancs

D. D. & L., London, E.C.
(10340) Wt W5300/P713 750,000 3/18 E 2688 Forms C/2118/16.

1/5 Bn Loyal N. Lancs Rgt (T.F.)

Instructions regarding War Diaries and Intelligence Summaries are contained in F. S. Regs., Part II. and the Staff Manual respectively. Title pages will be prepared in manuscript.

WAR DIARY
or
~~INTELLIGENCE SUMMARY.~~
(Erase heading not required.)

Army Form C. 2118.

1843

Place	Date	Hour	Summary of Events and Information	Remarks and references to Appendices
AGNEZ-LES-DUISANS	1/2/19.	Sun.	Church Parade. C.O. inspected the Camp. No 39 draft – 9 other Ranks demob. Capt. [illegible] appointed A/ADJT.	[illegible]
	2/2/19.	M.	Educational Classes & Salvage. No 40 draft 1 Officer and 18 other ranks demobilised.	[illegible]
FEBRUARY 1919	3/2/19.	T.	Educational Classes & Salvage. Nominal Roll of [illegible] issued with Bn. Routine Orders. The "FRAGMENTS" Concert Party gave a concert in the Concert Hall. No 41 draft [illegible] O.R. [illegible]	[illegible]
	4/2/19.	W.	[illegible] on Post [illegible] by Maj. [illegible] Education & Salvage. — Lieut. Col. D.B. [illegible] assumed command of the Brigade (140) vice Brig. Gen. [illegible] Maj. [illegible] The "TITS" Concert Party gave a concert to the Bn. No men demobilised	[illegible]
	5/2/19	THURS	Route March – [illegible] called for Army of Occupation. — No men demobilised	[illegible]
	6/2/19	FRI.	MUSTER PARADE. The "DOMINOS" gave a concert in the Concert Hall. (19 O.R. demob)	[illegible]
	7/2/19	SAT.	Coys at disposal of Coy Commanders. 26 O.R. demobilised	[illegible]

[signature] Lt Col
Comdg 1/5 Loyal N. Lancs Rgt

D. D. & L., London, E.C.
(10340. Wt W5300/P713 750,000 3/18 E 2688 Forms C/2118/16.

1/5 Loyal N Lancs Regt

Instructions regarding War Diaries and Intelligence Summaries are contained in F. S. Regs., Part II. and the Staff Manual respectively. Title pages will be prepared in manuscript.

WAR DIARY
or
INTELLIGENCE SUMMARY.
(Erase heading not required.)

Army Form C. 2118.

Place	Date	Hour	Summary of Events and Information	Remarks and references to Appendices
AGNEZ LES DUISANS	9/2/19	SUN.	Church Parades. 27 O.R. demobilised. The "Loyals" gave a concert.	[illegible]
	9/2/19	MON.	Men worked on the Camp. Notice for Brigade Knockout Football competition. We drew away against 170 Bde HQ	[illegible]
	10/2/19	TUES	Men worked on camp improvement – No demob	[illegible]
	11/2/19	WED.	Parade as yesterday – Result of first round 1/5 LNL. 5 goals. Bde HQ. 2 goals	[illegible]
	12/2/19	THURS.	New fire precautions issued: 3 O.R. demobilised Concert by "Stripes"	[illegible]
	13/2/19	FRI	Parades + work on camp 5. O.R. demobilised	[illegible]
	14/2/19	SAT.	Parades as yesterday 7 O.R. demobilised	[illegible]

[illegible] Lt Col.
Comdg 1/5 Loyal N Lancs Regt

D. D. & L., London, E.C.
(10340. Wt W5300/P713 750,000 3/18 E 2688 Forms C/2118/16.

1/5 Loyal N Lancs Regt

Instructions regarding War Diaries and Intelligence Summaries are contained in F. S. Regs., Part II. and the Staff Manual respectively. Title pages will be prepared in manuscript.

WAR DIARY
or
INTELLIGENCE SUMMARY.
(Erase heading not required.)

Army Form C. 2118.

Place	Date	Hour	Summary of Events and Information	Remarks and references to Appendices
AGNEZ-LES-DUISANS.	15/2/19.	SUN	Church Parade. Result of Semifinal of Brigade Competition 1/5 L N Lancs 3 goals 3/2 W. L (F A) 1 goal. 22 OR. demobilised	[illegible]
	16/2/19.	MON	Camp Cleaning Parades. 6 OR demobilised	[illegible]
	17/2/19	TUES	All rifles were inspected by Bde Armourer Sgt. FRAGMENTS gave a concert. Board of Enquiry was held to check Mobilisation Equipment	[illegible]
	18/2/19.	WED	Equipment Cleaning. Trial game & team selected for final	[illegible]
	19/2/19.	THURS	Court of Enquiry on 7 men overstayed leave 2 OR demobilised Result of FINAL 1/5 LN Lancs 4. 2/5 KORL Regt 1.	[illegible]
	20/2/19.	FRI	14 OR demobilised	[illegible]
	21/2/19.	SAT.	Notice from Division that the 1/5 LNL had won the Group Medals. 5 OR Demobilised	[illegible]

[illegible] Lt Col
Cmd. 1/5 Bn Loyal North Lancs Regt

D. D. & L., London, E.C.
(10340) Wt W5300/P713 750,000 3/18 E 2688 Forms C/2118/16.

1/5 Bn Loyal North Lancs Regt

WAR DIARY
or
INTELLIGENCE SUMMARY.
(*Erase heading not required.*)

Army Form C. 2118.

Instructions regarding War Diaries and Intelligence Summaries are contained in F. S. Regs., Part II. and the Staff Manual respectively. Title pages will be prepared in manuscript.

Place	Date	Hour	Summary of Events and Information	Remarks and references to Appendices
AGNEZ LES DUISANS	22/2/19	SUN	Church Parades. 11 OR Demobilised. Pickets sent out to Train Guards at ARRAS & AIGNY.	[initials]
	23/2/19	MON	Pte Sutcliffe awarded MILITARY MEDAL. 5 OR demobilised.	[initials]
	24/2/19	TUES	Working Party for ARTILLERY CORNER. No demobilisation.	[initials]
	25/2/19	WED	Lt Col Dawson relinquished command of the Brigade — Brig Gen Ransome returns from leave. Use of "IN THE FIELD" abolished.	[initials]
	26/2/19	THURS	Muster Parade for clothing Inspection. 11 OR demobilised.	[initials]
	27/2/19	FRI	One Company formed by amalgamating all men left in the Batt consequent on demobilisation. 20 OR demobilised.	[initials]
	28/2/19	SAT	MISS ADA WARD gave a concert to the Battalion. 1 Officer & 4 OR demobilised.	[initials]

[signature] Lt Col
Cmdg. 1/5 Loyal N Lancs Regt

D. D. & L., London, E.C.
(10340) Wt W5300/P713 750,000 3/18 E 2688 Forms/C/2118/16.

1/5 Bn Loyal N Lancs

Instructions regarding War Diaries and Intelligence Summaries are contained in F. S. Regs., Part II. and the Staff Manual respectively. Title pages will be prepared in manuscript.

WAR DIARY
or
INTELLIGENCE SUMMARY.

(Erase heading not required.)

Army Form C. 2118.

Place	Date	Hour	Summary of Events and Information	Remarks and references to Appendices
			SUMMARY. FEBRUARY	
AGNEZ LES DUISANS	FEB		The Ration Strength of the Battalion 1/3/19 is 149	[initials]
			No of men demobilised this month is 218	[initials]
			No of officers — — — — 2	[initials]
			The Battalion football team won the Brigade Football competition + Medals	[initials]
			Concerts were given on an average twice per week	[initials]
			Education Time Table attached	[initials]
			1/3/19	
			[signature] Lt Col, 1/5 Bn Loyal N Lancs Regt	

D. D. & L., London, E.C.
(10340) Wt W5300/P713 750,000 3/18 E 2688 FormsC/2118/16.

1/5th. Loyal North Lancs Regt.

Education Time Table.

Class	Monday		Tuesday		Wednesday		Thursday		Friday		Saturday	
	09·30 to 11·00	11·30 to 13·00	09·30 to 11·00	11·30 to 13·00	09·30 to 11·00	11·30 to 13·00	09·30 to 11·00	11·30 to 13·00	09·30 to 11·00	11·30 to 13·00	09·30 to 11·00	11·30 to 13·00
A 1.	English	Arithmetic	Arithmetic	Geography	Arithmetic	Civics	Arithmetic	History	Arithmetic	English.	Arithmetic	Civics
A 2.	Arithmetic	English	Geography	Arithmetic	Civics	Arithmetic	History	Arithmetic	English	Arithmetic	Civics	Arithmetic
A 3.	Reading	Arithmetic	Letter Writing	Arithmetic	Civics	Geography	Arithmetic	Reading	Arithmetic	English	Arithmetic	Civics
B 1.	Arithmetic & Mensuration	English, Reading & Civics	Arithmetic & Mensuration	English, Reading & Civics	Arithmetic & Mensuration	Geography	Arithmetic & Mensuration	Historical Essays & Civics	Metric System	Geography	Metric System	History & Civics
B 2.	English, Reading, & Civics.	Arithmetic & Mensuration	English, Reading & Civics.	Arithmetic & Mensuration	Geography	Arithmetic & Mensuration	Historical Essays & Civics	Arithmetic & Mensuration	Geography	Metric System.	History & Civics.	Metric System.
B 3.	Geography	Arithmetic & Mensuration	Arithmetic & Mensuration	History	Civics & History	Arithmetic & Mensuration	Arithmetic & Mensuration	Geography	English, Reading, & Civics	Arithmetic & Mensuration	Arithmetic & Mensuration	English, Reading & Civics.
C.	Algebra	English.	Arithmetic	Commercial Geography	Arithmetic	Civics.	Algebra	Commercial Correspondence	Arithmetic	Composition	Reading.	History

5/2/19.

[illegible] Lt.
Comdg 1/5 Loyal N. Lan Regt.

B. Kearney Lt.
Education Officer

Vol 44

1/5th Battallion Loyal North Lancashire Regiment

W A R D I A R _

Month ending 31st March , 1919.

Instructions regarding War Diaries and Intelligence Summaries are contained in F. S. Regs., Part II. and the Staff Manual respectively. Title pages will be prepared in manuscript.

WAR DIARY
or
INTELLIGENCE SUMMARY.
(*Erase heading not required.*)

1/5 Loyal N Lancs Regt

Army Form C. 2118.

MARCH - 1919

Place	Date	Hour	Summary of Events and Information	Remarks and references to Appendices
AGNEZ LES DUISANS	1/MARCH 1919	SAT	Salvage + clearing Battalion salvage dump. In future men going on leave must leave rifles + bayonets Box Resp. Steel Helmets + entrenching tool. Demob for 1/March/ — NIL.	GPS
	2nd	SUN	Church Parade - CO inspected entire Camp. Summer time comes into operation at midnight.	GPS
	3rd	MON.	Salvage. Lt Col Dawson assumed command of the Brigade (130) over Brig. Gen Ransome to England. Maj Suart assumed Cmd of Bn.	GPS
	4th	TUES.	Salvage Parades — Cash drawn for men's pay.	GPS
	5th	WED.	Muster Parade + Inspection by C.O. - Clothing Inspection	GPS
	6th	THUR.	Salvage Parade. Demob. NIL.	GPS
	7th	FRI.	Baths + Salvage	GPS

DEMOB. NIL

[signature] Lt Col.
Comdg 1/5 Bn Loyal North Lancs Regt

D. D. & L., London, E.C.
(10340) Wt W5300/P713 750,000 3/18 E 2688 Forms C/2118/16.

Instructions regarding War Diaries and Intelligence Summaries are contained in F. S. Regs., Part II. and the Staff Manual respectively. Title pages will be prepared in manuscript.

WAR DIARY
or
INTELLIGENCE SUMMARY.
(Erase heading not required.)

1/5 Loyal N Lancs Regt

Army Form C. 2118.

MARCH.

Place	Date	Hour	Summary of Events and Information	Remarks and references to Appendices
AGNEZ LES DUISANS.	8th.	SAT.	Letter of praise from Brig Dawson to Brigade on leaving for appointment in England. New Fire orders issued.	[illegible]
			Concert by Loyals	
	9th.	SUN.	Church Parade. Inspection of lines by C.O.	[illegible]
	10th	MON.	Salvage – Baths.	[illegible]
	11th	TUES	Cadre Coy Paraded for Inspection.	[illegible]
	12	WED	Cadre Coy Paraded	[illegible]
	13.	THURS	Inspection by Brigade Commander – Lena Ashwell Concert in Concert Hall	[illegible]
	14	FRI.	Salvage – Lena Ashwell Concert	[illegible]
			DEMOB. NIL.	

[signature]

Comdg 1/5 Loyal North Lancs Regt

D. D. & L., London, E.C.
(10340) Wt W5300/P713 750,000 3/18 E 2688 FormsC/2118/16.

Instructions regarding War Diaries and Intelligence Summaries are contained in F. S. Regs., Part II. and the Staff Manual respectively. Title pages will be prepared in manuscript. MARCH

WAR DIARY
or
INTELLIGENCE SUMMARY.

(Erase heading not required.)

1/5 L N L R A

Army Form C. 2118.

Place	Date	Hour	Summary of Events and Information	Remarks and references to Appendices
AGNEZ LES DUISANS.	15.	SAT.	Cadre Coy Paraded. Sera Astwell Concert	[illegible]
	16.	SUN.	Ceremonial Church Parade – Colours taken to Church. Colour Party. Capt H A Richardson. Sgt F A Niles. Sgt Topham. Pte Johnson. Pte Leaper. – Sera Astwell Concert. 3 O R Demobilised.	[illegible]
	17.	MON	Salvage – Cadre Coy Paraded.	[illegible]
	18.	TUES	Baths – Cash drawn – 1 O R demob.	[illegible]
	19.	WED	Audit board on Canteen Account	[illegible]
	20.	THURS	Salvage Parade 1 O R demobilised.	[illegible]
	21.	FRI		

[signature]

Comdg 1/5. Loyal N Lanc RA [illegible]

D. D. & L., London, E.C.
(10340) Wt W5300/P713 750,000 3/18 E 2688 Forms C/2118/16.

Instructions regarding War Diaries and Intelligence Summaries are contained in F. S. Regs., Part II. and the Staff Manual respectively. Title pages will be prepared in manuscript.

WAR DIARY
or
INTELLIGENCE SUMMARY.
(Erase heading not required.)

Army Form C. 2118.

MARCH.

1/5th L. N. L. Regt.

Place	Date	Hour	Summary of Events and Information	Remarks and references to Appendices
AGNEZ LES DUISANS	22	Sat.	Salvage work in camp. Cadre Coy parades.	
	23	Sun.	Church parade. Presentation of Medals to football teams, winners of Demob. knock out competition.	
	24	Mon.	General Barnes (Divisional Commander) publishes farewell address to the Division. This was repeated in orders. 50 OR dispatched to relieve prisoner guards on local dumps. Inspection of Mobilization stores ordered for tomorrow.	
	25	Tues.	Muster Parade	
	26.	Wed.	1 Ton of Salvage cleared from Bn Dump to Divisional Dump	
	27	Thurs.	Salvage work in camp. Letter acknowledging receipt of 15 (fifteen) Guineas for the benefit of Widows & Orphans of men of 5th Loyal N Lancs Regt from the Mayor of Bolton. Published in Bn Orders. Letter acknowledging receipt of 350 frs. proceeds of Lena Ashwell's Concert from YMCA H.23 1st Army. Published in Bn Orders.	

[illegible] Comdg.

D. D. & L., London, E.C.
(10340) Wt W5300/P713 750,000 3/18 E 2688 FormsC/2118/16.

1/5 Loyal N Lancs Regt

Army Form C. 2118.

Instructions regarding War Diaries and Intelligence Summaries are contained in F. S. Regs., Part II. and the Staff Manual respectively. Title pages will be prepared in manuscript.

WAR DIARY
or
INTELLIGENCE SUMMARY.

(*Erase heading not required.*)

Place	Date	Hour	Summary of Events and Information	Remarks and references to Appendices
Agny-les-Duisans.	1919 Mar 28	Friday	Salvage Work.	
	29.	Sat	Salvage Work	
	30	Sun.	Church Parade. Letter published in Bn Orders from Lena Ashwell thanking Battalion for donation of £10 (ten pounds) to Concerts at the Front Fund.	
	31.	Mon	Salvage Work.	
	Apr 1	Tues.	Salvage Work.	
	2	Wed	Clearing up of the Camp	
	3.	Thur	Lt L R Standen joined for duty and took over duties of Acting Adjutant. 2Lt C J Sollit took over duties of Transport Officer.	

[illegible] Lt Col
Commdg.

D. D. & L., London, E.C.
(10340. Wt W5300/P713 750,000 3/18 E 2688 Forms C/2118/16.

Instructions regarding War Diaries and Intelligence Summaries are contained in F. S. Regs., Part II. and the Staff Manual respectively. Title pages will be prepared in manuscript.

WAR DIARY
or
INTELLIGENCE SUMMARY.
(Erase heading not required.)

Army Form C. 2118.

98 4

Place	Date	Hour	Summary of Events and Information	Remarks and references to Appendices
	1919. April			
AGNEZ-LES-DUISANS.	4th	Fri.	Salvage Parades. Lieut. L.R. STANDEN appointed acting Adjutant, to date from 4.4.19. A/Lieut. C.J. SOLLITT assumes command of No. 1 Company from this date.	
	5th	Sat.	Cadre Company Parade – full marching order. Baths.	
	6th	Sun.	Divine Service Parade. Cash for pay drawn.	
	7th	Mon.	All ammunition of Cadre Company withdrawn. Baths.	
	8th	Tues.	Salvage parades.	
	9th	Wed.	Salvage parades. Baths.	
	10th	Thur.	Salvage work. 1 N.C.O. & 9 men detailed for detachment duty, Field Supply Depot, ARRAS. Lieut. A. FIELDEN reported for duty.	
			Demobilization: Rev. T.C.P. GOULD (C.F.), Lieut. F.A. WYLES & 2/Lt. H. WOOLLEY, proceeded for, on the 5th.	
			[signature] for Lieut. Col., commdg. 1/5th Bn. Loyal North Lancs. Regt.	

D. D. & L., London, E.C. (10340) Wt W5300/P713 750,000 3/18 E 2688 Forms C/2118/16.

Instructions regarding War Diaries and Intelligence Summaries are contained in F. S. Regs., Part II. and the Staff Manual respectively. Title pages will be prepared in manuscript.

WAR DIARY
or
INTELLIGENCE SUMMARY.

(Erase heading not required.)

Army Form C. 2118.

Place	Date	Hour	Summary of Events and Information	Remarks and references to Appendices
	1919. April.			
AGNEZ-LES-DUISANS.	11th	Fri.	Salvage work.	
	12th	Sat.	Salvage work. Baths allotted Brigade Concert given.	
	13th	Sun.	Divine Service Parade	
	14th	Mon.	Salvage parade Cash for pay drawn. 2 L.D. mules loaned to 171st Inf. Bde.	
	15th	Tues.	Salvage parades.	
	16th	Wed.	~~[illegible]~~ Salvage parades.	
	17th	Thur.	Salvage parades.	

[illegible signature]
Lieut. Col.
Commdg. 1/5th Bn. Loyal North Lancs. Regt.

D. D. & L., London, E.C.
(10340. Wt W5300/P713 750,000 3/18 E 2688 Forms C/2118/16.

Instructions regarding War Diaries and Intelligence Summaries are contained in F. S. Regs., Part II. and the Staff Manual respectively. Title pages will be prepared in manuscript.

WAR DIARY
or
INTELLIGENCE SUMMARY.
(Erase heading not required.)

Army Form C. 2118.

Place	Date	Hour	Summary of Events and Information	Remarks and references to Appendices
AGNEZ-LES-DUISANS.	1919 April			
	18th	Fri.	Divine Service F. G. C. M. assembled for trial of 25941 Pte. A. H. BLACKMAN, 1/5 L.N.L.	
	19th	Sat.	Battalion parade – full marching order.	
	20th	Sun.	Divine Service	
	21st	Mon.	Salvage parades.	
	22nd	Tues.	Battalion parade, drill order Cash for pay drawn	
	23rd	Wed.	Salvage work.	
	24th	Thur.	Salvage work.	

[signature] Lieut. Colonel, Comdg. 1/5 Loyal North Lanc. Regt.

D. D. & L., London, E.C. (10340. Wt W5300/P713 750,000 3/18 E 2688 Forms C/2118/16.

Instructions regarding War Diaries and Intelligence Summaries are contained in F. S. Regs., Part II. and the Staff Manual respectively. Title pages will be prepared in manuscript.

WAR DIARY
or
INTELLIGENCE SUMMARY.
(Erase heading not required.)

Army Form C. 2118.

Place	Date	Hour	Summary of Events and Information	Remarks and references to Appendices
AGNEZ-LES-DUISANS	1919. April			
	25th	Fri.	Salvage work.	
	26th	Sat.	Cadre Company parade - full marching order.	
	27th	Sun.	Divine Service.	
	28th	Mon.	Salvage work.	
	29th	Tue.	Salvage work.	
	30th	Wed.	Salvage work. Battalion parade for pay.	

[illegible signature] for [illegible]

VR 46

1/5th Bn Loyal North Lancs

War Diary

(Confidential)

Instructions regarding War Diaries and Intelligence Summaries are contained in F. S. Regs., Part II. and the Staff Manual respectively. Title pages will be prepared in manuscript.

WAR DIARY
or
INTELLIGENCE SUMMARY.
(Erase heading not required.)

Army Form C. 2118.

Place	Date	Hour	Summary of Events and Information	Remarks and references to Appendices
	1919. MAY.			
AGNEZ-LES-DUISANS.	22nd	Thu.	Salvage work.	
	23rd	Fri.	Salvage work.	
	24th	Sat.	Baths allotted to battalion.	
	25th	Sun.	Divine Service.	
	26th	Mon.	Salvage Parade.	
	27th	Tue.	Salvage Parade.	
	28th	Wed.	Salvage Work. Attack of men of battalion by two Chinese in village of DUISANS on night of 23rd/24th reported.	
	29th	Thu.	Salvage Work.	
	30th	Fri.	Salvage Work.	
	31st	Sat.	Loading for movement of cadre commenced.	

[signature] Comdg 1/5th L.N. Lancs. Regt.

D. D. & L., London, E.C. (10340) Wt W5300/P713 750,000 3/18 E 2688 Forms C/2118/16.

Instructions regarding War Diaries and Intelligence Summaries are contained in F. S. Regs., Part II. and the Staff Manual respectively. Title pages will be prepared in manuscript.

WAR DIARY
or
INTELLIGENCE SUMMARY.
(Erase heading not required.)

Army Form C. 2118.

1/5TH LOYAL NORTH LANCS. REGIMENT. No. A1/2655 Date 1/6/19

Place	Date	Hour	Summary of Events and Information	Remarks and references to Appendices
	1919. May.			
AGNEZ-LES-DUISANS.	15th	Thur	Salvage work.	
	16th	Fri.	Salvage work	
	17th	Sat	Baths allotted to battalion. Salvage work	
	18th	Sun	Divine Service.	
	19th	Mon	Salvage Parade.	
	20th	Tues	Salvage Work.	
	21st	Wed	Salvage Work.	

[signature] Lt Col
Commdg. 1/5th L. N. Lancs Regt.

D. D. & L., London, E.C.
(10340. Wt W5300/P713 750,000 3/18 E 2688 FormsC/2118/16.

Instructions regarding War Diaries and Intelligence Summaries are contained in F. S. Regs., Part II. and the Staff Manual respectively. Title pages will be prepared in manuscript.

WAR DIARY
or
INTELLIGENCE SUMMARY.
(*Erase heading not required.*)

Army Form C. 2118.

Place	Date	Hour	Summary of Events and Information	Remarks and references to Appendices
	1919 May.			
AGNEZ-LES-DUISANS.	8th	Thur.	Salvage Work.	
	9th	Fri.	Lieut.-Col. D. B. Dawson took over command of 57th Bde group of Cadres as from 7th. Lieut L. R. Standen took over command of battalion & Lieut A. Fielson acting Adjt as from 7th.	
	10th	Sat.	Salvage Work.	
	11th	Sun.	Div. Service.	
	12th	Mon.	Salvage Parade.	
	13th	Tues.	Salvage work.	
	14th	Wed.	Salvage work.	

[illegible] Lt. Col.
Comdg. 1/5th L. N. Lancs. Regt.

D. D. & L., London, E.C.
(10340. Wt W5300/P713 750,000 3/18 E 2688 Forms C/2118/16.

Instructions regarding War Diaries and Intelligence Summaries are contained in F. S. Regs., Part II. and the Staff Manual respectively. Title pages will be prepared in manuscript.

WAR DIARY
or
INTELLIGENCE SUMMARY.
(Erase heading not required.)

Army Form C. 2118.

Place	Date	Hour	Summary of Events and Information	Remarks and references to Appendices
AGNEZ-LES DUISANS	1919 May 1st	Thur	Salvage work.	
	2nd	Fri	Salvage work.	
	3rd	Sat.	Cadre Coy. parade. Salvage work.	
	4th	Sun.	Divine Service.	
	5th	Mon.	Salvage Parade.	
	6th	Tues	Salvage Parade	
	7th	Wed.	Salvage Parade	

[signature]
Comdg. 1/5th L. N. Lancs Regt.

D. D. & L., London, E.C.
(10340. Wt W5300/P713 750,000 3/18 E 2688 FormsC/2118/16.

57TH DIVISION
170TH INFY BDE

2-5TH LOY. NTH LANCS

~~FEB 1917-DEC 1917~~

1915 SEP – 1916 FEB
1917 FEB – 1917 DEC

TO DN PIONEERS

www.ingramcontent.com/pod-product-compliance
Lightning Source LLC
Chambersburg PA
CBHW081133220426
43649CB00038B/3334